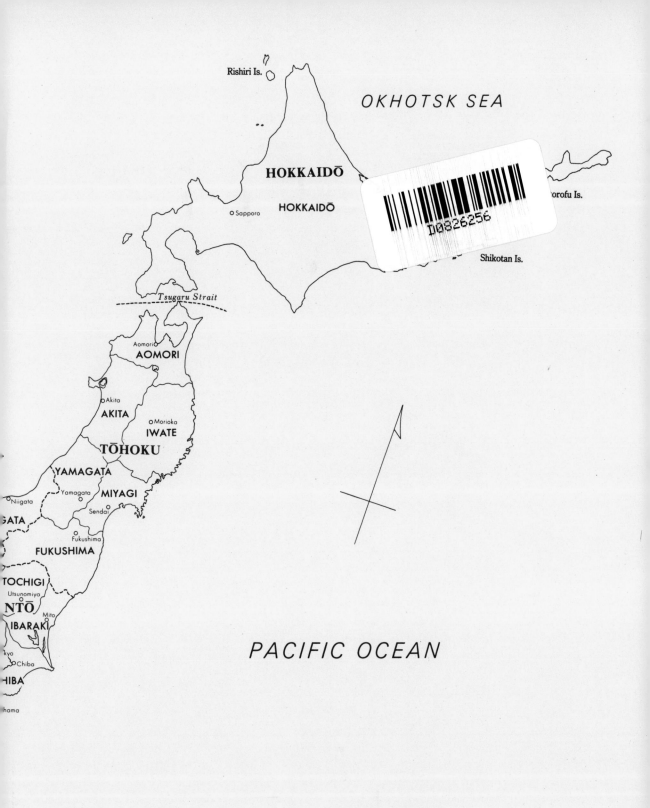

OKHOTSK SEA

HOKKAIDŌ

HOKKAIDŌ

O Sapporo

orofu Is.

Shikotan Is.

Tsugaru Strait

Aomori
AOMORI

Akita
AKITA

Morioka
IWATE

TŌHOKU

YAMAGATA

Niigata
Yamagata
MIYAGI

GATA
Sendai

Fukushima
FUKUSHIMA

TOCHIGI
Utsunomiya

NTŌ
Mito
IBARAKI

kyo
Chiba

HIBA

hama

PACIFIC OCEAN

Rishiri Is.

I0826256

0   40   80   120   160   200km

JAPANESE FOR BUSY PEOPLE

I

JAPANESE FOR BUSY PEOPLE

I

Kana Version

Association for Japanese-Language Teaching

KODANSHA INTERNATIONAL
Tokyo ▪ New York ▪ London

The Authors: The Association for Japanese-Language Teaching (AJALT) was recognized as a nonprofit organization by the Ministry of Education in 1977. It was established to meet the practical needs of people who are not necessarily specialists on Japan but who wish to communicate effectively in Japanese. In 1992 the Association was awarded the Japan Foundation Special Prize.

The Association maintains a web site on the Internet at www.ajalt.org and can be contacted over the Internet via info@ajalt.org by teachers and students who have questions about this textbook or any of the Association's other publications.

Distributed in the United States by Kodansha America, Inc., and in the United Kingdom and continental Europe by Kodansha Europe Ltd.

Published by Kodansha International Ltd., 17–14 Otowa 1-chome, Bunkyo-ku, Tokyo 112–8652, and Kodansha America, Inc.

Copyright © 1995 by the Association for Japanese-Language Teaching. All rights reserved. Printed in Japan.
ISBN-13: 978–4–7700–1987–5
ISBN-10: 4–7700–1987–4

First Edition, 1984
Revised Edition, 1994
Kana Version, 1995
10 09 08 07 06 05 04   20 19 18 17 16 15 14 13 12

www.kodansha-intl.com

CONTENTS

Preface for the *Kana Version* of *Japanese for Busy People*

When *Japanese for Busy People 1* was first published in 1984, many non-native learners, particularly from non-*kanji* cultures, considered Japanese one of the world's most difficult languages because of its seemingly inaccessible writing system. *Japanese for Busy People* was designed especially for such learners—be they business men from English-speaking countries or learners of Japanese-as-a-second language from other parts of the world—people wished to learn natural, spoken Japanese as effectively as possible in a limited amount of time. To this end, romanized Japanese was included in the *Japanese for Busy People* series so that learners both inside and outside Japan, as well as non-native instructors, could use the textbook to its full extent without the need to read Japanese script. As a measure, however, *kana* and *kanji* were progressively introduced through volumes *1* to *3*

But in the decade since *Japanese for Busy People's* first publication, there has been a growing increase in the number of people learning Japanese-as-a-second-language throughout the world. Many of them are now interested in studying Japanese in a more comprehensive way, and wish to learn to read and write as well as speak and understand what is said to them. Educationalists have pointed out the problems of teaching and learning accurate and natural pronunciation through romanization, as well as the inconvenience of not being able to read and write at an early stage. AJALT has received many requests to drop romanization and include more exercises in *kana* and *kanji*. In this, the *Kana Version* of *Japanese for Busy People*, all the romanization has been omitted so that the learner can now learn Japanese directly through the native script from volume *1*.

We sincerely hope that the book will be of much use for the many people interested in Japan and the Japanese language.

September 1995
Association for Japanese-Language Teaching (AJALT)

About the *Kana Version* of *Japanese for Busy People 1*

How can *Japanese for Busy People* help you learn Japanese?

The aim of *Japanese for Busy People* is to help you learn essential Japanese as quickly and as effectively as possible, so that you can actually communicate with native speakers in their own language. It has been prepared under the guidance of a working group of AJALT's experienced and specially-trained language instructors who have tested and revised the material in a working classroom environment. *Japanese for Busy People 1* aims to help you learn Japanese by increasing your awareness of just what *kind of language* Japanese actually is through basic conversational patterns.

The *Kana Version* is a basic textbook for students who intend to master the native *hiragana* and *katakana* scripts early on in their studies. This edition is designed so that it can be used by those attending a course in Japanese and for self-study in combination with either the cassette tapes or compact discs (and indeed all other components in the *Japanese for Busy People* series).

What does *Japanese for Busy People 1* cover?

Japanese for Busy People 1 covers "survival Japanese." This means all the language that you learn—conversation patterns, sentence structures, grammatical principles, and vocabulary—can be put to immediate use in conversational situations with native speakers.

Unlike many other textbooks that overwhelm the beginner with an excessive and all-too-often irrelevant amount of information, *Japanese for Busy People 1* limits vocabulary and grammar patterns to what is essential for the most common situations in which non-native speakers need to communicate in Japanese. Simplistic or even juvenile ways of expression that abound in most introductory texts have been abandoned in favor of uncomplicated *adult* speech. Much more than simple grammatical accuracy, emphasis has been placed on natural and authentic linguistic patterns actually used in Japanese communication. A table clearly showing all ten grammar sections and thirty different practical situations can be found at the end of this chapter.

These then are the specifications that, we believe, make *Japanese for Busy People 1* the essential textbook not only for busy, working people who want to learn basic Japanese, but also for people who already know a little Japanese but wish to review the phrases they know and reconfirm that they are using them in the correct situations.

What the *Kana Version* does not include

The *Kana Version* assumes that you are thoroughly familiar with *hiragana* and *katakana* or are currently working through *Kana for Busy People* or similar workbook. In any case, you should be able to read and recognize all forty-eight *hiragana* characters by the time you reach Lesson 10 of this textbook. Advice and instructions contained in *Kana for Busy People* are not generally repeated in the *Kana Version* of *Japanese for Busy People 1*.

Except for twenty *kanji* introduced in Appendix M, Chinese characters have not been covered in this textbook. *Japanese for Busy People 2* and *3* introduce many more *kanji,* as well as provide more advanced and specialist language skills necessary to function in a professional environment.

The structure of *Japanese for Busy People 1*

Japanese for Busy People 1 is divided into ten grammar sections, covering the most important and useful patterns in the Japanese language. Each grammar section is introduced, reinforced, and later reviewed through a number of different situations. Each lesson is based on one distinct conversational situation, and in the total of thirty lessons are included three revision lessons for reading practice and review. At the back of the book you will find twelve appendices covering, among other things, particles, verb conjugations, counters, and *kanji*. We have also included suggested answers to the Quiz sections, two glossaries, and a full index of the main grammatical items introduced in this book. Following this chapter, we have provided a brief summary of the Characteristics of Japanese Grammar, a page of Useful Daily Expressions, and three pages of Signs in Daily Life. The map of Japan printed on the front endpapers and the *hiragana* and *katakana* tables printed on the back endpapers should also prove useful to your studies.

Typically the lessons evolve around a practical topic or commonly encountered situations such as shopping in Lesson 4 and talking on the telephone in Lesson 12. The title of the lesson and the English topic sentence at the beginning of the lesson should give you a firm idea of the content of the dialogue or reading passage.

All dialogues appear in *kana* only. The type is large and clear enough for even the beginner to read. Without the hindrance of artificial romanized Japanese, which encourages English-style articulation, your pronunciation, intonation, and accent should develop naturally and fluently as you complete each lesson. From Lesson 3 onwards we have marked sentences that are more likely to be used in the written language with a black box symbol ■.

An idiomatic English translation of the dialogue or reading passage appears immediately after the Japanese text. New vocabulary and new usages of previously learned vocabulary are introduced in a list with their English equivalents. Note that new vocabulary is treated in exactly the same way when it appears for the first time in the Practice section.

More detailed analysis of important words and phrases is included in the Notes section of each lesson. Here, we aim to explain, as accurately and briefly as possible, points that many non-native learners commonly find difficult to grasp. Although we have concentrated chiefly on offering linguistic information, in some cases we thought it necessary to add some social or cultural references.

The Practice section reinforces the main points of the topic. Key Sentences are given in both Japanese and English to provide further examples of language patterns and vocabulary usage. Many non-native learners will find these examples useful for reference even after completing all thirty lessons. Exercises encourage you to learn new vocabulary, to practice conjugating verbs, and to acquire many other communication skills, such as telling the time. Short Dialogues summarize all new points introduced in the lesson through variations on the main situation.

Finally we have included a selection of problems in the Quiz section to enable you to check how well you have acquired the new language skills.

In ten special lessons, (Lessons 1, 6, 8, 10, 13, 15, 16, 18, and 19), you will find a grammar section offering explanation of the grammatical principles of the Japanese language. They will help you understand and apply the conversational patterns introduced in the lessons. The table at the end of this chapter illustrates more fully how the grammar is distributed in this textbook.

The three reading review lessons (Lessons 11, 25, and 30) are somewhat different from other lessons. First, there are no Notes, Practice, and Quiz sections. Second, they are presented in the form of written Japanese. In our experience, students learn Japanese most effectively when studying both conversational and written Japanese from the very beginning. The underlying rationale being that the two modes of communication, oral and written, are different, and it is thought best to highlight the difference at an early stage. When simply talking, speaker and listener share much information that could be omitted from the conversation without detriment to communication. In a story, a report, or a letter, however, it is essential to be more organized, structured, and explicit in order to communicate effectively.

Using *Japanese for Busy People 1* for self-study

The *Kana Version* has a number of features that promote ease of use and enable you to check your learning:

- The table on page xiv to helps you select the lessons you need to concentrate on.
- Tables and illustrations are often used to explain complex ideas. They are an essential part of the book and often contain information not explained elsewhere.
- Throughout the text you will find questions and activities in the Quiz sections. These are designed to help you check your understanding and assess your progress.

No romanized Japanese is used in the *Kana Version* of *Japanese for Busy People 1*. Mastering *hiragana* and *katakana* from the start will not only help you improve your pronunciation, it will also enable you to move smoothly and quickly to the study of *kanji*. Many educators believe this is the most effective way to learn Japanese.

Before beginning Lesson 1 of this textbook, it may be a good idea to go through *Kana for Busy People* or a similar workbook, if you do not already know *hiragana*. *Kana for Busy People* is particularly useful because the accompanying cassette tape ensures that you learn natural and accurate pronunciation of each *kana* syllable. *Kana for Busy People* will also help reinforce vocabulary and language patterns learned in *Japanese for Busy People 1*. Here are some tips for using *Kana for Busy People*.

- Concentrate first on reading the *kana*. Practice writing after you are able to recognize all the *kana* shapes.
- Listening to the cassette tape will improve your pronunciation.
- In addition to individual *kana* characters, commit to memory *hiragana* words and expressions.
- Read aloud as much as possible.

Within a space of several weeks, you should have completed the two *hiragana* sections in *Kana for Busy People* and mastered the *hiragana* syllabary. Remember your main objective at this stage is to be able to read and recognize the *kana*. Now you are ready to begin

Lesson 1 of the *Kana Version* of *Japanese for Busy People 1.*

To help you develop natural pronunciation, intonation, and accent, we suggest that you listen to the companion cassette tapes or compact discs for *Japanese for Busy People 1* and try to converse in Japanese with your Japanese friends. It also helps if you read out aloud from your textbook.

We suggest that you work through each lesson of *Japanese for Busy People 1* in the following manner:

(1) Read through the main dialogue or reading passage at the beginning of each lesson. Listening to the recording of the main dialogue on the cassette tape or compact disc is also recommended.

(2) Refer to the Notes, Vocabulary, and Grammar sections so that you fully understand the text.

(3) Check your understanding of the dialogue or reading passage with the English translation.

(4) The Practice section offers further example sentences of the patterns introduced in the main dialogue. Make new sentences based on the patterns, using words from the glossaries and appendices at the back of the book. Always try to read or speak aloud. Remember these patterns will only be useful when related to actual situations.

(5) Try out the Quiz at the end of each lesson to check your understanding and monitor your progress. Answers can be found at the back of the book.

Some learners may find it useful to memorize the main dialogue and key sentences.

Using the *Kana Version* of *Japanese for Busy People 1* in the classroom
Educators are advised to consult the teacher's manuals for *Japanese for Busy People 1,* available in both English (from late 1996) and Japanese, for a more comprehensive and structured approach to basing a Japanese-as-a-second-language course on this textbook, as well as for more details about the underlying rationale and methodology adopted in this series.

Since romanized Japanese is not used anywhere in the *Kana Version,* we strongly recommend that students master *hiragana* before starting Lesson 1 or at the latest by the time they reach Lesson 10 of this textbook. From our own classroom experience, we have found that the use of a *kana* workbook, such as *Kana for Busy People,* is often the most effective way of learning Japanese script, particularly as this means that more class time can be devoted to using Japanese. In our classes, we concentrate primarily on reading and recognition of *kana,* and postpone teaching writing skills until students are familiar with the *kana* script.

Kana for Busy People is particularly recommended, as the accompanying cassette tape allows students to practice accurate pronunciation of syllables outside the classroom. Here are a few ideas on how *Kana for Busy People* can be used in combination with this textbook.

- Inform students of the benefits of learning *kana* from the very beginning. *Kana* will help pronunciation, promote a better understanding of verb conjugations, and enable students to make a smooth and uninterrupted transition to the study of *kanji.*
- Try and complete the Hiragana 1 section in *Kana for Busy People* as the students work through Lessons 1–5 of this textbook. (More details are given below.)
- Make sure that students have completed the Hiragana 2 section in *Kana for Busy People* by the time they have reached Lesson 10 of this textbook.
- *Katakana* should be introduced gradually. Show students how to write their family name, given name, and school or company name in *katakana.*
- As well as methodically teaching each of the forty-eight *katakana* characters individually, introduce *katakana* words found in *Japanese for Busy People 1.*
- Focus on reading and recognizing *katakana* before attempting to teach writing.

At AJALT we have found the following to be a successful way of using *Kana for Busy People* with this textbook.

(1) Before tackling Lesson 1 of this textbook, focus class attention on pages 10–12 of *Kana for Busy People.* This covers the pronunciation of the basic syllables in Japanese. After reading the explanation, play the cassette tape and have students repeat as they look at the *kana.* Pages 13–16 of *Kana for Busy People* offers students an opportunity to familiarize themselves with the forms of *hiragana.*

(2) As students progress through Lessons 1–5 of *Japanese for Busy People 1,* they should work through pages 23–33 of *Kana for Busy People,* using the cassette tape as indicated above. Have students who show difficulty in recognizing individual *hiragana,* repeat the process until they have mastered the *kana.*

(3) For writing practice, students will find pages of 17–22 of *Kana for Busy People* helpful. Class time should focus on familiarizing students with the *kana* shapes. Actual writing practice is best done as a homework assignment.

(4) After completing Lesson 5 of this textbook, have the class practice reading the full *hiragana* sentences found in Lesson 1–5 of the Hiragana 2 section of *Kana for Busy People.* Attention should be given to reading more difficult *kana,* such as the particles は and を.

(5) At this stage, students may find it productive to review Lessons 1–5 of *Japanese for Busy People 1* by reading the dialogues and practice sentences without the assistance of teacher or cassette tape.

(6) Students should work through Lessons 6–8 of the Hiragana 2 section of *Kana for Busy People* at the same pace as they work through Lessons 6–8 of this textbook.

(7) Ideally, students should be able to read and understand the questions in the Quiz section by the time they reach Lesson 6 of *Japanese for Busy People 1.* All students should be able to this before tackling Lesson 10.

Japanese for Busy People 1 was designed to be taught in about fifty hours of classroom instruction. (At AJALT *Japanese for Busy People 1* is taught over a four-week period of five daily 150-minute classes every week.) Students will need to set aside two to three hours every day for preparation and review. Below we have listed a number of tips that may help teachers to use *Japanese for Busy People* more effectively in their classroom.

- The importance of student preparation cannot be overestimated. Before class, students should listen to the main dialogue, recorded on the companion cassette tapes or compact discs, to get a feel for the flow of the conversation. Students should then listen to the vocabulary for each lesson and memorize the English equivalents. Encourage students to review lessons after class, with emphasis on the dialogues, summary sentences, and key sentences.
- Apart from the three reading review lessons, each lesson has Short Dialogues and Practice sections designed to reinforce new patterns. Exercises offer relatively few examples. The emphasis, of course, is not on the number of example phrases or sentences, but rather on the number of possible substitutions which may or may not be provided by the teacher. A selection of additional words that may interest the students can be found in the appendices and bilingual glossaries at the back of this book. Oral proficiency can be boosted by using these new words in pattern practice.
- Increase vocabulary and improve weak points gradually over several lessons. Be careful not to overwhelm students with an excess of new words in any individual lesson or strive for perfection.
- Remember that some lessons require more time than others. For example, Lessons 13 and 14, which deal with adjectives, are relatively time-consuming.
- Quiz sections can be done either in class or at home. Teachers should look through student answers to check understanding, monitor progress, and identify individual problems.

Other publications in the *Japanese for Busy People* series

Teachers and learners alike will find the following publications useful supplementary materials.

- The opening dialogues, reading reviews, key sentences, and short dialogues for all thirty lessons in *Japanese for Busy People 1* have been recorded in authentic, natural Japanese on three forty-minute audio cassette tapes and two sixty-minute compact discs.
- A 184-page workbook for *Japanese for Busy People 1* provides drills to improve oral fluency. Learners may also find the two fifty-minute audio cassette tapes of the workbook particularly helpful to self-study.
- As outlined above, *Kana for Busy People* is particularly recommended for learners who have yet to master the two *kana* syllabaries. *Kana for Busy People* is the only *kana* workbook with a companion cassette tape, making it ideal for self-study
- *Kana Versions* of *Japanese for Busy People 2* and *3* are at present being prepared by an experienced group of instructors at AJALT. These titles will focus on the difficult transition to the study of *kanji*, seen by many non-native learners as being the major hurdle to mastering the Japanese language.

Table showing the structure of *Japanese for Busy People 1*

Grammatical structures	Situation(s)
Part 1 Nouns (noun 1) は (noun 2) です	Lesson 1 Introductions Lesson 2 Exchanging Business Cards Lesson 3 Dates and Times Lesson 4 Shopping 1 Lesson 5 Shopping 2
Part 2 Verbs 1 (direction) いきます・きます・かえります	Lesson 6 Movement of people and transport Lesson 7 Visiting 1—greeting a guest
Part 3 Verbs 2 (existence) あります・います	Lesson 8 Existence of people and things Lesson 9 Visiting a place
Part 4 Verbs 3 (activity) たべます・よみます, etc.	Lesson 10 Daily activities Lesson 11 Life in Tokyo (review) Lesson 12 Telephoning
Part 5 Adjectives ーい and ーな adjectives	Lesson 13 Visiting 2—offering refreshment Lesson 14 Giving one's opinion
Part 6 Verbs 4 (giving and receiving) あげます・もらいます	Lesson 15 Gifts
Part 7 Inviting and accepting ーましょう, ーませんか, ーませんか	Lesson 16 Invitation to go skiing Lesson 17 Inviting
Part 8 Ownership and events あります	Lesson 18 Invitation to the movies
Part 9 Inflection of verbs ーて form ーて ーてください ーてもいいです ーています ーない form ーない でください	Lesson 19 Talking about one's plans Lesson 20 Requests and orders Lesson 21 Using taxis and dry cleaning, services, making restaurant reservations Lesson 22 Using public transport Lesson 23 Asking permission Lesson 24 Refusing Lesson 25 Actions or events in progress Lesson 26 Part (review) Lesson 27 Talking about one's family
Part 10 (person) は (noun) が (adjectives) です ーたい です	Lesson 28 Expressing preferences Lesson 29 Dining out Lesson 30 Letter (review)

ACKNOWLEDGMENTS for *Japanese for Busy People 1*
Compilation of this textbook has been a cooperative endeavor, and we deeply appreciate the collective efforts and individual contributions of Mss. Sachiko Adachi, Nori Ando, Haruko Matsui, Shigeko Miyazaki, Sachiko Okaniwa, Terumi Sawada, and Yuriko Yobuko. For English translations and editorial assistance, we wish to thank Ms. Dorothy Britton.

ACKNOWLEDGMENTS for the *Revised Edition* of *Japanese for Busy People 1*
We would like to express our gratitude to the following people: Mss. Haruko Matsui, Junko Shinada, Keiko Ito, Mikiko Ochiai, and Satoko Mizoguchi.

ACKNOWLEDGMENTS for the *Kana Version* of *Japanese for Busy People 1*
We would like to express our gratitude to the following people: Mss. Haruko Matsui, Junko Shinada, Mikiko Ochiai, and Satoko Mizoguchi.

CHARACTERISTICS OF JAPANESE GRAMMAR

The grammar in this text is derived from a natural analysis of the Japanese language, rather than being an interpretation adapted to the syntax of Western languages. We have given as few technical terms as possible, choosing ones that will make for a smooth transition from the basic level to more advanced study.

The following points are basic and in most cases reflect differences between the grammar of Japanese and that of English, or other European languages. Specific explanations and examples are given in Grammar I through Grammar X, the notes and the appendices.

1. Japanese nouns have neither gender nor number. But plurals of certain words can be expressed by the use of a suffix.
2. The verb generally comes at the end of the sentence or clause.
    ex. わたしは　にほんじん<u>です</u>。I am a Japanese.
    わたしは　きょうとに<u>いきます</u>。I go to Kyoto.
3. Verb conjugation is not affected by the gender, number, or person of the subject.
4. Verb conjugation shows only two tenses, the present form and the past form. Whether use of the present form refers to habitual action or the future, and whether the past form is equivalent to the English past tense, present perfect, or past perfect can be determined from the context.
5. Japanese adjectives, unlike English ones, are inflected to show present and past, affirmative, and negative.
6. The grammatical function of nouns is indicated by particles. Their role is similar to English prepositions, but since they always come after the word, they are sometimes referred to as postpositions.
    ex. とうきょう<u>で</u>, at Tokyo
    15にち<u>に</u>, on the 15 (of the month)
7. Many degrees of politeness are expressable in Japanese. In this book the style is one which anyone may use without being rude.

Note: The following abbreviations are used in this book:

aff.	affirmative
neg.	negative
Aa:	Answer, affirmative
An:	Answer, negative
ex.	example
−い adj.	−い adjective
−な adj.	−な adjective

USEFUL DAILY EXPRESSIONS

1. おはようございます。Good morning! Used until about 10 A.M.
2. こんにちは。Hello. A rather informal greeting used from about 10 A.M. until sundown.
3. こんばんは。Good evening.
4. さようなら。Good-bye. On more formal occasions one uses しつれいします.
5. おやすみなさい。Good night. Said at night before going to bed. When parting at night outside the home, さようなら is more usual.
6. では　また。／じゃ　また。Well then... Said informally when parting from relatives or friends.
7. いってらっしゃい。So long. (*lit.* "Go and come back.") Said to members of a household as they leave the house.
8. いってまいります。So long. (*lit.* " [I'm] going and coming back.") This is the reply to いってらっしゃい.
9. ただいま。I'm back. (*lit.* " [I have returned] Just now.") Said by a person on returning home.
10. おかえりなさい。Welcome home. This is the reply to ただいま.
11. おげんきですか。How are you? (*lit.* "Are you well?")
12. ありがとうございます。げんきです。Fine, thank you.
13. おめでとうございます。Congratulations!
14. おだいじに。Take care of yourself.
15. どうも　ありがとうございます。Thank you very much.
16. どういたしまして。You're welcome.
17. すみません。Excuse me. I'm sorry.
18. ちょっと　まってください。Wait just a moment, please.
19. もう　いちどおねがいします。Once more, please.
20. おさきに。Pardon my going first (before you). Said when leaving the office or a meeting ahead of other people.
21. どうぞ　おさきに。Please, go ahead.
22. きをつけて。Take care!/Be careful!
23. あぶない。Look out! (*lit.* "It's dangerous.")
24. だめです。Out of the question./Impossible./No good.
25. がんばってください。Keep your chin up! Said to encourage someone.

あんない
Information

えいぎょうちゅう
Open

タクシーのりば
Taxi Stand

えき
(railway) Station

ちかてつ
Subway, Underground

じゅんびちゅう
Getting ready to open.
(May also indicate
　"Closed for the day.")

きっぷうりば
Ticket Office

かいさつぐち
Ticket Gate

せいさんじょ
(fare) Ajustment Office

きゅうぎょうちゅう
Closed

いりぐち
Entrance

でぐち
Exit

ひじょうぐち
Emergency Exit

おす
Push

ひく
Pull

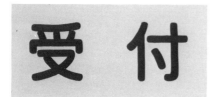

うけつけ
Reception

エレベーター
Elevator

エスカレーター
Escalator

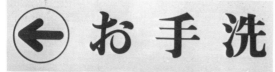

おてあらい
Toilet

おとこ
Men, Gentlemen

けしょうしつ
Powder Room

おんな
Women, Ladies

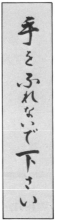

うせつきんし
No right turn

させつきんし
No left turn

ちゅうしゃきんし
No Parking

てをふれないで
ください
Do not touch.

いっぽうつうこうろ
One Way Street

しばふの なかに
はいらないでください
Please keep off the grass.

ちゅうしゃじょう
Parking lot

ゴミを すてないで
ください
Please don't litter.

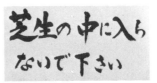

きんえん
No Smoking

こうじちゅう
Under Construction

きけん
Danger!

たちいりきんし
No Admittance

ちゅうい
Caution!

LESSON
1

はじめまして
INTRODUCTION

Mr. Hayashi introduces Mr. Smith to Mr. Tanaka.

はやし ： たなかさん、こちらは　スミスさんです。
スミス ： はじめまして。スミスです。どうぞ　よろしく。
たなか ： はじめまして。とうきょうでんきの　たなかです。
　　　　　どうぞ　よろしく。
はやし ： スミスさんは　ABCの　べんごしです。

Hayashi:　Mr. Tanaka, this is Mr. Smith.
Smith:　　How do you do. My name's Smith. I'm very glad to meet you.
Tanaka:　How do you do. I'm Tanaka from Tokyo Electric. I'm very glad to meet you.
Hayashi:　Mr. Smith is ABC's lawyer.

❏ Vocabulary

はやし	a surname
たなかさん	a surname with honorific
～さん	Mr., Mrs., Ms., Miss (suffix)
こちら	this one (implies this person)
は	as for (topic marker, particle)
スミス	Smith
です	is
はじめまして	How do you do
どうぞ　よろしく	*lit.* Please favor me.
とうきょうでんき	Tokyo Electric (company name)
の	= 's (possessive particle)
ABC（エービーシー）	ABC (company name)
べんごし	lawyer

GRAMMAR

Lesson 1–5 Identifying People and Things

1. noun 1 は　noun 2 です
2. noun 1 は　noun 2 ですか
   はい、（noun 1 は）noun 2 です
   いいえ、（noun 1 は）noun 2 ではありません／じゃありません

Present Form		Past Form	
aff.	*neg.*	*aff.*	*neg.*
です	ではありません	でした	ではありませんでした
is	is not	was	was not

- Particle は. Topic marker.
  は follows noun 1 indicating that it is the topic under discussion. Noun 2 is then identified and the phrase is concluded with です. The topic is often the same as the subject, but not necessarily. It is also possible for the object to be the topic. (See Note 2, p. 39; Grammar III, p. 52; Note 3, p. 178.) The ... は ... です structure is not affected by person or number.
  ex. A さんは　べんごしです。　"Mr. A is a lawyer."
  　　A さんと　B さんは　べんごしです。　"Mr. A and Mrs. B are lawyers."

- Particle か. Question marker.
  The formation of questions in Japanese is easy. Put か at the end of a sentence and it becomes a question. No change in word order is required even when the question contains interrogative words such as who, what, when, etc. Intonation normally rises on the particle か only, i.e., ...ですか. ↗

- はい and いいえ
  はい is virtually the same as "yes." いいえ is virtually the same as "no." It is better, however, to think of はい as meaning, "That's right," and いいえ as meaning, "That's wrong." Otherwise negative questions can be a problem. Namely, to the question, じゃ、バナナが　ありませんか, "So you have no bananas?" the reply is はい、ありません, "That's right, we have none." Or いいえ、あります, "That's wrong, we have some."

- Omission of topic (noun 1)
  When it is obvious to the other person what the topic is, it is generally omitted.
  ex. ［わたしは］スミスです。　"(As for me) I'm Smith."
  But when it is necessary to make the topic clear, it is not omitted.
  ex. こちらは　スミスさんです。　"This is Mr. Smith."

- ではありません。／じゃありません。
  Negative form of です. じゃ is more informal than では.

NOTES

1. たなかさん
   さん is a title of respect added to a name, so it cannot be used after one's own name. さん may be used with both male and female names, and with either surname or given name. It may even be suffixed to the name of an occupation.
   ex. べんごしさん, "Mr. Lawyer."

2. こちらは　スミスさんです。
   こちら, "this one," implies "this person here" and is a polite way of saying "this person."

3. はじめまして。
   Salutation used on meeting a person for the first time. It is a form of the verb はじめる, "to begin."

4. ［わたしは］スミスです。
   "My name's Smith." (*lit.* "I'm Smith.")
   Especially in conversational Japanese, わたし, "I," is hardly ever used. あなた, "you," is similarly avoided, especially when addressing superiors, in which case the person's surname, title, or occupation is used when necessary.

5. どうぞ　よろしく。
   A phrase used when being introduced, it is usually combined with はじめまして. It is also used when taking one's leave after having asked a favor. よろしく means "good" and is a request for the other person's favorable consideration in the future. It can also be used as follows: たなかさんに　よろしく. "Please give my regards to Mr. Tanaka."

6. とうきょうでんきの（たなかです。）
   The possessive particle の indicates ownership or attribution and comes after the noun it modifies, like " 's" in English. Here it shows that Mr. Tanaka belongs to, in the sense that he works for, Tokyo Electric. Japanese customarily give their company and position when being introduced.

7. だれ／どなた, "who?"
   The basic word for "who" is だれ, but どなた is more polite.
   ex. こちらは　だれですか。　"Who is this?"
   　　 こちらは　どなたですか。　"Might I ask who this is?"

PRACTICE

❏ KEY SENTENCES

1. ［わたしは］スミスです。
2. ［わたしは］ABCの　スミスです。
3. こちらは　たなかさんです。
4. たなかさんは　べんごしではありません。

1. My name's Smith.
2. I'm Smith from ABC.
3. This is Mr. Tanaka.
4. Mr. Tanaka is not a lawyer.

EXERCISES

I Practice the following pattern by changing the underlined part as in the example given.

  ex. ［わたしは］ スミスです。

   1. アメリカたいしかんの　スミス

   2. アメリカじん

   3. べんごし

II Make dialogues by changing the underlined parts as in the examples given.

  A. *ex.* Q: ［あなたは］ スミスさんですか。

       A: はい、スミスです。

         1. たなか

  B. *ex.* Q: ［あなたは］ にほんじんですか

      A*a*: はい、にほんじんです。

      A*b*: いいえ、にほんじんではありません。

         1. べんごし

         2. ひしょ

  C. *ex.* Q: ［あなたは］ にほんじんですか、ちゅうごくじんですか。

       A: にほんじんです。

         1. アメリカじん、ドイツじん

         2. がくせい、かいしゃいん

         3. べんごし、ひしょ

  D. *ex.* Q: ［あなたは］ どなたですか。

       A: スミスです。

         1. たなか

         2. アメリカたいしかんの　たなか

         3. にほんぎんこうの　たなか

  E. *ex.* Q: こちらは　どなたですか。

       A: スミスさんです。

         1. たなかさん

         2. にほんぎんこうの　たなかさん

❏ Vocabulary

わたし	I
アメリカたいしかん	American Embassy
アメリカ	America
たいしかん	embassy
アメリカじん	an American
～じん	person (suffix)
あなた	you
か	= ? (question marker, particle)
はい	yes, certainly
にほんじん	a Japanese
にほん	Japan
いいえ	no
ひしょ	secretary
ちゅうごくじん	a Chinese
ちゅうごく	China
ドイツじん	a German
ドイツ	Germany
がくせい	student
かいしゃいん	company employee
どなた	who
にほんぎんこう	Bank of Japan
ぎんこう	bank

SHORT DIALOGUES

1. スミス ： たなかさんですか。
   たなか ： はい、たなかです。
   スミス ： たなかさんは　がくせいですか。
   たなか ： いいえ、がくせいではありません。かいしゃいんです。

Smith:	Are you Mr. Tanaka?
Tanaka:	Yes, I am.
Smith:	Are you a student?
Tanaka:	No, I'm not a student. I'm a company employee.

2. Mr. Hayashi introduces Ms. Yamada to Mr. Tanaka.
   はやし ： ごしょうかいします。こちらは　やまださんです。スミスさ
   　　　　　んの　ひしょです。こちらは　たなかさんです。
   やまだ ： はじめまして。やまだです。どうぞ　よろしく。
   たなか ： はじめまして。たなかです。どうぞ　よろしく。

Hayashi:	Let me introduce you. This is Ms. Yamada. She is Mr. Smith's secretary. This is Mr. Tanaka.
Yamada:	How do you do. My name's Yamada. I'm very glad to meet you.
Tanaka:	How do you do. My name's Tanaka. I'm very glad to meet you.

❏ **Vocabulary**

ごしょうかいします   Let me introduce you.
やまだ   a surname

QUIZ

I Supposing you are Mr. Smith in the opening dialogue, answer the following questions.

   1. どなたですか。
      A.
   2. にほんじんですか。
      A.
   3. かいしゃいんですか、べんごしですか。
      A.

II Complete the questions so that they fit the answers.

   1. （　　　）ですか。
      はい、スミスです。
   2. スミスさんは（　　　）ですか。
      いいえ、ドイツじんではありません。
   3. スミスさんは（　　　）ですか、かいしゃいんですか。
      べんごしです。
   4. こちらは（　　　）ですか。
      たなかさんです。

III Put the appropriate particles in the parentheses.

   1. こちら（　　　）やまださんです。
   2. はやしさんは　べんごしです（　　　）、かいしゃいんです（　　　）。
      かいしゃいんです。
   3. スミスさんは　ABC（　　　）べんごしです。

IV Translate into Japanese.

   1. I'm Smith.
   2. How do you do. I'm glad to meet you.
   3. Ms. Yamada, this is Mr. Tanaka of Tokyo Electric.
   4. Is Mr. Smith American or German?

LESSON
2

わたしの　めいしです
ADDRESS AND TELEPHONE NUMBER

Mr. Tanaka gives Mr. Smith his business card. Mr. Smith cannot read *kanji.*

たなか　：　わたしの　めいしです。どうぞ。

スミス　：　どうも　ありがとうございます。これは　たなか
　　　　　　さんの　なまえですか。

たなか　：　ええ、そうです。たなかです。

スミス　：　これは？

たなか　：　かいしゃの　なまえです。とうきょうでんきです。

スミス　：　これは　かいしゃの　でんわばんごうですか。

たなか　：　はい、かいしゃのです。(03) 3400-9031です。うちの
　　　　　　でんわばんごうは　(045) 326-8871です。

Tanaka:　　This is my business card. Please...
Smith:　　Thank you very much. Is this (your) name?
Tanaka:　　Yes. That's right. Tanaka.
Smith:　　And this?
Tanaka:　　(That's) the name of my company, Tokyo Electric.
Smith:　　Is this the company's telephone number?
Tanaka:　　Yes, it's the company's (telephone number). (03) 3400-9031. (My) home telephone
　　　　　　number is (045) 326-8871.

❏ **Vocabulary**

わたしの	my
めいし	business card (*lit.* "name card")
どうぞ	please (accept)
どうも　ありがとう　ございます	Thank you very much.
どうも	very much

7

ありがとう　ございます	(I am) grateful
これ	this
なまえ	name
ええ	yes
そうです	That's right.
これは？	as for this?
かいしゃ	company
でんわばんごう	telephone number
でんわ	telephone
ばんごう	number
かいしゃのです	It is the company's.
うち	home

NOTES

1. めいし
Japanese, particularly professional people, carry business cards which they exchange during introductions. A few handwritten words on a business card can serve as a convenient introduction.

2. これは　たなかさんの　なまえですか。
Note that although addressing Mr. Tanaka, Mr. Smith uses his name rather than saying あなたの, "your." (See Note 4, p. 3.)

3. ええ。
"Yes." Less formal than はい.

4. そうです。
When replying to questions that end with ですか, そう can be used instead of repeating the noun.

5. これは？
A rising intonation on the particle は makes this informal phrase a question without using the question marker か.

6. かいしゃのです。
Short for かいしゃの　でんわばんごうです. This sort of abbreviated expression is often used in Japanese.

7. (03) 3400-9031
Spoken as ゼロ　さんの　さん　よん　ゼロ　ゼロの　きゅう　ゼロ　さん　いち. The area code (Tokyo's is 03), the exchange and the number are joined by the particle の. In telephone numbers 0 is often pronounced ゼロ in Japanese.

8. なに／なん, "What"
"What" is なに, but it often becomes なん, as in これは　なんですか. "What is this?"

9. なんばん, "What number?"

   ex. たなかさんの　でんわばんごうは　なんばんですか。"What is Mr. Tanaka's telephone number?"

PRACTICE

❏ KEY SENTENCES

1. これは　めいしです。
2. これは　めいしではありません。
3. これは　たなかさんの　とけいです。これは　たなかさんのです。
4. かいしゃの　でんわばんごうは　(03) 3400-9031です。

1. This is a business card. (These are business cards.)
2. This is not a business card.
3. This is Mr. Tanaka's watch. This is Tanaka's.
4. The company's telephone number is (03) 3400-9031.

❏ Vocabulary

とけい   clock, watch

EXERCISES

I Look at the pictures and practice the following pattern by changing the underlined parts as in the example given.

   ex. これは　<u>めいし</u>です。

     1. ほん
     2. しんぶん
     3. とけい
     4. かぎ
     5. でんわ
     6. くるま

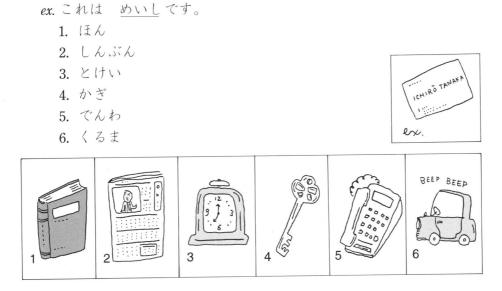

II Make dialogues by changing the underlined parts as in the examples given.

A. *ex.* Q: これは　<u>めいし</u>ですか。

A*a*: はい、<u>めいし</u>です。

A*b*: いいえ、<u>めいし</u>ではありません。<u>ほん</u>です。

   1. ほん、しんぶん

   2. じゅうしょ、でんわばんごう

B. *ex.* Q: これは　なんですか。

     A: <u>なまえ</u>です。

       1. とけい

       2. かぎ

       3. でんわ

C. *ex.* Q: これは　<u>たなかさん</u>の　くるまですか。

     A*a*: はい、<u>たなかさん</u>の　くるまです。<u>たなかさん</u>のです。

     A*b*: いいえ、<u>たなかさん</u>の　くるまではありません。<u>たなかさ</u>

     <u>ん</u>のではありません。

       1. スミスさん

       2. かいしゃ

D. *ex.* Q: これは　だれの　ほんですか。

     A: <u>たなかさん</u>のです。

       1. スミスさん

       2. かいしゃ

       3. わたし

III Numbers: Memorize the numbers from 0 to 20.

0 ゼロ／れい	7 しち／なな	14 じゅうし／じゅうよん
1 いち	8 はち	15 じゅうご
2 に	9 きゅう／く	16 じゅうろく
3 さん	10 じゅう	17 じゅうしち／じゅうなな
4 し／よん	11 じゅういち	18 じゅうはち
5 ご	12 じゅうに	19 じゅうきゅう／じゅうく
6 ろく	13 じゅうさん	20 にじゅう

IV Telephone numbers: Practice saying the following telephone numbers.

(03) 3742-8955. ゼロ　さんの　さん　なな　よん　にの　はち　き ゅ　ご　ご。

3401-5634. さん　よん　ゼロ　いちの　ご　ろく　さん　よん。

ゼロ, よん, なな and きゅう are used for 0, 4, 7 and 9 in telephone numbers.

V　Make dialogues by changing the underlined parts as in the example given.

ex. Q: かいしゃの　でんわばんごうは　なんばんですか。

A: 3742-8920です。

1. ぎんこう、3325-8871

2. がっこう、（03）3781-6493

3. たなかさんの　うち、3956-4158

❏ **Vocabulary**

ほん	book
しんぶん	newspaper
かぎ	key
くるま	car
じゅうしょ	address
なん	what
だれの	whose
なんばん	what number?
〜ばん	number (suffix).
がっこう	school

SHORT DIALOGUES

1. はやし：これは　スミスさんの　とけいですか。
   たなか：はい、スミスさんの　とけいです。

   Hayashi:　Is this Mr. Smith's watch?
   Tanaka:　Yes, it's Mr. Smith's watch.

2. はやし：これは　スミスさんの　とけいですか。
   スミス：はい、わたしの　とけいです。

   Hayashi:　Is this your watch?
   Smith:　Yes, it's my watch.

3. はやし：これは　たなかさんの　ほんですか。
   スミス：いいえ、たなかさんのではありません。わたしのです。

   Hayashi:　Is this Mr. Tanaka's book?
   Smith:　No, it's not Mr. Tanaka's. It's mine.

4. スミス： たいしかんの　でんわばんごうは　なんばんですか。
   ひしょ： 3325-7634です。
   スミス： ぎんこうの　でんわばんごうは？
   ひしょ： 3423-6502です。

Smith: What is the telephone number of the embassy?
Secretary: It's 3325-7634.
Smith: What about the telephone number of the bank?
Secretary: It's 3423-6502.

QUIZ

I   Look at the illustrated business card and the answer the questions.

   1. これは　なんですか。
   2. これは　かいしゃの　なまえですか。
   3. これは　たなかさんの　うちの　じゅうしょですか、かいしゃのですか。
   4. これは　たなかさんの　うちの　でんわばんごうですか。
   5. たなかさんの　かいしゃの　でんわばんごうは　なんばんですか。

II   Complete the questions so that they fit the answers.

   1. これは（　　）の　でんわばんごうですか。
      いいえ、かいしゃのではありません。うちのです。
   2. これは（　　）の　じゅうしょですか。
      たなかさんのです。
   3. これは（　　）ですか。
      とけいです。
   4. たなかさんの　うちの　でんわばんごうは　（　　）ですか。
      3325-7634です。

III Put the appropriate particles in the parentheses.

1. こちら（　　　）どなたですか。
2. これ（　　）なんです（　　　）。
   かいしゃ（　　）でんわばんごうです。
   これ（　　）？
   かいしゃ（　　）じゅうしょです。
3. これ（　　）わたし（　　　）くるまではありません。かいしゃ（　　　）です。

IV Translate into Japanese.

1. This is Mr. Tanaka.
2. This is Mr. Tanaka's business card.
3. This is not Mr. Tanaka's home telephone number. It is that of his company.
4. What is your company's telephone number?

LESSON
3

いま　なんじですか
DAY AND TIME

Mr. Smith goes to a department store. It is not open yet.

スミス：　　　　　　すみません。いま　なんじですか。
おんなの　ひと：　9じ50ぷんです。
スミス：　　　　　　デパートは　なんじからですか。
おんなの　ひと：　10じからです。
スミス：　　　　　　なんじまでですか。
おんなの　ひと：　ごご　6じまでです。
スミス：　　　　　　どうも　ありがとう。
おんなの　ひと：　どういたしまして。

■ デパートは　10じから　6じまでです。

Smith: Excuse me. What time is it now?
Woman: It's 9:50.
Smith: What time does the store open?
Woman: It opens at 10:00.
Smith: How late does it stay open?
Woman: It stays open until 6 P.M.
Smith: Thank you very much.
Woman: Don't mention it.

■The department store's hours are from 10:00 to 6:00.

❏ Vocabulary

すみません	Excuse me./I'm sorry.
いま	now
なんじ	what time?
〜じ	o'clock
おんなの　ひと	woman
おんな	woman, female
ひと	person
9じ	9 o'clock
50ぷん	50 minutes
〜ふん、〜ぷん	minute
デパート	department store
から	from (particle)
10じ	10 o'clock
まで	until (particle)
ごご	P.M.
6じ	6 o'clock
どう　いたしまして	Don't mention it./You're welcome. (*lit.* "What have (I) done?")

NOTES

1. すみません。
   すみません, "Excuse me," prefaces a request, such as asking a stranger for information. It can also mean "Thank you," "I'm sorry," or "Pardon me."

2. 10じからです。ごご　6じまでです。
   "From 10 o'clock." "Until 6 P.M."
   Particles follow words, rather than precede them. (See Grammar II, p. 38.)
   Note that instead of 10じから　ひらきます, "It is open from 10 o'clock," the word "open" is omitted. When the verb is understood, only the key words (here 10じから, 6 じまで) followed by です are used.

3. When
   Hour. なんじ, "what time?"
   Day of the week. なんようび, "which day of the week?"
   Day of the month. なんにち, "which day of the month?"
   Month. なんがつ, "which month?"
   Time in general. いつ, "when?"

PRACTICE

❏ KEY SENTENCES

1. いま　ごぜん　10 じです。
2. ひるやすみは　12 じから　1 じはんまでです。
3. きょうは　6 がつ 18 にちです。
4. あしたは　はやしさんの　たんじょうびです。
5. きのうは　きんようびでした。
6. きのうは　もくようびではありませんでした。

1. It's 10 A.M. now.
2. Lunch time is from 12:00 to 1:30.
3. Today is June 18.
4. Tomorrow is Mr. Hayashi's birthday.
5. Yesterday was Friday.
6. Yesterday was not Thurdsay.

❏ Vocabulary

ごぜん	A.M.
ひるやすみ	lunch time
ひる	noon
やすみ	rest (period)
1 じはん	half past (*lit.* "1 o'clock half")
はん	half
きょう	today
6 がつ 18 にち	June 18
6 がつ	June (*lit.* "sixth month")
〜がつ	month (See Exercise VII, p. 19.)
18 にち	18th day
〜にち	day (See Exercise VI, p. 19.)
あした	tomorrow
たんじょうび	birthday
きのう	yesterday
きんようび	Friday
〜ようび	day of the week (See Exercise V, p. 18.)
でした	was
もくようび	Thursday
ではありませんでした	was not

EXERCISES

I Numbers: Memorize the numbers from 20 to 100.

20 にじゅう　　50 ごじゅう　　　　　　80 はちじゅう
30 さんじゅう　60 ろくじゅう　　　　　90 きゅうじゅう
40 よんじゅう　70 しちじゅう／ななじゅう　100 ひゃく

Intermediate numbers are made by adding to the above numbers, the numbers from 1 to 9.

ex. 21, にじゅういち

II Look at the pictures and practice the following pattern as in the example given.

ex. いま　ごぜん　1じです。

1. 3じ
2. ごご　4じ10ぷん
3. ごぜん　6じ15ふん
4. 9じはん

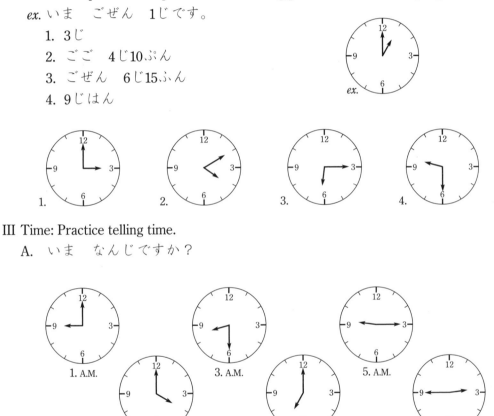

ex.

1.　　　2.　　　3.　　　4.

III Time: Practice telling time.

A.　いま　なんじですか？

1. A.M.　2. P.M.　3. A.M.　4. P.M.　5. A.M.　6. P.M.

B. なんじから　なんじまでですか？

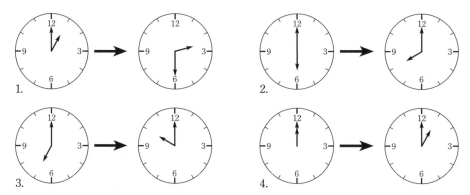

1.   2.

3.   4.

IV Make dialogues by changing the underlined parts as in the examples given.

A. *ex.* Q: いま　なんじですか。

A: 8じです。

1. 6:00
2. 3:00 P.M.
3. 9:30 A.M.

B. *ex.* Q: パーティーは　なんじからですか。

A: 7じからです。

1. ぎんこう、9:00
2. えいが、4:45
3. かいぎ、9:30

C. *ex.* Q: デパートは　なんじまでですか。

A. ごご　6じまでです。

1. ひるやすみ、1:30
2. ゆうびんきょく、ごご　5:00
3. しごと、5:15

D. *ex.* Q: ひるやすみは　なんじから　なんじまでですか。

A: 12じから　1じまでです。

1. えいが、3:30、4:45
2. ぎんこう、9:00、3:00

V Days of the week: Memorize the names of the days of the week.

にちようび	Sunday	すいようび	Wednesday	どようび	Saturday
げつようび	Monday	もくようび	Thursday		
かようび	Tuesday	きんようび	Friday		

VI Days of the month: Memorize the days of the month.

ついたち	1st	じゅういちにち	11th	にじゅういちにち	21st
ふつか	2nd	じゅうににち	12th	にじゅうににち	22nd
みっか	3rd	じゅうさんにち	13th	にじゅうさんにち	23rd
よっか	4th	じゅうよっか	14th	にじゅうよっか	24th
いつか	5th	じゅうごにち	15th	にじゅうごにち	25th
むいか	6th	じゅうろくにち	16th	にじゅうろくにち	26th
なのか	7th	じゅうしちにち	17th	にじゅうしちにち	27th
ようか	8th	じゅうはちにち	18th	にじゅうはちにち	28th
ここのか	9th	じゅうくにち	19th	にじゅうくにち	29th
とおか	10th	はつか	20th	さんじゅうにち	30th
				さんじゅういちにち	31st

VII Months: Memorize the names of the months.

いちがつ	January	ごがつ	May	くがつ	September
にがつ	February	ろくがつ	June	じゅうがつ	October
さんがつ	March	しちがつ	July	じゅういちがつ	November
しがつ	April	はちがつ	August	じゅうにがつ	December

VIII Make dialogues by changing the underlined parts as in the examples given.

A. *ex.* Q: きょうは　なんにちですか。
　　　A: 15にちです。
　　　　1. 19にち
　　　　2. 23にち
　　　　3. 27にち

B. *ex.* Q: あしたは　なんようびですか。
　　　A: かようびです。
　　　　1. すいようび
　　　　2. もくようび

C. *ex.* Q: きのうは　なんにちでしたか。
　　　A: 11にちでした。
　　　　1. 12にち
　　　　2. 13にち

D. *ex.* Q: [あなたの]　たんじょうびは　いつですか。
　　　A: 3がつです。
　　　Q: 3がつ　なんにちですか。
　　　A: 3がつ26にちです。

1. 4がつ、15にち
2. 9がつ、21にち
3. 12がつ、18にち

E. *ex.* Q: きのうは　<u>もくようび</u>でしたか。

A: いいえ、<u>もくようび</u>ではありませんでした。<u>きんようび</u>でした。

1. げつようび、かようび
2. すいようび、もくようび
3. どようび、にちようび

❏ **Vocabulary**

パーティー	party
えいが	movie
かいぎ	conference, meeting
ゆうびんきょく	post office
しごと	work
なんにち	which day (of the month)
なんようび	which day (of the week)
いつ	when

SHORT DIALOGUES

1. スミス：いま　なんじですか。
   ひしょ：9じはんです。
   スミス：かいぎは　なんじからですか。
   ひしょ：10じからです。

   Smith: 　What time is it now?
   Secretary: It's 9:30.
   Smith: 　What time does the meeting begin?
   Secretary: It's from 10:00.

2. たなか：なつやすみは　いつからですか。
   スミス：7がつ15にちからです。
   たなか：7がつ15にちは　なんようびですか。
   スミス：どようびです。

   Tanaka: 　When does summer vacation begin?
   Smith: 　　It's from July 15.
   Tanaka: 　What day is July 15?
   Smith: 　　It's Saturday.

QUIZ

I　Read this lesson's opening dialogue and answer the following questions.

1. いま　10じですか。
2. デパートは　なんじからですか。
3. デパートは　7じまでですか。

II　Complete the questions so that they fit the answers.

1. ひるやすみは（　　　　）からですか。
   12じはんからです。
2. きょうは（　　　　）ですか。
   かようびです。
3. きのうは（　　　　）でしたか。
   11にちでした。

III　Put the appropriate particles in the parentheses.

1. きのう（　　　　）きんようびでした。
2. わたし（　　　）かいしゃの　ひるやすみ（　　　）12じからです。
3. デパート（　　　）なんじ（　　　）なんじ（　　　）ですか。

IV　Translate into Japanese.

1. Thank you very much.
2. You're welcome.
3. Excuse me. Until what time does the post office stay open?
4. Today is the 15. Tomorrow is the 16.
5. Today is Thursday. Yesterday was Wednesday.

LESSON
4

いくらですか
HOW MUCH?

Mr. Smith goes shopping in the department store.

デパートの　てんいん：いらっしゃいませ。
スミス：　　　　　　それを　みせてください。
デパートの　てんいん：はい、どうぞ。
スミス：　　　　　　これは　いくらですか。
デパートの　てんいん：3,000えんです。
スミス：　　　　　　それは　いくらですか。
デパートの　てんいん：これも　3,000えんです。
スミス：　　　　　　じゃ、それを　ください。
デパートの　てんいん：はい、ありがとうございます。

Store Clerk:	May I help you, sir? (*lit.* "Welcome!")
Smith:	Would you show me that, please?
Store Clerk:	Certainly, sir. Here you are.
Smith:	How much is this?
Store Clerk:	3,000 yen.
Smith:	How much is that one?
Store Clerk:	This one's 3,000 yen, too.
Smith:	Well then, please give me that one.
Store Clerk:	Very well, sir. Thank you.

❏ Vocabulary

てんいん	store clerk
いらっしゃいませ	Come in!/Welcome! (greeting to customers in stores/restaurants)
それ	that, that one
を	(object marker, particle)
みせて　ください	Please show me.

みせます（みせる）	show
いくら	how much
3,000えん	3,000 yen
〜えん	yen (¥)
も	too (particle)
じゃ	Well then ...
ください	Please give me ...

NOTES

1. これ、それ

Whereas English has only "this" and "that," Japanese has three separate indicators: これ, それ, and あれ. (See Note 5, p. 31.)

これ indicates something near the speaker.

それ indicates something near the person spoken to.

あれ indicates something not near either person.

ex. これは　わたしの　めいしです。 "This is my business card."

2. も

The particle も means "too, also, either." It is used in both affirmative and negative sentences.

ex. それは　3,000えんです。これも　3,000えんです。 "That one is ¥3,000. This one is ¥3,000, too."

これは　わたしの　かさじゃありません。それも　わたしのじゃありません。 "This is not my umbrella. That's not mine either."

3. じゃ、それを　ください。

では and じゃ correspond to "well" or "well then," an interjection expressing conclusion or resignation.

4. それを　ください。

ください, "please give me," follows the object (a noun referring to concrete things only) + object marker を. In this case, おねがいします can be used instead of ください.

ex. バナナを　ください。 "Please give me some bananas."

5. いくら、 "how much"

ex. このフィルムは　いくらですか。 "How much is this film?"

❏ KEY SENTENCES

1. これは　とけいです。
2. それも　とけいです。
3. あれは　3,000えんです。
4. これを　ください。
5. あれも　ください。

1. This is a watch.
2. That is a watch, too.
3. That one (over there) is ¥3,000.
4. Give me this one, please.
5. Give me that one (over there), too, please.

❏ Vocabulary

あれ 　　　　　　　　　　　　that (over there)

EXERCISES

I 　Look at the pictures on the next page and practice the following patterns.

A.　Imagine you are Mr. A and say the following.
1. これは　とけいです。
2. それは　かさです。
3. あれは　テレビです。

B.　Now imagine you are Mr. B and say the following.
1. これは　かさです。
2. それは　とけいです。
3. あれは　テレビです。

C.　Imagine you are the clerk and state the prices of the objects illustrated.
1. これは　3,000えんです。
2. それは　3,500えんです。
3. あれも　3,500えんです。

II Numbers: Memorize the numbers from 100 to 1,000,000,000,000 and note how decimals and fractions are read.

100	ひゃく	1,000	せん	10,000	いちまん
200	にひゃく	2,000	にせん	100,000	じゅうまん
300	さんびゃく	3,000	さんぜん	1,000,000	ひゃくまん
400	よんひゃく	4,000	よんせん	10,000,000	せんまん
500	ごひゃく	5,000	ごせん	100,000,000	いちおく
600	ろっぴゃく	6,000	ろくせん	1,000,000,000	じゅうおく
700	ななひゃく	7,000	ななせん	10,000,000,000	ひゃくおく
800	はっぴゃく	8,000	はっせん	100,000,000,000	せんおく
900	きゅうひゃく	9,000	きゅうせん	1,000,000,000,000	いっちょう

Intermediate numbers are made by combining the numbers composing them.

ex. 135 ひゃくさんじゅうご   1,829 せんはっぴゃくにじゅうきゅう

Decimals. (The word for "decimal point" is てん.)

     0 れい, ゼロ

   0.7 れいてんなな

  0.29 れいてんにきゅう

0.538 れいてんごさんはち

Fractions. (ぶん means "part.")

1/2 にぶんの　いち　　1/4 よんぶんの　いち　　2/3 さんぶんの　に

III Make dialogues by changing the underlined parts as in the examples given.

  A. *ex.* Q: これは　いくらですか。

       A:　[それは] <u>2,000えん</u>です。

         1. 1,800えん

2. 1,200えん

3. 7,500えん

B. *ex.* Q: それは　<u>ほん</u>ですか。

A: はい、これは　<u>ほん</u>です。

Q: あれも　<u>ほん</u>ですか。

A: はい、あれも　<u>ほん</u>です。

1. とけい

2. ラジオ

C. *ex.* Q: これは　<u>いくら</u>ですか。

A: それは　<u>3,500えん</u>です。

Q: あれも　<u>3,500えん</u>ですか。

A: はい、あれも　<u>3,500えん</u>です。

1. いくら、5,000えん

2. なん、ラジオ

D. *ex.* Q: それは　<u>3,000えん</u>ですか。

A: はい、これは　<u>3,000えん</u>です。

Q: あれも　<u>3,000えん</u>ですか。

A: いいえ、あれは　<u>3,000えん</u>ではありません。3,500えんです。

1. テープレコーダー、ラジオ

2. たなかさんの　ほん、スミスさんの　ほん

IV Practice the following pattern by changing the underlined part as in the example given.

ex. <u>これ</u>を　ください。

1. それ

2. はいざら

3. みず

4. りんご

5. レシート

❏ **Vocabulary**

かさ	umbrella
テレビ	TV (set)
ラジオ	radio
テープレコーダー	tape recorder
はいざら	ashtray
みず	water
りんご	apple
レシート	receipt

SHORT DIALOGUES

スミス：　すみません。あれは　ラジオですか。
てんいん：いいえ、ラジオではありません。テープレコーダーです。
スミス：　これは　ラジオですか。
てんいん：はい、ラジオです。
スミス：　いくらですか。
てんいん：28,000えんです。
スミス：　では、これを　ください。

Smith: Excuse me. Is that a radio?
Clerk: No, it's not a radio. It's a tape recorder.
Smith: Is this a radio?
Clerk: Yes, it's a radio.
Smith: How much is it?
Clerk: It's ¥28,000.
Smith: Then, I'll take this.

❏ **Vocabulary**

では   well then

QUIZ

I   Imagine you are B in the illustration and answer A's questions.

    1. これは　とけいです。
      それも　とけいですか。
    2. あれは　なんですか。
    3. あれは　いくらですか。
    4. これも　50,000えんですか。
    5. これは　いくらですか。
    6. それも　50,000えんですか。

II Complete the questions so that they fit the answers.

    1. それは　（　　　）ですか。

これは　テープレコーダーです。
2. これは（　　）ですか。
それは　13,000えんです。
3. こちらは（　　）ですか。
たなかさんです。
4. （　　）は　いくらですか。
あれは　3,500えんです。

III Put the appropriate particles in the parentheses.

1. これ（　　）ください。
2. これ（　　）いくらですか。
5,000えんです。
それ（　　）5,000えんですか。
はい、これ（　　）5,000えんです。
あれ（　　）5,000えんですか。
いいえ、あれ（　　）5,000えんではありません。あれ（　　）3,500
えんです。

IV Answer with the appropriate expressions in Japanese.

1. When you want a store clerk to show you an article that is near him, what do you say?
2. When you have decided to buy an article that is near you, what do you say to the clerk?
3. When you want to know the price of an article near you, what do you say?
4. What does a store clerk say when a customer enters the store?

LESSON
5

ひとつ　ください
COUNTING OBJECTS

Mr. Smith buys a camera at a camera shop.

スミス　：　すみません。その　カメラは　いくらですか。
カメラや：　どれですか。
スミス　：　その　ちいさい　カメラです。
カメラや：　これですか。25,000えんです。どうぞ。
スミス　：　これを　ください。それから　フイルムを　みっ
　　　　　　つ　ください。

■ ちいさい　カメラは　25,000えんです。

Smith:　　　Excuse me. How much is that camera?
Salesman: Which one, sir?
Smith:　　　That small camera.
Salesman: This one? It's ¥25,000. Here you are.
Smith:　　　I'll take this. And please let me have three (rolls of) film.

■The small camera is ¥25,000.

❏ Vocabulary

その	that
カメラ	camera
カメラや	camera store, camera seller
～や	store, seller
どれ	which
ちいさい	small (－い adj.)
それから	and
フイルム	film
みっつ	3

NOTES

1. カメラや

   カメラや means not only "camera store" but also the store owner or store clerk. や is added to many things to mean the store or the person selling something.

   ex. はなや, "flower shop, florist"; さかなや, "fish shop, fish seller"; ほんや, "book store, book seller."

2. それから

   それから, "and, and also, and then, after that, in addition," is a connective placed at the beginning of a new sentence to connect it to the previous one.

3. みっつ

   In Japanese there are two numerical systems, the ひとつ, ふたつ, みっつ system and the abstract いち, に, さん system. Counting things can be done in two ways:

   1.   Using the ひとつ, ふたつ, みっつ system independently. (See Exercise III, p. 33.)
   ex. フイルムを　みっつ　ください。 "Please give me three (rolls of) film."

   2.   Using the いち, に, さん system combined with a counter. Two counters are ～まい, for thin, flat objects such as paper, records, etc., and ～ほん (～ぼん, ～ぽん), for long, slender objects such as pencils, bottles, etc. Other counters appear in the appropriate place in the text, and they are listed comprehensively in Appendix I.

～まい （how many ... なんまい）		～ほん （how many ... なんぼん）	
いちまい	しちまい／ななまい	いっぽん	ななほん
にまい	はちまい	にほん	はっぽん
さんまい	きゅうまい	さんぼん	きゅうほん
よんまい	じゅうまい	よんほん	じゅっぽん
ごまい	じゅういちまい	ごほん	じゅういっぽん
ろくまい	じゅうにまい	ろっぽん	じゅうにほん

ex. はがきを　さんまい　ください。 "Please give me three postcards." (*lit.* "three 'sheets of' ")

Note: The ひとつ, ふたつ, みっつ system only goes as far as とお (10), after which the いち, に, さん system is used: じゅういち, じゅうに, じゅうさん, etc.

4. フィルムを　みっつ　ください。
   Note the word order: thing + を + numeral (or numeral and counter) + ください.

5. この　ちいさい　カメラ
   ちいさい is an adjective. Adjectives will be treated in detail in Lesson 13 and Lesson 14. In Lesson 4 it was pointed out that there are three words for this and that: これ, それ, and あれ. The demonstratives この, その, and あの are used with nouns and have similar meanings from the viewpoint of the speaker. Study the following diagram and the chart (see Appendix F) to understand the meaning of these words.

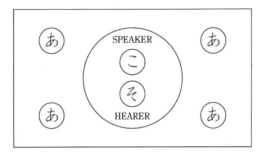

6. いくつ、 "How many?"
   ex. フィルムを　ください。 "Please give me some film."
   はい、いくつですか。 "Certainly sir, how many would you like?"

PRACTICE

❏ KEY SENTENCES

1. この　カメラは　25,000えんです。
2. この　りんごは　ひとつ　200えんです。
3. これは　にほんの　カメラです。
4. その　ちいさい　でんちを　みっつ　ください。

1. This camera is ¥25,000.
2. One of these apples is ¥200.
3. This is a Japanese camera.
4. Please give me three of those small batteries.

❑ Vocabulary

この	this
ひとつ	1
でんち	battery

EXERCISES

I Look at the picture and practice how to use これ／この, それ／その, and あれ／あの.

　　1. これは　30,000えんです。
　　　　この　カメラは　30,000えんです。
　　2. それは　20,000えんです。
　　　　その　とけいは　20,000えんです。
　　3. あれは　10,000えんです。
　　　　あの　テープレコーダーは　10,000えんです。

II Make dialogues by changing the underlined parts as in the examples given.
　　A. *ex.* Q: <u>その　カメラ</u>は　いくらですか。
　　　　　　　A: <u>これ</u>は　30,000えんです。
　　　　　　　　1. この　ラジオ、それ
　　　　　　　　2. あの　テープレコーダー、あれ

B. *ex.* Q: これは　にほんの　くるまですか。
　　　　A: いいえ、にほんのではありません。ドイツのです。
　　　　　　1. アメリカ、イギリス
　　　　　　2. イタリア、フランス

C. *ex.* Q: これは　どこの　カメラですか。
　　　　A: にほんの　カメラです。
　　　　　　1. ドイツ
　　　　　　2. アメリカ

D. *ex.* Q: あの　あかい　かさは　いくらですか。
　　　　A: あれは　5,000えんです。
　　　　　　1. ちいさい　カメラ、20,000えん
　　　　　　2. ドイツの　とけい、10,000えん

E. *ex.* Q: はやしさんの　かさは　これですか。
　　　　A: はい、それです。
　　　　　　1. それ、これ
　　　　　　2. あれ、あれ

F. *ex.* Q: はやしさんの　かさは　どれですか。
　　　　A: これです。
　　　　　　1. にほんごの　テープ
　　　　　　2. スミスさんの　くるま

III Practice how to count things.

1 ひとつ	4 よっつ	7 ななつ	10 とお
2 ふたつ	5 いつつ	8 やっつ	11 じゅういち
3 みっつ	6 むっつ	9 ここのつ	12 じゅうに

IV Look at the pictures on the next page and practice the following pattern by changing the underlined parts as in the example given.

　ex. この　フイルムを　ふたつ　ください。
　　　1. この　でんち、ひとつ
　　　2. その　おおきい　りんご、いつつ
　　　3. この　みかん、2キロ
　　　4. 100えんの　きって、10まい
　　　5. ビール、12ほん

ex.

❏ **Vocabulary**

あの	that, that one (over there)
イギリス	United Kingdom
イタリア	Italy
フランス	France
どこ	where, belonging to or coming from what place?
あかい	red (－い adj.)
にほんご	Japanese language
〜ご	language
テープ	tape
ふたつ	2
おおきい	big (－い adj.)
いつつ	5
みかん	tangerine
2キロ	2 kilograms
〜キロ	kilogram
きって	postage stamp
10まい	*lit.* 10 (sheets)
〜まい	(counter)
ビール	beer
12ほん	12 bottles
〜ほん、〜ぼん、〜ぽん	(counter)

SHORT DIALOGUES

1. スミス：　すみません。ラジオを　みせてください。
   てんいん：どの　ラジオですか。
   スミス：　あの　ちいさい　ラジオです。
   てんいん：はい、どうぞ。

Smith:	Excuse me. Would you show me that radio?
Clerk:	Which radio?
Smith:	That small radio (over there).
Clerk:	Certainly, sir. Here you are.

2. スミス： 　あの　かさは　いくらですか。

てんいん：　どれですか。

スミス： 　あの　あおい　かさです。

てんいん：　あれは　5,000えんです。

スミス： 　あの　くろい　かさも　5,000えんですか。

てんいん：　いいえ、あれは　7,000えんです。

スミス： 　じゃ、あの　あおい　かさを　ください。

Smith:	How much is that umbrella (over there)?
Clerk:	Which one?
Smith:	That blue one.
Clerk:	That's ¥5,000.
Smith:	Is that black umbrella ¥5,000, too?
Clerk:	No, it's ¥7,000.
Smith:	Well then, I'll take that blue one.

❏ **Vocabulary**

どの	which
あおい	blue (− い adj.)
くろい	black (− い adj.)

QUIZ

I　Supposing you are the store clerk in the illustration. Answer the customer's questions.

　1. この　ドイツの　カメラは　いくらですか。

　2. その　カメラも　ドイツのですか。

　3. その　カメラは　いくらですか。

　4. あの　ちいさい　ラジオは　どこのですか。

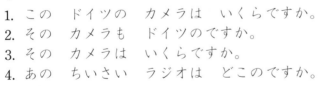

にほんの　ラジオ

にほんの　カメラ

¥50000　¥35000

ドイツの　カメラ

II Complete the questions so that they fit the answers.

1. この　でんちは　（　　　）　ですか。
   100えんです。
2. （　　　）は　いくらですか。
   あれは　30,000えんです。
3. あれは（　　　）の　きってですか。
   いいえ、イギリスのではありません。
   （　　　）のですか。
   アメリカのです。

III Put the appropriate particles in the parentheses. (If a particle is not required, put an X in the parentheses.)

1. これ（　　　）にほん（　　　）テープレコーダーです。その　テープ
   レコーダー（　　　）にほん（　　　）です。
2. カメラ（　　　）みせてください。
3. ビール（　　　）15ほん（　　　）ください。
4. これ（　　　）150えんです。
5. この（　　　）りんご（　　　）ひとつ（　　　）200えんです。

IV Translate into Japanese.

1. How much is this?
2. How much is this radio?
3. My watch is not Japanese. It is American.
4. Please show me that small tape recorder.
5. Please give me 3 (rolls of) film.
   Which film?
   That film.

LESSON

きょうとに いきます
GOING AND COMING

Mr. Tanaka meets Mr. Hayashi at Tokyo Station. Mr. Hayashi looks as if he is going on a trip.

たなか： あ、はやしさん。しゅっちょうですか。

はやし： ええ。

たなか： どこに いきますか。

はやし： きょうとの ししゃに いきます。

たなか： ひとりで いきますか。

はやし： いいえ、かいしゃの ひとと いきます。

たなか： おおさかにも いきますか。

はやし： いいえ、おおさかには いきません。

たなか： いつ とうきょうに かえりますか。

はやし： あさって かえります。

■ はやしさんは かいしゃの ひとと きょうとの ししゃ
　 に いきます。そして あさって とうきょうに かえり
　 ます。

Tanaka:	Ah, Mr. Hayashi, is it a business trip (you're going on)?
Hayashi:	Yes.
Tanaka:	Where are you going?
Hayashi:	I'm going to our branch office in Kyoto.
Tanaka:	Are you going alone?
Hayashi:	No, I'm going with a person from the company.
Tanaka:	Are you going to Osaka, too?
Hayashi:	No, we're not going to Osaka.
Tanaka:	When are you coming back to Tokyo?
Hayashi:	We're returning the day after tomorrow.

37

■ Mr. Hayashi is going to the company's branch office in Kyoto with a colleague. They will return to Tokyo the day after tomorrow.

❑ **Vocabulary**

あ	ah
しゅっちょうですか	Is it a business trip (you're going on)?
しゅっちょう	business trip
に	to (particle)
いきます（いく）	go, is going
きょうと	Kyoto (city and prefecture)
ししゃ	branch office
ひとりで	alone
と	with (particle)
おおさか	Osaka (city and prefecture)
とうきょう	Tokyo (city and prefecture)
かえります（かえる）	return, come back
あさって	the day after tomorrow
そして	and then

GRAMMAR II

Lessons 6-7 に／へ verb

1. noun は　place に／へ　いきます
2. noun は　place に／へ　いきますか
   はい、（noun は　place に）いきます
   いいえ、（noun は　place に）いきません

● Particles に／へ

Particles are an important part of Japanese sentence structure. They resemble English prepositions in the way they connect words, but unlike English prepositions, which come before nouns, Japanese particles are postpositions, always coming after nouns. Particles show the grammatical role of nouns in Japanese.

The role of the preposition "to" in English is played by the particles に and へ in Japanese, placed after the noun — something like the English suffix "-ward," as in "northward."

ex. とうきょうに／へ　いきます。 "I am going to Tokyo." (*lit.* " 'Tokyo-ward' I am going.")

Theoretically the use of に and へ are divided as given below, but in actual practice they are interchangeable. In this book, in situations where either might occur, we use に.

へ： expresses direction

ex. ひがしへ　いきます。 "(I) am going toward the east."

に： expresses arrival at a destination

ex. きょねんの　12がつに　にほんに　きました。 "(I) came to Japan last December."

Note that some particles, like か, may come at the end of phrases, clauses, or sentences. See Lesson 1, か; Lesson 9, から, よ, ね; Lesson 10, ね; Lesson 12, が; and Lesson 16, に.

- Verbs

Japanese sentences end with the verb. (です in Grammar I is not strictly speaking a verb, but its use in sentences is similar to that of a verb and so it comes at the end.) The endings of verbs show the tense and whether they are positive or negative.

Tenses of Japanese verbs can be divided roughly into two large categories:

1. Present Form
   Habitual action: *ex.* たなかさんは　まいにち　かいしゃに　いきます。
   "Mr. Tanaka goes to the office (*lit.* company) every day."
   Future: *ex.* ［わたしは］あした　かえります。 "I return/am returning/will return tomorrow."

2. Past Form
   Past: *ex.* ［わたしは］せんしゅう　きょうとに　いきました。 "Last week (I) went to Kyoto."
   Present perfect: *ex.* いま　きました。 "(He) has just come."

In simple sentences like the above, tenses of Japanese verbs closely resemble those in English. However, verbs that occur within a sentence in addition to the main verb at the end (i.e., Before I left home, I turned off the TV), do not necessarily take the same form they would in English. But that kind of sentence is outside the scope of this book and must be studied in Book II.

Note: The − **u** form of the verb given in the vocabulary lists (− **u** (う), − **ku** (く), − **su** (す), − **ru** (る), etc.) is the form found in dictionaries, so it is often called the dictionary form. Used at the end of a sentence, it is less formal in conversations than the − ます form. This book uses only the more polite − ます form.

NOTES

1. A. ひとりで　いきます。
   Number of people takes the particle で.
   ex. ひとりで, "alone, by oneself"
   　　さんにんで, "three of us/them"
   B. かいしゃの　ひとと　いきます。
   Individual or individuals take the particle と, "with."
   ex. たなかさんと, "with Mr. Tanaka"

2. おおさかにも　いきますか。
   いいえ、おおさかには　いきません。
   Mr. Hayashi says he is going to Kyoto, which is close to the important industrial city of Osaka, so Mr. Tanaka asks him if he is going to Osaka too. おおさかにも ...? Note the position after the noun of the particles に, "to, towards," and も, "too, also."
   In his reply, Mr. Hayashi uses the topic marker particle は to show that おおさかに is the topic, "As for Osaka, I am not going there." (See Grammar III, p. 51.) Note that while two particles may normally follow one another, as do にも and には above, は and も never follow the particles が and を, but simply take their place. Similarly, は and も are never used together. One or the other is used.
   ex. スミスさんは　べんごしです。 "Mr. Smith is a lawyer." ブラウンさんも

べんごしです。"Mr. Brown, too, is a lawyer."
も can follow any of the other particles such as に, から, で, etc.

3. あさって　かえります。
Relative time expressions like "yesterday," "next week," "this month" and "last year" do not take particles.

4. そして、あさって　とうきょうに　かえります。
In Japanese many sentences begin with connectives, like そして, meaning "and then," which link them to the previous sentence.

5. A.　どこ, "where"
   ex. どこに　いきますか。"Where are you going?"
   B.　いつ, "when" Time in general.
   ex. いつ　きますか。"When are you coming?"
   C.　だれ／どなた（が）, "who"
   ex. だれが　おおさかに　いきますか。"Who is going to Osaka?"
When the subject is unknown, the particle が should be used after だれ／どなた instead of the topic marker は. (see Grammar III, p. 51.)

PRACTICE

❏ KEY SENTENCES

1. わたしは　あした　ぎんこうに　いきます。
2. この　でんしゃは　とうきょうえきに　いきません。
3. わたしは　きのう　ゆうびんきょくに　いきました。
4. わたしは　せんしゅう　がっこうに　いきませんでした。
5. スミスさんは　きょねん　アメリカから　にほんに　きました。
6. スミスさんは　らいねん　アメリカに　かえります。

1. I'm going to the bank tomorrow.
2. This train doesn't go to Tokyo Station.
3. I went to the post office yesterday.
4. I didn't go to school last week.
5. Mr. Smith came to Japan from America last year.
6. Mr. Smith will go back to America next year.

❏ Vocabulary

でんしゃ	(electric) train
とうきょうえき	Tokyo Station
えき	station
せんしゅう	last week
きょねん	last year
から	from (particle)

きました	came
きます（くる）	come
らいねん	next year

EXERCISES

I Verbs: Memorize the following verbs in their present and past forms.

	Present Form		Past Form	
	aff.	*neg.*	*aff.*	*neg.*
go	いきます	いきません	いきました	いきませんでした
come	きます	きません	きました	きませんでした
return	かえります	かえりません	かえりました	かえりませんでした

II Practice the following by changing the underlined part as in the example given.

    ex.   [わたしは] ぎんこうに いきます。

      1. かいしゃ

      2. アメリカ

III Make dialogues by changing the underlined part as in the examples given.

  A. *ex.* Q: [あなたは] あした かいしゃに いきますか。

        A*a*: はい、いきます。

        A*n*: いいえ、いきません。

          1. ともだちの うち

          2. デパート

          3. たいしかん

  B. *ex.* Q: この でんしゃは とうきょうえきに いきますか。

        A*a*: はい、いきます。

        A*n*: いいえ、いきません。

          1. バス

          2. ちかてつ

  C. *ex.* Q: スミスさんは きのう アメリカに かえりましたか。

        A*a*: はい、かえりました。

        A*n*: いいえ、かえりませんでした。

          1. せんしゅう

          2. せんげつ

          3. きょねん

  D. *ex.* Q: だれが きょう たいしかんに いきますか。

A: たなかさんが　いきます。
　　　1. ともだち
　　　2. たなかさんの　ひしょ

E. *ex.* Q: ［あなたは］いつ　にほんに　きましたか。
　　　A: せんげつ　きました。
　　　　1. せんしゅう
　　　　2. きょねん

F. *ex.* Q: たなかさんは　きのう　どこに　いきましたか。
　　　A: デパートに　いきました。
　　　　1. ゆうびんきょく
　　　　2. ともだちの　うち
　　　　3. ぎんこう

G. *ex.* Q: スミスさんは　だれと　なりたくうこうに　いきましたか。
　　　A: たなかさんと　いきました。
　　　　1. ともだちと
　　　　2. かいしゃの　ひとと
　　　　3. ひとりで

❏ Vocabulary

ともだち	friend
バス	bus
ちかてつ	subway, *lit.* "underground railway"
せんげつ	last month
が	(subject marker, particle)
なりたくうこう	Narita Airport
くうこう	airport

SHORT DIALOGUES

1. たなか：きょう　ぎんこうに　いきますか。
　ひしょ：はい、いきます。
　たなか：ゆうびんきょくにも　いきますか。
　ひしょ：いいえ、ゆうびんきょくには　いきません。

Tanaka:　　Are you going to the bank today?
Secretary: Yes, I am.
Tanaka:　　Will you go to the post office, too?
Secretary: No, I'm not going to the post office.

2. スミス： 　　　　　この　でんしゃは　とうきょうえきに　いきますか。
おとこの　ひと： いいえ、いきません。
スミス： 　　　　　どの　でんしゃが　いきますか。
おとこの　ひと： あの　あおい　でんしゃが　いきます。

Smith:　　　Does this train go to Tokyo Station?
Man:　　　No, it doesn't.
Smith:　　　Which train goes there?
Man:　　　That blue train over there does.

❏ **Vocabulary**

おとこの　ひと	man
おとこ	man, male

QUIZ

I　Read this lesson's opening dialogue and answer the following questions.

  1. はやしさんは　おおさかの　ししゃに　いきますか、きょうとの
ししゃに　いきますか。

  2. はやしさんは　だれと　きょうとの　ししゃに　いきますか。

  3. はやしさんは　いつ　とうきょうに　かえりますか。

II　Complete the questions so that they fit the answers.

  1. （　　　）に　いきますか。
はい、ぎんこうに　いきます。
（　　　）にも　いきますか。
いいえ、ゆうびんきょくには　いきません。

  2. （　　　）にほんに　きましたか。
きょねん　きました。

  3. （　　　）に　いきましたか。
くうこうに　いきました。
（　　　）と　いきましたか。
ひとりで　いきました。

III　Put the appropriate particles in the parentheses. (If a particle is not required,
put an X in the parentheses.)

  1. たなかさんは　あした（　　　）おおさか（　　　）いきます。

  2. やまださんは　かいしゃの　ひと（　　　）くうこう（　　　）いきま
した。

  3. たなかさん（　　　）いつ（　　　）おおさかから　かえりますか。

4. ともだちは　せんしゅう　ひとり　（　　　）アメリカに　かえりました。
5. あした　きょうと　（　　　）いきます。
   おおさかに　（　　　）いきますか。
   いいえ、おおさかに　（　　　）いきません。
6. だれ　（　　　）きましたか。
   やまださんが　きました。

IV Translate into Japanese.

1. Excuse me, does this bus go to Tokyo Station?
2. Mr. Tanaka went to Osaka yesterday with a person from his company. And he will return to Tokyo the day after tomorrow.
3. Mr. Smith came to Japan alone last year.
4. Who went to the airport?
   Mr. Tanaka's secretary went.

LESSON
7

よく いらっしゃいました
GOING BY TAXI

Mr. Smith visits Mr. Tanaka on Sunday.

たなか ： スミスさん、よく いらっしゃいました。
スミス ： こんにちは。
たなか ： どうぞ おはいりください。
スミス ： しつれいします。
たなか ： どうぞ こちらへ。バスで きましたか。
スミス ： いいえ、タクシーで きました。
たなか ： どうぞ おかけください。
スミス ： ありがとうございます。

■スミスさんは にちようびに タクシーで たなかさんの
うちに いきました。

Tanaka: Mr. Smith, how nice of you to come.
Smith: Hello.
Tanaka: Do come in.
Smith: May I?
Tanaka: This way, please. Did you come by bus?
Smith: No. I came by taxi.
Tanaka: Do sit down.
Smith: Thank you.

■ Mr. Smith went to Mr. Tanaka's house by taxi on Sunday.

❑ Vocabulary

よく　いらっしゃいました	How nice of you to come. (*lit.* "Welcome!")
よく	well
いらっしゃいました	came
いらっしゃいます	
（いらっしゃる）	come (polite word for くる)
おはいり　ください	Do come in.
はいります（はいる）	enter
しつれいします	May I? (I'm afraid I'll be disturbing you.)
こちらへ	this way
こちら	this direction
で	by (particle)
タクシー	taxi
おかけ　ください	Please have a seat. (*lit.* "Please sit down.")
かけます（かける）	sit
に	on (particle)

NOTES

1. しつれいします。
"May I?" (*lit.* "I'll be so bold as to do so.")
しつれい essentially means "rudeness" and is used when entering a house or room, passing in front of someone, leaving in the middle of a gathering and so on, in other words, when creating some sort of disturbance and interrupting the status quo. Some people use it as a form of "good-bye," instead of さようなら, when leaving a house or room.

2. バスで　きましたか。
The particle で follows nouns to express means.
ex. バスで, (travel) "by bus"
ペンで, (write) "with a pen"
にほんごで, (speak) "in Japanese"
イヤホーンで, (listen) "with earphones"
ふなびんで, (send) "by sea mail"

3. にちようびに　いきました。
Specific expressions of time take the particle に as in the following:
ex. 5じに, "at 5 o'clock"
どようびに, "on Saturday"
12にちに, "on the 12th"
1960ねんに, "in 1960"

4. なに／なんで, "how"
ex. なんで　いきますか。"How will you go?"
バスで　いきます。"I'll go by bus."
An exception to this pattern is あるいて　いきます, "I'll walk."

PRACTICE

❏ KEY SENTENCES

1. クラークさんは 5がつ18にちに カナダから にほんに きました。
2. クラークさんは らいねんの 3がつに カナダに かえります。
3. わたしは ちかてつで かいしゃに いきます。

1. Mr. Clark came to Japan on May 18 from Canada.
2. Mr. Clark will go back to Canada in March of next year.
3. I go to the office by subway.

❏ Vocabulary

クラーク	Clark
カナダ	Canada

EXERCISES

I Practice the following pattern by changing the underlined part as in the example given.

    ex. ホワイトさんは <u>5がつ18にちに</u> にほんに きました。

      1. 15にちに
      2. 1980ねんに
      3. せんしゅうの もくようびに
      4. せんげつ
      5. おととい
      6. せんしゅう

II Make dialogues by changing the underlined part as in the examples given.

    A. *ex.* Q: ホワイトさんは いつ にほんに きますか。
        A: <u>5がつ18にちに</u> きます。

        1. げつようび
        2. らいしゅうの どようび
        3. らいげつの 15にち
        4. らいねんの 10がつ

    B. *ex.* Q: たなかさんは なんで うちに かえりましたか。
        A: <u>くるまで</u> かえりました。

        1. タクシー
        2. バス
        3. でんしゃ

C. *ex.* Q: はやしさんは　なんねんに　イギリスに　いきましたか。
   A: <u>1981ねんに</u>　いきました。
   　　1. 1975ねん
   　　2. 1982ねん
D. *ex.* Q: だれが　きょう　きょうとの　ししゃに　いきますか。
   A: <u>はやしさんが</u>　いきます。
   Q: <u>はやしさんは</u>　いつ　とうきょうに　かえりますか。
   A: あさって　かえります。
   　　1. たなかさん
   　　2. スミスさん

❏ **Vocabulary**

ホワイト	White
1980ねん	(the year) 1980
〜ねん	year (See Appendix K.)
おととい	the day before yesterday
らいしゅう	next week
らいげつ	next month
なんで	how, by what means
なんねん	what year?

SHORT DIALOGUE

たなか：　クラークさんは　いつ　にほんに　きましたか。
クラーク：きょねんの　5がつ18にちに　きました。
たなか：　きょうとに　いきましたか。
クラーク：ええ、せんしゅう　しんかんせんで　いきました。きんようび
　　　　　に　とうきょうに　かえりました。

Tanaka:	When did you come to Japan?
Clark:	I came on May 18 last year.
Tanaka:	Did you go to Kyoto?
Clark:	Yes, I went (there) by Shinkansen last week. I returned to Tokyo on Friday.

❏ **Vocabulary**

しんかんせん	Shinkansen, New Trunk Line

I Read this lesson's opening dialogue and answer the following questions.

1. だれが　たなかさんの　うちに　いきましたか。
2. スミスさんは　いつ　たなかさんの　うちに　いきましたか。
3. スミスさんは　たなかさんの　うちに　でんしゃで　いきましたか。
4. スミスさんは　たなかさんの　うちに　なんで　いきましたか。

II Complete the questions so that they fit the answers.

1. にちようびに　（　　）に　いきましたか。
   ともだちの　うちに　いきました。
2. たなかさんは　（　　）きょうとから　かえりましたか。
   せんしゅうの　どようびに　かえりました。
3. クラークさんは　（　　）に　おおさかに　いきますか。
   18にちに　いきます。
   （　　）で　いきますか。
   しんかんせんで　いきます。
   （　　）と　いきますか。
   ひとりで　いきます。

III Put the appropriate particles in the parentheses. (If a particle is not required, put an X in the parentheses.)

1. わたしは　バス（　　）かいしゃ（　　）きます。あなた（　　）バスで　きますか。
2. いつ（　　）にほんに　きましたか。
   5がつ18にち（　　）きました。

IV Answer with the appropriate expressions in Japanese.

1. How does one greet a person one meets in the daytime?
2. What does one say to a guest who has just arrived?
3. How does one offer a chair to a guest?

V Translate into Japanese.

1. Please come this way.
2. Do come in.
3. Mr. Tanaka went home yesterday by taxi.
4. Ms. White is going to the Osaka branch office on Friday.

LESSON

にわに　たなかさんが　います

EXISTENCE OF PEOPLE AND THINGS

Let's have a look at Mr. Tanaka's house.

いまに　いすや　テーブルや　テレビが　あります。テーブ
ルの　うえに　しんぶんと　はなが　あります。いまに　た
なかさんの　おくさんが　います。にわに　たなかさんと
おとこの　こが　います。だいどころに　だれも　いません。

There is a chair, a table, a TV set (etc.) in the living room. There are some flowers and a newspaper on (top of) the table. Mrs. Tanaka is in the living room. Mr. Tanaka and a boy are in the
garden. There isn't anybody in the kitchen.

❏ Vocabulary

いま	living room
に	in (particle)
いす	chair
や	and (etc.) (particle)
テーブル	table
あります（ある）	are (for inanimate things)
うえ	top
と	and (particle)
はな	flower
おくさん	(his) wife (See Note 2, p. 161.)
います（いる）	is (for living things)
にわ	garden
おとこの　こ	boy (*lit.* "male child")
こ	child
だいどころ	kitchen
だれも　－ません	nobody is

GRAMMAR III

Lessons 8-9 Existence of People and Things

1. place に　noun が　あります／います
2. noun は　place に　あります／います
3. place には　noun が　あります／います

● あります／います
Both verbs express "being." あります is used for inanimate things (books, buildings, trees, etc.) and います for animate things (people, animals, insects, etc.)

● Particle に
Existence in a place is indicated by the particle に, not へ.
ex. にわに　たなかさんが　います。 "Mr. Tanaka is in the garden."

● Particle が. Subject marker.
When a subject is introduced for the first time, or when the speaker believes the information to be new to the listener, the subject marker が is used after the noun.
ex. バスが　きます。 "The bus is coming."
　　　きのう　やまださんが　きました。 "Mr. Yamada came yesterday."
が is also used when the subject is unknown, i.e., with question words like "who" and "what." (See Note 4, below.)
ex. だれが　きましたか。 "Who came?"
が is used similarly in the reply.
ex. はやしさんが　きました。 "Mr. Hayashi came."

- が→は / に→には

For a neutral description, the following pattern is used.

ex. いっかいに　レストランが　あります。 "There is a restaurant on the first floor."

When you want to talk about the restaurant, "the restaurant" becomes the topic.

ex. レストランは　いっかいに　あります。 "The restaurant is on the first floor."

When you want to talk about what is on the first floor, "on the first floor" becomes the topic.

ex. いっかいには　レストランが　あります。 "On the first floor, there is a restaurant."

- Verb→です

When the verb is understood, です sometimes takes its place at the end of the sentence. In Lesson 6 we see the sentence, "しゅっちょうですか?" and です here is used in place of します.

ex. テレビは　どこに　ありますか。 "Where is the TV set?"
テーブルの　うえです。(for テーブルの　うえに　あります.) "It's on the table."

If it is not certain whether there is a TV or not, です cannot be substituted and あります must be repeated to make the meaning clear.

ex. テーブルの　うえに　テレビが　ありますか。 "Is there a TV set on the table?"
はい、あります。 / はい、テレビが　あります。 "Yes, there is./Yes, there is a TV set."

In this case, one may not say: はい、テレビです。 / はい、テーブルの　うえです。

NOTES

1. いまに　いすや　テーブルや　テレビが　あります。
The particle や is used for "and" when listing two or more things or people and implying the existence of others as well.

2. テーブルの　うえに　しんぶんと　はなが　あります。
The particle と is used for "and" when the existence of nothing or nobody else is implied. From the Japanese sentence it is clear that there is nothing on the table besides the newspaper and the flowers. Note that unlike "and," both と and や are used only to connect nouns. They cannot be used to connect verbs or clauses.

3. だれも　いません。
だれ, "who," combines with the particle も to mean "nobody" when followed by a verb with the negative ending －ません. Similarly, なにも, "nothing," and どこにも, "nowhere," take the negative verb ending －ません.

ex. だれも　きませんでした。 "Nobody came."
たなかさんは　あした　どこにも　いきません。 "Mr. Tanaka is not going anywhere tomorrow."

4. なにが

Like だれ, "who" (see Note 5, p. 40), なに, "what," is never followed by the topic marker は. It always takes the subject marker が.

ex. いすの うえに なにが ありますか。 "What is there on the chair?"
ほんが あります。 "There is a book."

PRACTICE

❏ KEY SENTENCES

1. いっかいに いまが あります。
2. はこの なかに きってと はがきが あります。
3. たなの うえに しゃしんや ほんが あります。
4. まどの ちかくに おんなの こが います。
5. げんかんに だれも いません。
6. とだなの まえに なにも ありません。

1. There is a living room on the first floor.
2. There are stamps and postcards in the box.
3. There are pictures, books (etc.) on the shelf.
4. There is a girl near the window.
5. There isn't anybody in the entrance hall.
6. There isn't anything in front of the cabinet.

❏ Vocabulary

いっかい	first floor, ground floor
〜かい	floor (See Appendix I.)
はこ	box
なか	inside
はがき	postcard
たな	shelf
しゃしん	photograph
まど	window
ちかく	near, close to
おんなの こ	girl (*lit.* "female child")
げんかん	entrance hall
とだな	cabinet
まえ	in front of, before

I Verbs: Memorize the following verbs and their present and past forms.

	Present Form		Past Form	
	aff.	*neg.*	*aff.*	*neg.*
be	あります	ありません	ありました	ありませんでした
be	います	いません	いました	いませんでした

II Practice the following pattern by changing the underlined parts as in the examples given.

    A. *ex.* いまに　テレビが　あります。
        1. とだな
        2. いす
        3. でんわ

    B. *ex.* いまに　こどもが　います。
        1. おとこの　こ
        2. おんなの　こ

III Make dialogues by changing the underlined parts as in the examples given.

    A. *ex.* Q: いっかいに　なにが　ありますか。
           A: いまが　あります。
        1. だいどころ
        2. しょくどう
        3. おてあらい

    B. *ex.* Q: はこの　なかに　なにが　ありますか。
           A: はがきと　きってが　あります。
        1. テーブルの　うえ、はなと　しんぶん
        2. たなの　うえ、しゃしんや　ほん

    C. *ex.* Q: にわに　だれが　いますか。
           A: おとこの　こが　います。
        1. おとこの　こと　おんなの　こ
        2. たなかさん

    D. *ex.* Q: だいどころに　だれが　いますか。
           A: だれも　いません。
        1. げんかん
        2. しょくどう

E. *ex.*　　Q: <u>とだなの　まえに</u>　なにが　ありますか。

　　　　　A: なにも　ありません。

　　　　　　1. いすの　うえ

　　　　　　2. いすの　した

❏ Vocabulary

こども	child
しょくどう	dining room
おてあらい	lavatory
お〜	(Traditionally added to certain words to give them elegance.) (prefix)
なにも　〜ません	nothing is
した	under

SHORT DIALOGUE

おとこの　ひと：　この　ビルには　でんわが　ありますか。

おんなの　ひと：　はい、あります。あそこに　うけつけが　あります
　　　　　　　　　ね。あの　うけつけの　まえに　あります。

おとこの　ひと：　どうも　ありがとう。

Man:　　　Is there a telephone in this building?

Woman:　Yes, there is. There's a reception desk over there, you see? It's in front of the reception desk.

Man:　　　Thank you.

❏ Vocabulary

ビル	building
あそこ	over there, that place (over there)
うけつけ	reception (desk)
ね	You see ... (*lit.* ... "isn't there?")

QUIZ

I　Read this lesson's opening text and answer the following questions.

　1. いまに　なにが　ありますか。

　2. テーブルの　うえに　なにが　ありますか。

　3. いまに　だれが　いますか。

　4. だいどころに　だれが　いますか。

II Complete the questions so that they fit the answers.

1. にわに（　　）が　いますか。
   たなかさんが　います。
2. いまに（　　）が　ありますか。
   いすや　テーブルが　あります。
3. だいどころに（　　）が　いますか。
   だれも　いません。
4. いすの　うえに（　　）が　ありますか。
   なにも　ありません。

III Circle the correct verb of the two in parentheses.

1. たなの　うえに　しゃしんや　ほんが（あります、います）。
2. にわに　たなかさんが（あります、います）。
3. だいどころに　だれも（います、いません）。
4. テレビの　うえに　なにも（あります、ありません）。

IV Put the appropriate particles in the parentheses. (If a particle is not required, put an X in the parentheses.)

1. はこ（　　）なか（　　）きって（　　）あります。
2. テーブル（　　）うえに　はな（　　）しんぶん（　　）あります。
   (There is nothing else there besides the flowers and the newspapers.)
3. はこの　なかに　はがき（　　）きって（　　）あります。(There are other things besides postcards and stamps.)
4. げんかんに　だれ（　　）いますか。
   だれ（　　）いません。

V Translate into Japanese.

1. There are chairs, tables (etc.) in the living room.
2. In the garden (there) are Mr. Tanaka and a boy.
3. Who is in the kitchen?
   There isn't anybody (there).
4. There isn't anything on the chair.

LESSON
9

ゆうびんきょくは　どこに　ありますか
PLACE, LOCATION

Mr. Smith wants to send a parcel home. He is in front of the apartment building asking the superintendent how to go about it.

スミス：　　　この　ちかくに　ゆうびんきょくが　あり
　　　　　　　ますか。
かんりにん：ええ、ありますよ。
スミス：　　　どこですか。
かんりにん：あそこに　スーパーが　ありますね。ゆう
　　　　　　　びんきょくは　あの　スーパーの　となり
　　　　　　　です。あかい　ポストが　ありますから、
　　　　　　　わかりますよ。
スミス：　　　どうも　ありがとう。

■ゆうびんきょくは　スーパーの　となりです。

Smith:	Is there a post office near here?
Superintendent:	Yes, there is.
Smith:	Where is it?
Superintendent:	See that supermarket over there? The post office is next to that supermarket. There's a red mail box, so you can't miss it.
Smith:	Thank you.

■The post office is next to the supermarket.

かんりにん	superintendent
よ	I tell you (particle)
スーパー	supermarket
となり	next to
ポスト	mail box, post box
から	so, because (particle)
わかります（わかる）	understand, see

NOTES

1. ええ、ありますよ。
The particle よ is added to the end of a sentence to call attention to information the speaker thinks the other person does not know.

2. どこですか。
The same as どこに ありますか. です is used in place of に あります. (See Grammar III, p. 51.)

3. あそこに スーパーが ありますね。
"See that supermarket over there?" (*lit.* "There's a supermarket over there, isn't there?")
The particle ね comes at the end of a sentence or phrase and, like "you see?" or "isn't there/it?" in English, seeks the confirmation and agreement of the other person. The particle よ tells, while the particle ね asks.

4. あかい ポストが ありますから
The particle から means "because, so, therefore" and comes after the phrase or clause. The Japanese meaning can be expressed in English in two ways:
"Because there's red mail box," or "there's a red mail box, so ..."

5. どうして, "why"
ex. どうして びょういんは　12じまでですか。"Why is the hospital (only open) until 12 o'clock?"
きょうは　どようびですから。"Because today is Saturday."

PRACTICE

❏ KEY SENTENCES

1. えきの　ちかくに　たてものが　たくさん　あります。
2. ほんやの　まえに　こどもが　5にん　います。
3. タクシーのりばは　えきの　まえです。
4. きょうは　どようびですから、びょういんは　12じまでです。

1. There are many buildings near the station.
2. There are 5 children in front of the book store.
3. The taxi stand is in front of the station.
4. Today is Saturday, so the hospital is (only open) until 12:00.

❏ **Vocabulary**

たてもの	building
たくさん	many, lots of
ほんや	book store
5にん	5 people
～にん	(counter for people) (see Appendix. I.)
タクシーのりば	taxi stand
のりば	*lit.* "boarding place'
びょういん	hospital

EXERCISES

I Practice the following patterns by changing the underlined parts as in the examples given.

A. *ex.* テーブルの　うえに　<u>りんごが</u>　<u>いつつ</u>　あります。

    1.　はがき、3まい

    2.　ビール、2ほん

    3.　はな、たくさん

B. *ex.* にわに　<u>おとこの　こが</u>　<u>ふたり</u>　います。

    1.　おんなの　こ、3にん

    2.　おとこの　ひと、ひとり

II Make dialogues by changing the underlined parts as in the examples given.

A. *ex.* Q: テーブルの　うえに　<u>りんごが</u>　<u>いくつ</u>　ありますか。

    A: <u>みっつ</u>　あります。

    1. はがき、なんまい、3まい

    2. ビール、なんぼん、2ほん

    3. はな、なんぼん、たくさん

B: *ex.* Q: にわに　<u>おとこの　ひとが</u>　なんにん　いますか。

    A: <u>ひとり</u>　います。

    1. おんなの　こ、3にん

    2. おとこの　こ、ふたり

C. *ex.* Q: この　ちかくに　<u>タクシーのりばが</u>　ありますか。

    A: はい、あります。<u>タクシーのりばは</u>　<u>えきの　まえに</u>　あ
ります。

    1. きっぷうりば、えきの　なか

    2. ちかてつの　いりぐち、デパートの　まえ

    3. びょういん、あそこ

    4. くすりや、そこ

D. *ex.* Q: <u>くるまの　かぎは</u>　どこに　ありますか。

    A: <u>ここに</u>　あります。

    1. わたしの　めがね

    2. この　へやの　かぎ

E. *ex.* Q: たなかさんは　どこに　いますか。
A: <u>2かいに</u>　います。
1. にわ
2. となりの　へや
F. *ex.* Q: <u>バスのりばは</u>　どこですか。
A: <u>えきの　まえ</u>です。
1. ほんや、デパートの　となり
2. かいさつぐち、えきの　なか
3. くすりや、こうばんの　となり
4. びょういん、えきの　ちかく

III A. Connect the following sentences using から, "because," as in the example given.
ex. きょうは　やすみです。わたしは　がっこうに　いきません。
きょうは　やすみですから、わたしは　がっこうに　いきません。
1. きょうは　にちようびです。わたしは　かいしゃに　いきません。

B. Read the short dialogues and make the appropriate statements (S) using から.
ex. Q: どうして　きょう　びょういんは　12じまでですか。
A: きょうは　どようびですから。
S: きょうは　どようびですから、びょういんは　12じまでです。
1. Q: どうして　あなたは　きょう　がっこうに　いきませんか。
A: きょうは　にちようびですから。
S:
2. Q: どうして　スミスさんは　くうこうに　いきますか。
A: おくさんが　ひこうきで　きますから。
S:

❏ Vocabulary

ふたり	2 people (See Appendix I.)
ひとり	1 person
いくつ	how many
なんまい	how many sheets
なんぼん	how many bottles
なんにん	how many people
きっぷうりば	ticket office
きっぷ	ticket
〜うりば	*lit.* "selling place"
いりぐち	entrance
びょういん	hospital
くすりや	pharmacy, drug store
くすり	medicine
にくや	meat store
にく	meat
やおや	vegetable store
さかなや	fish store
さかな	fish
パンや	bread store, bakery
パン	bread
さかや	liquor store
そこ	there, that place
ここ	here, this place
めがね	(eye) glasses
へや	room
バスのりば	bus terminal
かいさつぐち	ticket gate
こうばん	police box
やすみ	holiday
どうして	why
ひこうき	airplane

スミス：　きょうの　しんぶんは　どこに　ありますか。
やまだ：　ここに　あります。はい、どうぞ。

Smith:　　　Where is today's paper?
Yamada:　　It's here. Here you are.

QUIZ

I Read this lesson's opening dialogue and answer the following questions.

1. スミスさんは　どこに　いきますか。
2. ゆうびんきょくは　スーパーの　まえですか。

II Complete the questions so that they fit the answers.

1. タクシーのりばは（　　　）ですか。
   あそこです。
2. えきの　ちかくに（　　　）が　ありますか。
   バスのりばや　ゆうびんきょくや　デパートが　あります。
3. ほんやは（　　　）に　ありますか。
   スーパーの　となりに　あります。
4. （　　　）なりたくうこうに　いきますか。
   ともだちが　きますから。
5. テーブルの　うえに　りんごが（　　　）ありますか。
   みっつ　あります。
6. えきの　まえに　おとこの　ひとが（　　　）いますか。
   ふたり　います。

III Put the appropriate particles in the parentheses. (If a particle is not required, put an X in the parentheses.)

1. バスのりば（　　　）どこ（　　　）ですか。
   デパート（　　　）まえ（　　　）あります。
2. テーブルの　うえ（　　　）ビールが　なんぼん（　　　）あります
   か。
   2ほん（　　　）あります。
3. どうして　きょう　かいしゃ（　　　）いきませんか。
   どようびです（　　　）。
4. おてあらい（　　　）どこ（　　　）ありますか。
   あそこです。

IV Translate into Japanese.

1. The liquor store is next to the vegetable store.
2. Excuse me, where is the lavatory?
   It's over there.
3. Ms. White went to Osaka, so she isn't in the office today.
4. Why is the hospital (only open) until 12:00 today?
   Because it's Saturday.
5. There are five children in front of the book store.

LESSON
10

しゅうまつに　なにを　しますか

TICKETS BOUGHT

Mr. Smith and Mr. Tanaka are talking about their plans for the weekend.

たなか：　しゅうまつに　なにを　しますか。
スミス：　にちようびに　ともだちと　かぶきを　みます。
たなか：　いいですね。もう　きっぷを　かいましたか。
スミス：　ええ、せんしゅう　ぎんざの　プレイガイドで
　　　　　かいました。

■ スミスさんは　せんしゅう　ぎんざの　プレイガイドで
　かぶきの　きっぷを　かいました。にちようびに　とも
　だちと　かぶきを　みます。

Tanaka:　　What are you doing this weekend?
Smith:　　 I'm going to see the Kabuki with friends on Sunday.
Tanaka:　　How nice. Have you bought your tickets yet?
Smith:　　 Yes, I bought them last week at a theater booking agency in the Ginza.

■ Mr. Smith bought tickets for the Kabuki at a theater booking agency in the Ginza last week. He is going to see the Kabuki with friends on Sunday.

❏ **Vocabulary**

しゅうまつ	weekend
します（する）	do
かぶき	Kabuki (Japanese theater)
みます（みる）	see
いいですね	*lit.* "It's nice (good, all right)."
いい	good (－い adj.)
もう	already

かいました	bought
かいます（かう）	buy
ぎんざ	Ginza (place name)
プレイガイド	theater booking agency
で	at (particle)

GRAMMAR IV

Lessons 10-12 ... を verb/ ... に ... を verb

1. person は　noun を　verb
2. person は　person に　noun を　verb

● Verbs

	Present Form		Past Form	
	aff.	*neg.*	*aff.*	*neg.*
see	みます	みません	みました	みませんでした
buy	かいます	かいません	かいました	かいませんでした
read	よみます	よみません	よみました	よみませんでした
show	みせます	みせません	みせました	みせませんでした
telephone	でんわを します	でんわを しません	でんわを しました	でんわを しませんでした

● Particle を. Object marker.
Placed after a noun, を indicates that the noun is the object. を is used with verbs such as "see," "read," "drink," "buy," and many others.
ex. テレビを　みます, "(I) watch TV."

● Particle に. Indirect object marker.
In Japanese, the indirect object, or recipient, in the case of verbs such as "give," "teach," "telephone," and so on is indicated by the particle に.
ex. はやしさんは　スミスさんに　でんわを　しました。 "Mr. Hayashi telephoned Mr. Smith."

NOTES

1. いいですね。
Here the particle ね does not seek confirmation or agreement. It is a sharing of the other person's pleasure. Nuances can be conveyed by the amount of stress given any syllable. Compare this ね with the ね in Lesson 9.

2. ぎんざの　プレイガイドで　かいました。
Nouns and place names concerned with actions such as where things are bought, seen, eaten, and so on take the particle で.

3. どこ, "where"

   ex. どこで　テレビを　みますか。"Where do you watch television?"
      いまで　みます。"I watch it in the living room."

4. なに, "what"

   ex. なにを　かいましたか。"What did you buy?"
      きっぷを　かいました。"I bought a/some ticket/tickets."

PRACTICE

❏ KEY SENTENCES

1. ［わたしは］あした　えいがを　みます。
2. たなかさんは　まいにち　うちで　べんきょうを　します。
3. ［わたしは］きのう　レストランで　ひるごはんを　たべました。
4. ［わたしは］きのう　デパートで　なにも　かいませんでした。

1. I am going to see a movie tomorrow.
2. Mr. Tanaka studies at home every day.
3. I had lunch at a restaurant yesterday.
4. I didn't buy anything yesterday at the department store.

❏ Vocabulary

まいにち	every day
まい〜	every (See Appendix K.)
べんきょうを　します	study
（べんきょうを　する）	
レストラン	restaurant
ひるごはん	lunch
ごはん	meal
たべました	ate
たべます（たべる）	eat

I Verbs: Memorize the following verbs and their present and past forms.

	Present Form		Past Form	
	aff.	*neg.*	*aff.*	*neg.*
see	みます	みません	みました	みませんでした
listen	ききます	ききません	ききました	ききませんでした
eat	たべます	たべません	たべました	たべませんでした
drink	のみます	のみません	のみました	のみませんでした
buy	かいます	かいません	かいました	かいませんでした
read	よみます	よみません	よみました	よみませんでした
study	べんきょうを します	べんきょうを しません	べんきょうを しました	べんきょうを しませんでした
shop	かいものを します	かいものを しません	かいものを しました	かいものを しませんでした
give a party	パーティーを します	パーティーを しません	パーティーを しました	パーティーを しませんでした
work	しごとを します	しごとを しません	しごとを しました	しごとを しませんでした
play tennis	テニスを します	テニスを しません	テニスを しました	テニスを しませんでした

II Practice the following patterns by changing the underlined part as in the examples given.

A. *ex.* ［わたしは］えいがを みます。

    1. テレビ

    2. かぶき

    3. え

B. *ex.* ［わたしは］ラジオを ききます。

    1. ニュース

    2. おんがくの テープ

    3. レコードや CD

C. *ex.* ［わたしは］ひるごはんを たべます。

    1. あさごはん

2. ばんごはん
　　　3. サンドイッチと　サラダ

D. *ex.* ［わたしは］<u>おちゃ</u>を　のみます。
　　　1. おさけ
　　　2. スープ
　　　3. くすり

E. *ex.* ［わたしは］<u>はな</u>を　かいます。
　　　1. ざっし
　　　2. きって
　　　3. にほんの　ちず

F. *ex.* ［わたしは］<u>ほん</u>を　よみます。
　　　1. てがみ
　　　2. にほんごの　しんぶん

G. *ex.* ［わたしは］<u>べんきょう</u>を　します。
　　　1. かいもの
　　　2. パーティー
　　　3. しごと
　　　4. テニス

III Make dialogues by changing the underlined parts as in the examples given.
　　Convert verbs to their appropriate form as necessary.

A. *ex.* Q: ［あなたは］こんばん　<u>えいが</u>を　<u>みます</u>か。
　　A*a*: はい、<u>みます</u>。
　　A*n*: いいえ、<u>みません</u>。
　　　1. ほん、よみます
　　　2. にほんごの　べんきょう、します

B. *ex.* Q: ［あなたは］きのう　<u>ほんや</u>で　<u>ほん</u>を　<u>かいました</u>か。
　　A*a*: はい、<u>かいました</u>。
　　A*n*: いいえ、<u>かいませんでした</u>。
　　　1. かいしゃ、しごと、します
　　　2. きっさてん、コーヒー、のみます

C. *ex.* Q: ［あなたは］まいあさ　なにを　のみますか。
　　A: <u>コーヒー</u>を　のみます。
　　　1. こうちゃ
　　　2. ミルク
　　　3. ジュースと　コーヒー

D. *ex.* Q: ［あなたは］きのう　なにを　しましたか。

      A: うちで　ほんを　よみました。

        1. デパートで　くつを　かいます

        2. うちで　にほんごの　べんきょうを　します

        3. びょういんに　いきます

E. *ex.* Q: ［あなたは］きょう　どこで　ひるごはんを　たべますか。

      A: うちで　たべます。

        1. えきの　ちかくの　レストラン

        2. ともだちの　うち

F. *ex.* Q: ［あなたは］いつ　にほんごの　べんきょうを　しますか。

      A: まいにち　します。

        1. まいばん

        2. げつようびと　かようびに

        3. まいしゅう　かようびに

G. *ex.* Q: ［あなたは］しゅうまつに　だれと　テニスを　しますか。

      A: たなかさんと　します。

        1. ともだち

        2. かぞく

H. *ex.* Q: ［あなたは］デパートで　なにを　かいましたか。

      A: なにも　かいませんでした。

        1. たべます

        2. のみます

❏ Vocabulary

え	picture
ききます（きく）	listen
ニュース	news
おんがく	music
レコード	record
CD（シーディー）	CD, compact disc
あさごはん	breakfast (*lit.* "morning meal")
あさ	morning
ばんごはん	dinner (*lit.* "evening meal")
ばん	evening
サンドイッチ	sandwich
サラダ	salad
おちゃ	tea
ちゃ	tea

おさけ	Japanese rice wine
さけ	Japanese rice wine
スープ	soup
ざっし	magazine
ちず	map
よみます（よむ）	read
てがみ	letter
かいもの	shopping
テニス	tennis
こんばん	this evening
きっさてん	coffee shop
コーヒー	coffee
のみます（のむ）	drink
まいあさ	every morning
こうちゃ	black tea
ミルク	milk
ジュース	juice
くつ	shoes
まいばん	every evening
まいしゅう	every week
かぞく	(my) family

SHORT DIALOGUE

はやし ：きのう　にほんごの　べんきょうを　しましたか。
ホワイト ：いいえ、しませんでした。
はやし ：どうして　べんきょうを　しませんでしたか。
ホワイト ：ともだちが　うちに　きましたから。

Hayashi:	Did you study Japanese yesterday?
White:	No, I didn't.
Hayashi:	Why didn't you study?
White:	Because some friends came to my house.

QUIZ

I Read this lesson's opening dialogue and answer the following quesitons.

1. スミスさんは　にちようびに　えいがを　みますか、かぶきを　みますか。
2. スミスさんは　ひとりで　かぶきを　みますか。
3. スミスさんは　いつ　かぶきの　きっぷを　かいましたか。
4. スミスさんは　どこで　かぶきの　きっぷを　かいましたか。

II Complete the questions so that they fit the answers.

1. （　　　）に　えいがを　みましたか。
   にちようびに　みました。
2. きょう（　　　）で　ひるごはんを　たべますか。
   えきの　ちかくの　レストランで　たべます。
3. どようびに（　　　）を　しますか。
   ともだちの　うちに　いきます。そして　ともだちの　うちで　ば
   んごはんを　たべます。
4. デパートで（　　　）を　かいましたか。
   なにも　かいませんでした。

III Put the appropriate particles in the parentheses. (If a particle is not required, put an X in the parentheses.)

1. スミスさんは　しょくどう（　　　）います。
2. ホワイトさんは　ちかてつ（　　　）かいしゃ（　　　）いきます。
3. たなかさんは　かいしゃの　ちかくの　レストラン（　　　）ひるご
   はん（　　　）たべました。
4. わたしは　きのう　デパート（　　　）なに（　　　）かいませんでし
   た。
5. しゅうまつに　なに（　　　）しますか。
6. わたしは　まいあさ（　　　）うち（　　　）しんぶん（　　　）よみま
   す。

IV Translate into Japanese.

1. I bought a camera at the department store on Sunday. It was ¥45,000.
2. What did you do yesterday?
   I listened to a tape of Japanese at home in the morning. I went to the Ginza in the afternoon and bought a camera (there).
3. Ms. White doesn't eat anything in the morning.

ブラウンさんの　いちにち
READING REVIEW

　ブラウンさんは　ABCの　べんごしです。そして　スミス
さんの　ともだちです。ブラウンさんは　ことしの　6がつ
に　ひとりで　にほんに　きました。おくさんは　らいしゅ
う　にほんに　きます。

　ブラウンさんの　かいしゃは　とうきょうえきの　ちかく
に　あります。しごとは　げつようびから　きんようびまで
です。

　ブラウンさんは　まいあさ　コーヒーを　のみますが、な
にも　たべません。そして　しんぶんを　よみます。ちかて
つで　かいしゃに　いきます。ときどき　ちかてつで　ほん
や　ざっしを　よみます。

　かいしゃは　9じから　5じはんまでです。レストランや
かいしゃの　しょくどうで　ひるごはんを　たべます。ひる
やすみは　12じはんから　2じまでですから、ときどき　か
いしゃの　ひとと　デパートや　きっさてんに　いきます。

　うちに　7じごろ　かえります。きのうは　かいしゃから
スミスさんの　うちに　いきましたから　11じごろ　うちに
かえりました。

　ブラウンさんは　あした　しんかんせんで　きょうとに
いきます。きょうとの　ししゃで　かいぎを　します。そし
て　きんようびに　とうきょうに　かえります。

Mr. Brown is a lawyer with ABC. And he is a friend of Mr. Smith's. Mr. Brown came to Japan alone this June. His wife will come to Japan next week.

Mr. Brown's company is near Tokyo Station. He works from Monday to Friday.

Mr. Brown drinks coffee every morning, but he doesn't eat anything. And he reads the paper. He goes to his office by subway. Sometimes he reads a book or a magazine on the subway.

His office hours are from 9:00 to 5:30. He has lunch at a restaurant or in the company cafeteria. Lunch time is from 12:30 to 2:00, so sometimes he goes to a department store or a cafe with people from the office.

He gets home about 7:00. Last night he got home about 11:00 because he went from the office to the Smiths' house.

Mr. Brown is going to Kyoto tomorrow on the Shinkansen. He is holding a meeting at the branch office in Kyoto. He will return to Tokyo on Friday.

❏ Vocabulary

ブラウン	Brown
ことし	this year
が	but (particle)
ときどき	sometimes (See Appendix J.)
しょくどう	cafeteria
7じごろ	about 7:00
〜ごろ	about
かいぎを　します	hold a meeting/conference
（かいぎを　する）	

LESSON
12

もしもし、スミスさんの　おたくですか
TELEPHONING

Mr. Kato telephones Mr. Smith.

かとう　：　もしもし、スミスさんの　おたくですか。

スミス　：　はい、そうです。

かとう　：　かとうですが、ごしゅじんは　いらっしゃいます
　　　　　　か。

スミス　：　いま　いません。9じごろ　かえります。

かとう　：　そうですか。では　また　あとで　でんわを　し
　　　　　　ます。

スミス　：　はい、おねがいします。

かとう　：　しつれいします。

スミス　：　さようなら。

■かとうさんは　スミスさんの　うちに　でんわを　しまし
　た が、スミスさんの　ごしゅじんは　いませんでした。

Kato:　　　Hello. Is that Mr. Smith's residence?
Smith:　　Yes, it is.
Kato:　　　This is Kato. Is your husband there?
Smith:　　He's not here now. He'll be back about 9:00.
Kato:　　　I see. Then I'll call again later.
Smith:　　Yes. Please do.
Kato:　　　Good-bye.
Smith:　　Good-bye.

■ Mr. Kato telephoned the Smiths' house but Mr. Smith was not there.

❏ Vocabulary

かとう	a surname
もしもし	hello
おたく	(his) residence
が	(particle) (See Note 3 below.)
ごしゅじん	(your) husband
ご〜	(honorific, referring to someone else's ...)
いらっしゃいます（いらっしゃる）	is (polite word for います)
そうですか	I see.
また	again
あとで	afterwards
おねがいします	Please (do).
しつれいします	good-bye (*lit.* "I'll be rude.")
に	to (particle)

NOTES

1. もしもし。
   This is the conventional beginning of a telephone conversation and may be repeated during the call to confirm whether the other party is still on the line. It is sometimes also like "I say!" used to attract the attention of someone one does not know. (See Lesson 24.) It is best to confine its use to the telephone.

2. スミスさんの　おたく
   The honorific お (or ご as in ごしゅじん) is often prefixed to nouns to mean "your," i.e., おなまえ, "your name." Similarly, おたく means "your house," or, as here, "Mr. Smith's residence." It is very polite.
   The word たく alone is seldom used. うち, "house," is more common. I.e., あれは だれの　うちですか。"Whose house is that?" うち is also used to mean "my/our house" or simply "our," as in うちの　くるま, "our car."

3. A. かとうですが、ごしゅじんは　いらっしゃいますか。
   B. かとうさんは　スミスさんに　でんわを　しましたが、スミスさんは いませんでした。
   This が is a connective, joining two clauses. It can usually be translated as "but," as in B, but sometimes it cannot, as in A. In A, it has no particular meaning. It is just a kind of courteous hesitation and indicates that the phrase before it is merely a preliminary to the principal matter.

4. 9じごろ
   The suffix ごろ, "about," is used to indicate approximate time.
   ex. 3じごろ, "about 3 o'clock"
   9がつごろ, "about September"

5. そうですか。
   When そうですか means "I see," as here, it is said with a falling intonation. It can also mean "Oh, really?" or "Is that so?" and be a question expecting an answer. In that case, it is said with a rising intonation.

6. おねがいします

A very convenient phrase, used when making a request. Literally, it means "I beg you," and the verb may be simply implied, as here, where it means "I beg you (to do that)."

ex. タイプを おねがいします。 "Could you type this, please?"
ぎんざまで おねがいします。 "Please take me to the Ginza." (Said to a taxi driver.)
The replay to おねがいします is often はい、わかりました。 "Certainly./I see."

PRACTICE

❏ KEY SENTENCES

1. ［わたしは］あした べんごしに あいます。
2. ［わたしは］はやしさんに でんわを します。
3. ［わたしは］よく ともだちに てがみを かきます。
4. ［わたしは］あまり えいがを みません。
5. ［わたしは］スミスさんの かいしゃに でんわを しましたが、スミスさんは いませんでした。

1. I am going to see the lawyer tomorrow.
2. I will telephone Mr. Hayashi.
3. I often write to (my) friends.
4. I don't see movies very often.
5. I telephoned Mr. Smith's office, but he wasn't there.

❏ Vocabulary

あいます（あう）	meet
でんわを します	make a phone call
（でんわを する）	
よく	often (See Appendix. J.)
かきます（かく）	write
あまり －ません	does not ... often (See Appendix J.)

EXERCISES

I Verbs: Memorize the following verbs and their present and past forms.

	Present Form		Past Form	
	aff.	*neg.*	*aff.*	*neg.*
telephone	でんわを します	でんわを しません	でんわを しました	でんわを しませんでした
write	かきます	かきません	かきました	かきませんでした
ask	ききます	ききません	ききました	ききませんでした
tell	おしえます	おしえません	おしえました	おしえませんでした
meet	あいます	あいません	あいました	あいませんでした

II Practice the following pattern by changing the underlined part as in the example given.

    ex. ［わたしは］はやしさんに でんわを します。

      1. スミスさん

      2. がっこう

      3. かいしゃ

III Make dialogues by changing the underlined parts as in the examples given.

  A. *ex.* Q: ［あなたは］まいねん ともだちに クリスマスカードを かきますか。

      A*a*: はい、かきます。

      A*n*: いいえ、かきません。

      1. ねんがじょう

  B. *ex.* Q: ［あなたは］だれに でんわを しますか。

      A: たなかさんに します。

      1. ともだち

      2. はは

  C. *ex.* Q: ［あなたは］どこに でんわを しますか。

      A: かいしゃに します。

      1. がっこう

      2. ホテル

D. *ex.* Q: たなかさんは　スミスさんに　なにを　おしえましたか。

    A. <u>たなかさんの　うちの　でんわばんごう</u>を　おしえました。

    1. みせの　なまえ

    2. ないせんばんごう

E. *ex.* Q: たなかさんは　だれに　はやしさんの　じゅうしょを　ききましたか。

    A: <u>ひしょ</u>に　ききました。

    1. スミスさん

    2. かいしゃの　ひと

F. *ex.* Q: ［あなたは］あした　だれに　あいますか。

    A: <u>ともだち</u>に　あいます。

    1. がっこうの　せんせい

    2. はやしさんの　おとうさんと　おかあさん

G. *ex.* Q: ［あなたは］よく　ともだちに　てがみを　かきますか。

    A*a*: <u>はい、よく</u>　かきます。

    A*n*: <u>いいえ、あまり</u>　かきません。

    1. はい、ときどき　　いいえ、ぜんぜん

IV Connect the following sentences using が, "but," as in the example given.

    ex. あしたは　にちようびです。［わたしは］かいしゃで　しごとを　します。

    あしたは　にちようびですが、［わたしは］かいしゃで　しごとを　します。

    1. わたしは　きのう　たなかさんの　うちに　いきました。たなかさんは　いませんでした。

    2. わたしは　きのう　デパートに　いきました。デパートは　やすみでした。

❏ **Vocabulary**

まいねん	every year
クリスマスカード	Christmas card
ねんがじょう	New Year's card
はは	(my) mother
ホテル	hotel
おしえます（おしえる）	tell
みせ	store, shop
ないせんばんごう	extension number
ききます（きく）	ask

せんせい	teacher
おとうさん	(your) father
おかあさん	(your) mother
ぜんぜん　－ません	never (do) (See Appendix J.)

SHORT DIALOGUES

1. On the telephone.

おとこの　ひと：　もしもし、たなかさんの　おたくですか。
おんなの　ひと：　いいえ、ちがいます。
おとこの　ひと：　どうも　すみません。
おんなの　ひと：　いいえ。どういたしまして。

Man:	Hello. Is this Mr. Tanaka's residence?
Woman:	No, you have the wrong number.
Man:	Sorry to have troubled you.
Woman:	That's quite all right.

2. On the telephone.

こうかんしゅ：とうきょうでんきでございます。
はやし：　　　たなかさんを　おねがいします。
こうかんしゅ：はい、しょうしょう　おまちください。

Operator:	This is Tokyo Electric.
Hayashi:	May I speak to Mr. Tanaka, please?
Operator:	Just a moment, please.

3. スミス：［わたしは］まいあさ　ジョギングを　しますが、はやし
　　　　さんも　ジョギングを　しますか。
はやし：はい、わたしも　よく　します。

Smith:	I jog every morning. Do you jog, too?
Hayashi:	Yes, I often do.

❏ Vocabulary

ちがいます（ちがう）	That's wrong.
こうかんしゅ	switchboard operator
とうきょうでんきでございます	This is Tokyo Electric.
でございます	(polite word for です)
しょうしょう	a moment
おまちください	Please wait.
まちます（まつ）	wait
ジョギングを　します	jog
（ジョギングを　する）	

I Read this lesson's opening dialogue and answer the following questions.

1. だれが　スミスさんの　うちに　でんわを　しましたか。
2. スミスさんの　ごしゅじんは　うちに　いましたか、いませんでしたか。
3. スミスさんの　ごしゅじんは　なんじごろ　うちに　かえりますか。
4. かとうさんは　また　あとで　スミスさんに　でんわを　しますか。

II Complete the questions so that they fit the answers.

1. きのう　（　　）を　しましたか。
てがみを　かきました。
（　　）に　かきましたか。
ははに　かきました。
2. はやしさんは（　　）に　クラークさんの　じゅうしょを　ききましたか。
ホワイトさんに　ききました。
3. （　　）が　きょうとの　ししゃに　でんわを　しましたか。
スミスさんが　しました。

III Circle the correct word of the two in parentheses.

1. よく　この　レストランに　きますか。
（はい、いいえ）、あまり（きます、きません）。
2. よく　テレビを（みます、みません）か。
（はい、いいえ）、ぜんぜん（みます、みません）。
3. やまださんは　（よく、あまり）ともだちに　でんわを　します。
4. スミスさんは　よく　でんしゃで　しんぶんを　（よみます、よみません）が、クラークさんは　ぜんぜん（よみます、よみません）。

IV Put the appropriate particles in the parentheses. (If a particle is not required, put an X in the parentheses.)

1. スミスさんは　はやしさん（　　）でんわを　しました。
2. どこ（　　）でんわを　しますか。
がっこうに　します。
3. よく（　　）だれ（　　）テニスを　しますか。
かぞくと　します。
4. たなかさんは　ホワイトさん（　　）やまださんの　うちの　でんわばんごう（　　）おしえました。
5. もしもし、スミスです（　　）、はやしさん（　　）いらっしゃいますか。

V Translate into Japanese.

1. Hello. Is this the Tanaka residence?
2. This is Tanaka of Tokyo Electric. Is Mr. Hayashi there?
3. I'll call again later.
4. I asked Mr. Clark for his office telephone number.
5. Mr. Clark doesn't write letters to his friends very often but Ms. White does (write often).

LESSON
13

きれいな　おかしですね
DELICIOUS CAKES

Mr. Tanaka is offering Mr. Smith a cup of tea.

たなか： おちゃを　どうぞ。

スミス： ありがとうございます。

たなか： おかしは　いかがですか。

スミス： はい、いただきます。きれいな　おかしですね。
　　　　 にほんの　おかしですか。

たなか： ええ、そうです。どうぞ　めしあがってください。

スミス： とても　おいしいです。

たなか： おちゃを　もう　いっぱい　いかがですか。

スミス： いいえ、もう　けっこうです。

■スミスさんは　たなかさんの　うちで　きれいな　にほん
　の　おかしを　たべました。おちゃを　いっぱい　のみま
　した。

Tanaka:　Do have some tea.
Smith:　Thank you.
Tanaka:　Will you have a cake?
Smith:　Yes, I'd love one. What pretty cakes! Are they Japanese cakes?
Tanaka:　Yes, they are. Please, help yourself.
Smith:　They are delicious.
Tanaka:　Will you have another cup of tea?
Smith:　No (thank you). That was enough.

■ Mr. Smith ate (some) pretty Japanese cakes at Mr. Tanaka's house. He drank a cup of tea.

❏ Vocabulary

おかし	cake
いかがですか	How about ...?
いかが	how
いただきます（いただく）	eat (polite word for たべます)
きれい（な）	pretty, clean（ー な adj.）
めしあがって　ください	Please eat/have (some)
とても	very (See Appendix J.)
おいしい	good, tasty（ー い adj.）
もう	more (another)
1ぱい	1 cupful
～はい, ばい, ぱい	(counter. See Appendix I.)
いいえ、もう　けっこうです	No (thank you). That was enough.

GRAMMAR V

Lessons 13-14 Adjectives

1. ADJECTIVE + noun
2. noun は　ADJECTIVE です

	1. Modifying Nouns: Adjective + Noun	
ー い adj.	おおきい　こうえん	big park
ー な adj.	ゆうめいな　こうえん	famous park

	2. Adjective as Predicate: Adjective + です			
	Present Form		Past Form	
	aff.	*neg.*	*aff.*	*neg.*
ー い adj.	おおきいです	おおきく ないです	おおき かったです	おおきく なかったです
ー な adj.	ゆうめいです	ゆうめいでは ありません	ゆうめいでした	ゆうめいでは ありませんでした

- Japanese adjectives can either modify nouns by immediately preceding them or act as predicates. In this they resemble English.

  There are two kinds of adjectives: ー い adjectives and ー な adjectives. Unlike English adjectives, Japanese adjectives are inflected as shown above. Either ー い or ー な adjectives can take the place of noun 2 in the noun 2 + です construction given in Grammar I.

1. どうぞ。
   どうぞ, "please (accept/do)," is used when making an offer to someone or when begging their kindness and consideration.

2. いかがですか。
   A politer way of saying どうですか, *lit.* "How is it?" This phrase is often used when offering things like food and drink, meaning "Would you like one?" or "How about some?" It can be used in a variety of situations, such as when enquiring about a person's preferences or circumstances, when asking whether the person is free to do something (Lesson 18), or his state of health (Lesson 22).

3. いただきます。
   A polite equivalent of たべます, "I eat," and もらいます, "I receive." Said when taking something that is offered, implying both acceptance and gratitude.
   Japanese mealtime conventions:
   Before eating: いただきます. "I gratefully partake."
   After eating: ごちそうさま. "Thank you for a lovely meal." (*lit.* "It was indeed a feast!")

4. いいえ、もう けっこうです。
   The polite way of refusing something offered. けっこう means "good, fine, splendid." もう in this case means "already." The expression けっこうです implies, "I am all right as I am," or "What I've had was fine. It was enough."

5. どんな, "what kind of"
   When one wants to know more about things, people, or places, one uses どんな + noun. Answers can be given in various ways.
   ex. Q: どんな おかしを たべましたか。 "What kind of cakes did (you) eat?"
   　　 A1: おいしい おかしを たべました。 "(I) had (some) delicious cakes."
   　　 A2: きれいな おかしを たべました。 "(I) ate (some) pretty cakes."
   　　 A3: にほんの おかしを たべました。 "(I) ate Japanese cakes."
   　　 A4: クッキーを たべました。 "(I) ate cookies."

PRACTICE

❏ KEY SENTENCES

1. この りんごは とても おいしいです。
2. あの りんごは あまり おいしくないです。
3. [わたしは] おいしい りんごを たべました。
4. この へやは しずかです。
5. あの へやは しずかではありません。
6. [わたしは] しずかな へやで べんきょうをします。

1. This apple is very good.
2. That apple doesn't taste very good.

3. I ate some delicious apples.
4. This room is quiet.
5. That room is not quiet.
6. I study in a quiet room.

❏ Vocabulary

あまり－ない／－ません	not very ... (See Appendix J.)
しずかな	quiet (－な adj.)

EXERCISES

I －い adjective: Memorize the following －い adjectives.

	As Predicate: Present Form		Modifying Noun
	aff.	*neg.*	
big	おおきいです	おおきくないです	おおきい
expensive	たかいです	たかくないです	たかい
good	いいです	よくないです*	いい
new, fresh	あたらしいです	あたらしくないです	あたらしい
small	ちいさいです	ちいさくないです	ちいさい
cheap	やすいです	やすくないです	やすい
bad	わるいです	わるくないです	わるい
old	ふるいです**	ふるくないです	ふるい
interesting	おもしろいです	おもしろくないです	おもしろい
difficult	むずかしいです	むずかしくないです	むずかしい
far	とおいです	とおくないです	とおい
good, tasty	おいしいです	おいしくないです	おいしい
busy	いそがしいです	いそがしくないです	いそがしい
boring	つまらないです	つまらなくないです	つまらない
easy	やさしいです	やさしくないです	やさしい
near	ちかいです	ちかくないです	ちかい

* All inflected forms of いい come from the －い adjective よい, which also means "good."

** Not used for people.

II Practice the following patterns by changing the underlined parts in the examples given.

A. *ex.* <u>この　カメラ</u>は　おおきいです。
   <u>あの　カメラ</u>は　ちいさいです。
   1. この　くるま、あの　くるま
   2. この　たまご、あの　たまご

B. *ex.* <u>この　ラジオ</u>は　たかいです。
   <u>あの　ラジオ</u>は　やすいです。
   1. この　とけい、あの　とけい
   2. ぎゅうにく、とりにく

C. *ex.* これは　あたらしい　<u>うち</u>です。
   あれは　ふるい　<u>うち</u>です。
   1. テレビ
   2. さかな
   3. やさい

III Make dialogues by changing the underlined part as in the examples given.

A. *ex.* Q: にほんごは　<u>やさしい</u>ですか。
   A*a*: はい、<u>やさしい</u>です。
   A*n*: いいえ、<u>やさしく</u>ないです。
   1. むずかしい
   2. おもしろい

B. *ex.* Q: この　ほんは　<u>おもしろい</u>ですか。
   A*a*: はい、<u>おもしろい</u>です。
   A*n*: いいえ、あまり　<u>おもしろく</u>ないです。
   1. たかい
   2. いい

C. *ex.* Q: これは　<u>いい</u>　ほんですか。
   A*a*: はい、とても　<u>いい</u>　ほんです。
   A*n*: いいえ、あまり　<u>いい</u>　ほんではありません。
   1. おもしろい
   2. むずかしい

D. *ex.* Q: <u>こうえん</u>は　ここから　とおいですか。
   A: いいえ、とおくないです。ちかいです。
   1. バスのりば
   2. がっこう
   3. ちかてつの　えき

IV －な adjective: Memorize the following －な adjectives.

	As Predicate: Present Form		Modifying Noun
	aff.	*neg.*	
pretty, clean	きれいです	きれいではありません	きれいな
quiet	しずかです	しずかではありません	しずかな
famous	ゆうめいです	ゆうめいではありません	ゆうめいな
kind, helpful	しんせつです	しんせつではありません	しんせつな
free	ひまです	ひまではありません	ひまな
lively	にぎやかです	にぎやかではありません	にぎやかな
convenient	べんりです	べんりではありません	べんりな
well, healthy	げんきです	げんきではありません	げんきな

V Practice the following patterns by changing the underlined parts as in the examples given.

A. *ex.* この はなは きれいです。
1. ホワイトさん
2. あの きっさてん

B. *ex.* この だいどころは べんりです。
1. この カメラ
2. とうきょうの ちかてつ

C. *ex.* わたしたちは きれいな レストランで しょくじを しました。
1. しずかな
2. ゆうめいな

VI Make dialogues by changing the underlined part as in the examples given.

A. *ex.* Q: たなかさんは げんきですか。
A*a*: はい、げんきです。
A*n*: いいえ、げんきではありません。
1. しんせつ

B. *ex.* Q: あれは ゆうめいな レストランですか。
A*a*: はい、とても ゆうめいな レストランです。
A*n*: いいえ、あまり ゆうめいな レストランではありません。
1. きれいな
2. しずかな

C. *ex.* Q: ［あなたは］あした ひまですか。

      A: いいえ、ひまではありません。いそがしいです。

      1. あしたの ごご

      2. らいしゅうの きんようび

D. *ex.* Q: とうきょうホテルは どんな ホテルですか。

      A: あたらしい ホテルです。

      1. おおきい

      2. しずかな

      3. とても いい

E. *ex.* Q: はやしさんは どんな ひとですか。

      A: しんせつな ひとです。

      1. おもしろい

      2. げんきな

❏ Vocabulary

たまご	egg
たかい	expensive (− い adj.)
やすい	cheap (− い adj.)
ぎゅうにく	beef
とりにく	chicken meat
あたらしい	new, fresh (− い adj.)
ふるい	old, not fresh (− い adj.)
やさい	vegetable
やさしい	easy (− い adj.)
むずかしい	difficult (− い adj.)
おもしろい	interesting (− い adj.)
こうえん	park
べんりな	convenient (− な adj.)
わたしたち	we
〜たち	(plural suffix for people)
しょくじを します	have a meal
（しょくじを する）	
しょくじ	meal
ゆうめいな	famous (− な adj.)
げんきな	well, healthy (− な adj.)
しんせつな	kind, helpful (− な adj.)
ひまな	free (− な adj.)
いそがしい	busy (− い adj.)
とうきょうホテル	Tokyo Hotel
どんな	what kind of

SHORT DIALOGUES

1. たなか：スミスさん、おげんきですか。
   スミス：ええ、ありがとうございます。げんきです。

   Tanaka:　　How are you, Mr. Smith?
   Smith:　　Fine, thank you.

2. たなか：きょうは　いい　てんきですね。
   スミス：ええ、ほんとうに　いい　てんきですね。
   たなか：きょうは　いそがしいですか。
   スミス：いいえ、あまり　いそがしくないです。

   Tanaka:　　It's a fine day today, isn't it?
   Smith:　　Yes, it really is lovely weather.
   Tanaka:　　(Are you) busy today?
   Smith:　　No, (I'm) not so busy.

3. たなか：スミスさんの　うちは　かいしゃから　とおいですか。
   スミス：いいえ、とおくないです。ちかいです。ちかてつで　20ぷんぐ
   　　　　らいです。
   たなか：そうですか。べんりですね。

   Tanaka:　　Is your house far from your office?
   Smith:　　No, it isn't. It's near by. It's about 20 minutes by subway.
   Tanaka:　　I see. How convenient.

4. ホワイト：ここは　しずかな　こうえんですね。
   やまだ：　ええ、おおきい　きや　きれいな　はなが　たくさん　あ
   　　　　　りますね。ホワイトさんは　よく　こうえんに　いきます
   　　　　　か。
   ホワイト：ええ、にちようびの　あさ　ときどき　うちの　ちかくの
   　　　　　こうえんに　いきます。

   White:　　This is a quiet park, isn't it?
   Yamada:　　Yes. There are lots of big trees and beautiful flowers (etc.), aren't there?
   　　　　　Do you go to parks often?
   White:　　Yes. I sometimes go to the park near my house on Sunday morning.

❏ Vocabulary

てんき	weather
ほんとうに	really, truly
20ぷんぐらい	about 20 minutes (for about 20 minutes)
ぐらい	about, approximately
き	tree

I Read this lesson's opening dialogue and answer the following questions.

   1. スミスさんは　おかしを　たべましたか。

   2. スミスさんは　どこの　おかしを　たべましたか。

   3. スミスさんは　なにを　のみましたか。

II Complete the questions so that they fit the answers.

   1. たなかさんは（　　　）ですか。

     はい、げんきです。

   2. その　ほんは（　　　）ですか。

     いいえ、あまり　おもしろくないです。

   3. あの　ひとは（　　　）ですか。

     たなかさんです。

   4. あの　ひとは（　　　）ひとですか。

     しんせつな　ひとです。

III Circle the correct adjective in the parentheses.

   1. あの　きっさてんの　コーヒーは　あまり（おいしいです、おいしくないです）。

   2. うちの　ちかくに（きれい、きれいな）こうえんが　あります。

   3. この　ほんは（おもしろくないです、おもしろいではありません）。

   4. わたしの　ラジオは（いくないです、よくないです、いいではありません）。

   5. あれは（ゆうめい、ゆうめいな）レストランです。

   6. やまださんの　うちは　ここから　とても（ちかいです、ちかくないです）。

IV Translate into Japanese.

   1. Would you like some coffee?

     Thank you, I'll have some.

   2. Would you like another cup of coffee?

     No, thank you. That was enough.

   3. We had dinner at a famous restaurant.

   4. That cafe is clean, but it isn't quiet.

   5. I am busy today.

LESSON
14

かぶきは　どうでしたか
YESTERDAY'S ENJOYABLE KABUKI

Mr. Tanaka is asking Mr. Smith about the kabuki he saw.

たなか：　かぶきは　どうでしたか。

スミス：　とても　きれいでした。

たなか：　にほんごが　わかりましたか。

スミス：　いいえ、ぜんぜん　わかりませんでしたから、イ
　　　　　ヤホーンで　えいごの　せつめいを　ききました。
　　　　　とても　おもしろかったです。

■スミスさんは　かぶきを　みました。イヤホーンで　えい
　ごの　せつめいを　ききました。かぶきは　とても　おも
　しろかったです。

Tanaka:	How was the Kabuki?
Smith:	It was very beautiful.
Tanaka:	Did you understand the Japanese?
Smith:	No, I didn't understand it at all, so I listened to the English explanation with earphones. It was fascinating.

■ Mr. Smith saw a Kabuki play. He listened to the English explanation with earphones. He enjoyed the Kabuki very much.

❏ **Vocabulary**

どうでしたか	How was it?
どう	how
わかりました	understood
わかります（わかる）	understand
ぜんぜん　－ません	(not) at all (See Appendix E.)

イヤホーン	earphones
えいご	English language
せつめい	explanation

NOTES

1. どうでしたか。

   Used when asking a person his impression of something.

   ex. えいがは　どうでしたか。"How was the movie?"
   おもしろかったです。"It was delightful."

2. にほんごが　わかりましたか。

   Note that with the verb わかります, the noun usually takes the particle が rather than を. (See Grammar X, p. 168.)

PRACTICE

❏ KEY SENTENCES

1. きのうは　さむかったです。
2. きのうは　あつくなかったです。
3. きのうの　パーティーは　にぎやかでした。
4. ［わたしは］せんしゅう　ひまではありませんでした。

1. It was cold yesterday.
2. It wasn't hot yesterday.
3. Yesterday's party was lively.
4. I had no free time last week.

❏ Vocabulary

さむかった	was cold
さむい	cold (－い adj.)
あつくなかった	was not hot
あつい	hot (－い adj.)
にぎやかな	lively (－な adj.)

EXERCISES

I A.　－い adjectives: Memorize the following　－い　adjectives and their present and past forms.

	Present Form		Past Form	
	aff.	*neg.*	*aff.*	*neg.*
cold	さむいです	さむくない です	さむかった です	さむくなかった です
hot	あついです	あつくない です	あつかった です	あつくなかった です
enjoyable	たのしいです	たのしくない です	たのしかった です	たのしくなかった です
good	いいです	よくないです	よかったです	よくなかったです
interesting	おもしろい です	おもしろく ないです	おもしろかっ たです	おもしろくなかった です
tasty	おいしい です	おいしくない です	おいしかった です	おいしくなかった です
expensive	たかいです	たかくない です	たかかった です	たかくなかった です

B.   － な adjectives: Study the following － な adjectives.

	Present		Past	
	aff.	*neg.*	*aff.*	*neg.*
quiet	しずかです	しずかでは ありません	しずかでした	しずかではありません でした
well, healthy	げんきです	げんきでは ありません	げんきでした	げんきではありません でした

II Practice the following patterns by changing the underlined part as in the examples given.

A. *ex.* きのうの　えいがは　おもしろかったです。

　　1. いい

　　2. たのしい

B. *ex.* きのう　まちは　しずかでした。

　　1. にぎやか

III Make dialogues by changing the underlined parts as in the examples given.

A. *ex.* Q: <u>きのうの　パーティー</u>は　<u>たのしかった</u>ですか。
    A*a*: はい、<u>たのしかった</u>です。
    A*n*: いいえ、<u>たのしくなかった</u>です。
     1. りょこう
     2. ゴルフ

B. *ex.* Q: <u>たなかさん</u>は　<u>げんき</u>でしたか。
    A*a*: はい、とても　<u>げんき</u>でした。
    A*n*: いいえ、あまり　<u>げんき</u>ではありませんでした。
     1. せんせい
     2. たなかさんの　ひしょ

C. *ex.* Q: この　ほんは　<u>よかった</u>ですか。
    A*a*: はい、<u>よかった</u>です。
    A*n*: いいえ、<u>よくなかった</u>です。
     1. おもしろい
     2. むずかしい

D. *ex.* Q: きのうの　パーティーは　どうでしたか。
    A*a*: とても　<u>たのしかった</u>です。
    A*n*: あまり　<u>たのしくなかった</u>です。
     1. おもしろい
     2. にぎやか

E. *ex.* Q: <u>りょこう</u>は　どうでしたか。
    A: とても　<u>たのしかった</u>です。
     1. えいが、おもしろい
     2. りょうり、おいしい

❏ **Vocabulary**

たのしい	enjoyable（－い adj.）
まち	town, street
りょこう	trip
ゴルフ	golf
りょうり	food, cooking

SHORT DIALOGUE

たなか：　きのう　えきの　ちかくの　レストランに　いきました。
スミス：　どんな　レストランでしたか。
たなか：　しずかな　レストランでした。

スミス： りょうりは どうでしたか。
たなか： とても おいしかったです。
スミス： よかったですね。

Tanaka: Yesterday I went to the restaurant near the station.
Smith: What was the restaurant like?
Tanaka: It was a quiet restaurant.
Smith: How was the food?
Tanaka: It was very good.
Smith: It turned out well (then), didn't it?

QUIZ

I Read this lesson's opening dialogue and answer the following questions.

1. スミスさんは なにを みましたか。
2. かぶきは おもしろかったですか、おもしろくなかったですか。
3. スミスさんは なんで えいごの せつめいを ききましたか。

II Give the antonyms of the following.

1. むずかしい
2. とおい
3. おもしろい
4. ちいさい
5. やすい
6. ひまな
7. さむい
8. にぎやかな
9. あたらしい
10. いい

III Complete the questions so that they fit the answers.

1. しゅうまつに （　　　） を しましたか。
   きょうとに いきました。
   きょうとは （　　　） でしたか。
   とても きれいでした。
   てんきは （　　　） ですか。
   ええ、とても よかったです。
2. （　　　） ひるごはんを たべませんか。
   いそがしいですから。
3. あの ひとは （　　　） ひとですか。
   おもしろい ひとです。

IV Circle the correct words in the parentheses.

1. きのうの　てんきは　とても（よかったです、いいでした、いかったです）。

2. りょこうは（なん、どう）でしたか。
   たのしかったです。

3. どようびの　パーティーは（にぎやかったです、にぎやかでした）。

4. あの　レストランは　あまり（きれくないです、きれいです、きれいではありません）。

5. きのう　えいがを　みましたが、ぜんぜん（おもしろかったです、おもしろくないでした、おもしろくなかったです）。

6. たなかさんは　せんしゅう（げんきかったです、げんきでした）。

V Translate into Japanese.

1. How was yesterday's meeting?

2. Yesterday's weather was good.

3. That restaurant's food was not very good.

LESSON
15

ともだちに　かびんを　もらいました
GIVING AND RECEIVING

Mr. Tanaka and Mr. Smith are talking about a vase Mr. Tanaka received from Mr. Clark.

スミス：　きれいな　かびんですね。

たなか：　ええ、たんじょうびに　ともだちの　クラークさ
　　　　　んに　もらいました。

スミス：　いい　いろですね。

たなか：　ええ、わたしの　すきな　いろです。

■たなかさんは　クラークさんに　かびんを　もらいました。
　クラークさんは　たなかさんに　かびんを　あげました。

Smith:　　What a lovely vase!
Tanaka:　Yes. My friend Mr. Clark gave it to me on my birthday.
Smith:　　It's a nice color, isn't it?
Tanaka:　Yes, it's a favorite color of mine.

■ Mr. Tanaka received a vase from Mr. Clark. Mr. Clark gave Mr. Tanaka a vase.

❏ **Vocabulary**

かびん	vase
に	from (particle)
もらいました	received
もらいます（もらう）	receive
いろ	color
すき（な）	likeable, favorite (－な adj.)
に	to (particle)
あげました	gave
あげます（あげる）	give

Lesson 15 Giving and Receiving

…に …を verb

1. person は   person に   noun を   あげます
2. person は   person に   noun を   もらいます

- あげます／くれます, "give"
  もらいます, "receive"

There are two words in Japanese meaning "give," and great care must be taken in their correct use. あげます, *lit.* "to raise up," implies "to humbly present," and can never be used when speaking of something that someone gives you.

くれます, on the other hand, literally means "to hand down" and must only be used in connection with things given to you.

ex. わたしは   たなかさんに   かびんを   あげました。
   "I gave Mr. Tanaka a vase."
   クラークさんは   わたしに   かびんを   くれました。
   "Mr. Clark gave me a vase."
   わたしは   クラークさんに   かびんを   もらいました。
   "I received a vase from Mr. Clark."

Note: くれます is not used in this book since もらいます, "receive," is more frequently used. Also, から is often used with もらいます instead of に.

あげます may also be freely used when the speaker is not involved in the giving.

ex. クラークさんは   たなかさんに   かびんを   あげました。 "Mr. Clark gave Mr. Tanaka a vase."

NOTE

1. ともだちの   クラークさん
   This is not the possessive の. It is the appositive, "my friend, Mr. Clark."

PRACTICE

❏ KEY SENTENCES

1. はやしさんは   スミスさんに   ほんを   あげました。
2. スミスさんは   はやしさんに   ほんを   もらいました。

1. Mr. Hayashi gave Mr. Smith a book.
2. Mr. Smith received a book from Mr. Hayashi.

EXERCISES

I Verbs: Memorize the following verbs and their present and past forms.

	Present Form		Past Form	
	aff.	*neg.*	*aff.*	*neg.*
give	あげます	あげません	あげました	あげません でした
receive	もらいます	もらいません	もらいました	もらいません でした

II Practice the following pattern by changing the underlined parts as in the example given.

 ex. はやしさんは　スミスさんに　ほんを　あげます。スミスさんは はやしさんに　ほんを　もらいます。

 1. スミスさん、スミスさんの　ひしょ

 2. にほんごの　せんせい、クラークさん

III Make dialogues by changing the underlined part as in the examples given.

 A. *ex.* Q: ［あなたは］クラークさんに　ほんを　あげましたか。

   A*a*: はい、あげました。

   A*n*: いいえ、あげませんでした。

   1. きれいな　きって

   2. あたらしい　じしょ

   3. りょこうの　しゃしん

 B. *ex.* Q: だれが　クラークさんに　あたらしい　じしょを　あげますか。

   A: たなかさんが　あげます。

   1. はるこさん

   2. かいしゃの　ひと

 C. *ex.* Q: ［あなたは］だれに　えいがの　きっぷを　もらいましたか。

   A: ともだちに　もらいました。

   1. ちち

   2. あね

 D. *ex.* Q: ［あなたは］おとうさんの　たんじょうびに　なにを　あげますか。

   A: ネクタイを　あげます。

   1. とけい

   2. れきしの　ほん

❏ Vocabulary

じしょ	a dictionary
はるこ	a given name (female)
ちち	(my) father
あね	(my) elder sister
ネクタイ	necktie
れきし	history

SHORT DIALOGUES

1. はやし：　いい　ネクタイですね。
   クラーク：どうも　ありがとう。きのう　かないに　もらいました。
   きのうは　わたしの　たんじょうびでした。

   Hayashi:　What a nice necktie.
   Clark:　Thank you. I received it from my wife yesterday. Yesterday was my birthday.

2. スミス：わたしは　アメリカで　にほんごの　べんきょうを　しました。
   たなか：ひらがなや　かんじの　べんきょうも　しましたか。
   スミス：はい、しました。かんじは　とても　おもしろいです。わたしは　よく　にほんごの　ほんを　よみます。にほんごの　せんせいに　この　ほんを　もらいました。とても　おもしろい　ほんです。

   Smith:　I studied Japanese in America.
   Tanaka:　Did you study *hiragana*, *kanji* (and so on), too?
   Smith:　Yes, I did. *Kanji* is fascinating. I often read books in Japanese. I was given this book by my Japanese teacher. It's a very entertaining book.

❏ Vocabulary

かない	(my) wife
ひらがな	*hiragana* (Japanese script)
かんじ	*kanji* (Chinese characters)

QUIZ

I　Read this lesson's opening dialogue and answer the following questions.

1. たなかさんは　いつ　きれいな　かびんを　もらいましたか。
2. たなかさんは　だれに　きれいな　かびんを　もらいましたか。
3. だれが　たなかさんに　きれいな　かびんを　あげましたか。
4. クラークさんは　だれに　きれいな　かびんを　あげましたか。

II Complete the questions so that they fit the answers.

1. たなかさんは（　　）に　りょこうの　しゃしんを　あげました
   か。
   クラークさんに　あげました。

2. はやしさんは（　　）に　えいがの　きっぷを　もらいましたか。
   スミスさんに　もらいました。

3. ともだちに（　　）を　あげましたか。
   にほんごの　じしょを　あげました。

III Put the appropriate particles in the parentheses. (If a particle is not required,
put an X in the parentheses.)

1. わたしは　この　かびんを　かいませんでした。ともだち（　　）
   もらいました。

2. だれ（　　）はやしさんに　えいがの　きっぷ（　　）あげました
   か。

3. スミスさんは　ともだち（　　）アメリカの　きれいな　きって
   （　　）あげました。

4. たんじょうび（　　）なに（　　）もらいましたか。
   なに（　　）もらいませんでした。

IV Translate into Japanese.

1. Mr. Tanaka received a pretty vase from Mr. Clark.

2. Mr. Hayashi gave Mr. Smith a map of Kyoto.

3. Did you give that person a business card?
   Yes, I did (give him one).

LESSON
16

スキーに　いきませんか
ASKING PREFERENCES

Mr. Hayashi invites Mr. Smith to go skiing.

はやし　：　どようびに　にっこうに　スキーに　いきます。
　　　　　　スミスさん、いっしょに　いきませんか。

スミス　：　いいですね。いきましょう。なんで　いきますか。

はやし　：　でんしゃで　いきます。とうきょうえきで　あい
　　　　　　ません か。

スミス　：　はい。なんじに　あいましょうか。

はやし　：　あさの　7じに　とうきょうえきの　かいさつぐち
　　　　　　で　あいましょう。

スミス　：　はい、わかりました。じゃ、どようびに。

■はやしさんは　スミスさんと　にっこうに　スキーに　い
　きます。　どようびの　あさ　7じに　とうきょうえきの
　かいさつぐちで　スミスさんに　あいます。

Hayashi:　　I'm goting to Nikko on Saturday to ski. Mr. Smith, wouldn't you like to go with me?
Smith:　　　How nice! I'd love to go. (*lit.* "Let's go.") How do we get there?
Hayashi:　　We'll go by train. Shall we meet at Tokyo Station?
Smith:　　　All right. What time shall we meet?
Hayashi:　　Let's meet by the ticket gate in Tokyo Station at 7:00 in the morning.
Smith:　　　Sure. That's fine. Well, see you Satruday!

■ Mr. Hayashi is going skiing in Nikko with Mr. Smith. He is meeting Mr. Smith at 7:00 on
　Saturday morning by the ticket gate at Tokyo Station.

❏ **Vocabulary**

にっこう	Nikko (city name)
スキー	skiing
に	to (particle)
いっしょに	together with
あいましょうか	Shall we meet ...
わかりました	sure, certainly

GRAMMAR VII

Lessons 16-17 Inviting and Offering to Do Something

1. verb －ましょう
2. verb －ましょうか
3. verb －ませんか

- Inviting and Suggesting
verb －ましょう

ex. 12じに えきの まえで あいましょう。
  "Let's meet at 12:00 in front of the station."
  Verb －ましょう is generally translatable as "let's," "we'll," "I'll."

verb －ましょうか

ex. なんじに あいましょうか。 "What time shall we meet?"
  Verb －ましょうか is used when you are inviting someone to decide a time, place, etc., for something.

verb －ませんか

ex. いっしょに にっこうに いきませんか。 "Won't you go to Nikko with me?"
  にちようびに うちに きませんか。
  "Won't you come to my house on Sunday?"
  Verb －ませんか is used to invite someone to do something. Appropriate replies are as follows.
  Acceptance: 1. ええ／はい、verb －ましょう。 "Yes, let's."
  　　　　　2. ええ／はい、ありがとうございます。 "Yes, thank you."
  　　　　　3. ええ／はい、ぜひ。 "Yes, I'd love to."
  Refusal: 1. ざんねんですが、つごうが わるいです。 "I'm sorry, I'm afraid it's not convenient." (*lit.* "Unfortunately the circumstances are unfavorable.")
  　　　　2. ありがとうございます。でも（もう よみました）。 "Thank you. But (I've already read it.)" (State your reason after でも.)
  　　　　3. いいえ、けっこうです。 "No, thank you." (See Note 4, p. 85)
- Offering to do something
verb －ましょうか

ex. ちずを かきましょうか。 "Shall I draw you a map?"
  Verb －ましょうか is used when offering to do something for someone.
  Appropriate replies are as follows.

Acceptance: はい、おねがいします。 "Yes, please."
Refusal: いいえ、けっこうです。 "No, thank you."

NOTES

1. スキーに いきます。
   スキー, "skiing," is a purpose, not a place. Therefore it takes the particle に, not へ.

2. スミスさん、いっしょに いきませんか。
   スミスさん is simply being addressed by name and hence is not the topic of the sentence. In this case, the name, or title, usually comes at the beginning of the Japanese sentence.
   ex. たなかさん、どうぞ こちらに。 "This way, please, Mr. Tanaka."

3. じゃ、どようびに。
   どようびに is short for どようびに あいましょう。 "Let's meet on Saturday." Japanese often refer to the next meeting rather than saying "Goodbye."
   ex. じゃ、また あした。 "Well then, (see you) again tomorrow."

PRACTICE

❏ KEY SENTENCES

1. どようびに いっしょに テニスを しませんか。
2. いっしょに しょくじに いきませんか。
3. 12じに えきの まえで あいましょう。

1. Won't you play tennis with me on Saturday?
2. Won't you go out for a meal with me?
3. Let's meet at 12:00 in front of the station.

EXERCISES

I Verbs: Memorize the following －ましょう, －ましょうか, and －ませんか forms.

	go	see	do	meet
V-ます	いきます	みます	します	あいます
V-ましょう	いきましょう	みましょう	しましょう	あいましょう
V-ましょうか	いきましょうか	みましょうか	しましょうか	あいましょうか
V-ませんか	いきませんか	みませんか	しませんか	あいませんか

II Practice the following patterns:

   ex. えいがに　いきます→えいがに　いきましょう。
   　　　　　　　　　　　　えいがに　いきましょうか。
   　　　　　　　　　　　　えいがに　いきませんか。

   1. しょくじを　します
   2. コーヒーを　のみます

III Make dialogues by changing the underlined parts as in the examples given.

   A. *ex.* A: Bさん、あした　いっしょに　<u>しょくじ</u>に　いきませんか。
   　　　B*a*: ええ、いきましょう。
   　　　B*n*: ざんねんですが、つごうが　わるいです。
   　　　　1. かいもの
   　　　　2. ハイキング
   　　　　3. ドライブ

   B. *ex.* A: Bさん、いっしょに　<u>えいがを　みません</u>か。
   　　　B: ええ、<u>みましょう</u>。
   　　　　1. さんぽを　します
   　　　　2. タクシーで　かえります
   　　　　3. あの　レストランで　ひるごはんを　たべます

   C. *ex.* A: なんで　かえりましょうか。
   　　　B: <u>タクシーで</u>　かえりませんか。
   　　　A: ええ、そう　しましょう。
   　　　　1. ちかてつ
   　　　　2. バス

   D. *ex.* A: なんじに　あいましょうか。
   　　　B: <u>12じ</u>ごろは　どうですか。
   　　　A: ええ、いいです。
   　　　　1. 3じ
   　　　　2. 5じはん

   E. *ex.* A: どこに　<u>ドライブ</u>に　いきましょうか。
   　　　B: <u>うみの　ちかく</u>に　いきませんか。
   　　　A: ええ、いきましょう。
   　　　　1. かいもの、ぎんざ
   　　　　2. スキー、にっこう

   F. *ex.* A: なにを　しましょうか。
   　　　B: <u>テニスを　しましょう</u>。
   　　　　1. さんぽに　いきます
   　　　　2. えいがを　みます

ざんねんですが	I'm sorry, but ...
ざんねんな	regrettable (− な adj.)
つごうが わるいです	(I) am unable (*lit.* "Conditions are bad.")
つごう	condition
ハイキング	hiking
ドライブ	driving/a drive
さんぽを します	take a walk
（さんぽを する）	
さんぽ	a walk
うみ	sea

SHORT DIALOGUES

1. スミス： はやしさん、さんぽに いきませんか。
   はやし： ええ、いきましょう。
   スミス： この ちかくに おおきい こうえんが あります。こうえんに いきましょう。

   Smith:　　Mr. Hayashi, wouldn't you like to go for a walk?
   Hayashi:　Yes, let's go.
   Smith:　　There is a big park near here. Let's go to the park.

2. Discussing what to give the Tanakas for their new baby.
   やまだ：　 たなかさんの あかちゃんに なにを あげましょうか。
   ホワイト： スプーンと コップは どうですか。
   やまだ：　 いいですね。あした デパートで かいませんか。
   ホワイト： ええ、そう しましょう。

   Yamada:　What shall we give the Tanakas for their (new) baby?
   White:　　How about a spoon and a mug?
   Yamada:　All right. Shall we buy them tomorrow at the department store?
   White:　　Yes, let's do that.

❏ **Vocabulary**

あかちゃん	baby (other than speaker's own)
スプーン	spoon
コップ	mug

I Read this lesson's opening dialogue and answer the following questions.

 1. はやしさんは どこに スキーに いきますか。
 2. はやしさんは ひとりで スキーに いきますか。
 3. はやしさんは スミスさんに どこで あいますか。
 4. はやしさんは スミスさんに 7じに あいますか、8じに あいますか。
 5. はやしさんと スミスさんは なんで いきますか。

II Complete the questions so that they fit the answers.

 1. どようびに えいがに いきませんか。
  ええ、いきましょう。(　　　)で あいましょうか。
  とうきょうえきの かいさつぐちで あいましょう。
  (　　　)に あいましょうか。
  4じに あいませんか。
  ええ、いいです。4じに あいましょう。
 2. きのう テニスに いきました。
  そうですか。(　　　)と しましたか。
  スミスさんと しました。

III Put the appropriate particle in the parentheses. (If a particle is not required, put an X in the parentheses.)

 1. いっしょ (　　　) テニス (　　　) しませんか。
 2. いっしょ (　　　) テニス (　　　) いきませんか。
 3. らいしゅうの どようび (　　　) ドライブ (　　　) いきませんか。
 4. しょくじ (　　　) いきませんか。
  ええ。どこ (　　　) たべましょうか。

IV Translate into Japanese.

 1. I went shopping at a department store on Saturday.
 2. Won't you have a meal with me?
  Yes, let's (do that). Where shall we go?
  Wouldn't you like to go to the new restaurant near the station?
  Yes, let's do that.

LESSON
17

ちずを　かきましょうか
INVITATION TO A PARTY

Mr. Tanaka invites Mr. Smith to a farewell party for Mr. Clark.

たなか：　どようびの　ばん　うちで　クラークさんの　そ
　　　　　うべつかいを　します。スミスさん、きませんか。

スミス：　ええ、ぜひ。ありがとうございます。おたくは
　　　　　どちらですか。

たなか：　あざぶです。ちずを　かきましょうか。

スミス：　ええ、おねがいします。

■スミスさんは　どようびの　ばん　クラークさんの　そう
　べつかいに　いきます。

Tanaka:　　I'm giving a farewell party for Mr. Clark at my house on Saturday evening. Won't
　　　　　you come, Mr. Smith?
Smith:　　Yes, I'd like to. Thank you very much. Where is your house?
Tanaka:　　It's in Azabu. Shall I draw you a map?
Smith:　　Yes, please.

■ Mr. Smith is going to a farewell party for Mr. Clark on Saturday evening.

❏ **Vocabulary**

そうべつかい	farewell party
ぜひ	I'd like to. (*lit.* "by all means")
どちら	where (polite word for どこ)
あざぶ	Azabu (place name)
かきましょうか	Shall (I) draw ...

---

1. そうべつかいを　します。

Since Mr. Tanaka is the host, he says そうべつかいを　します, "I'm giving a farewell party," rather than そうべつかいが　あります, "There will be a farewell party." (See Grammar VIII, p. 114.)

PRACTICE

❏ **KEY SENTENCES**

1. にちようびに　うちに　きませんか。
2. まどを　あけましょうか。

1. Won't you come to my house on Sunday?
2. Shall I open the window?

❏ **Vocabulary**

あけましょうか	Shall I open ...?
あけます（あける）	open

EXERCISES

I Verbs: Memorize the following verbs and their －ましょう forms.

	open	close	turn on	turn off	make a copy
V-ます	あけます	しめます	つけます	けします	コピーを します
V-ましょう	あけま しょう	しめま しょう	つけま しょう	けしま しょう	コピーを しましょう
V-ましょうか	あけま しょうか	しめま しょうか	つけま しょうか	けしま しょうか	コピーを しましょうか

II Practice the following patterns.

ex. まどを　あけます→まどを　あけましょう。
　　　　　　　　　　　まどを　あけましょうか。

1. ラジオを　けします
2. ドアを　しめます

III Make dialogues by changing the underlined parts as in the examples given.

A. *ex.* A: どようびに　うちで　<u>クラークさんの　そうべつかいを</u>
　　　　　　します。うちに　きません。

　　Ba: ええ、ぜひ。

　　Bn: ざんねんですが、つごうが　わるいです。

　　　1. パーティー

　　　2. クラークさんの　かんげいかい

B. *ex.* A: この　<u>ほん</u>は　おもしろいですよ。<u>よみません</u>か。

　　Ba: ええ、ありがとうございます。

　　Bn: ありがとうございます。でも　もう　よみました。

　　　1. ざっし、よみます

　　　2. ビデオ、みます

C. *ex.* A: <u>あつい</u>ですね。<u>まどを　あけましょう</u>か。

　　Ba: ええ、おねがいします。

　　Bn: いいえ、けっこうです。

　　　1. くらい、でんきを　つけます

　　　2. うるさい、ドアを　しめます

　　　3. あつい、ヒーターを　けします

❏ **Vocabulary**

けします（けす）	turn off
ドア	door
しめます（しめる）	close
かんげいかい	welcome party
でも	but
ビデオ	video
くらい	dark (－い adj.)
でんき	(electric) light
つけます（つける）	turn on
うるさい	noisy (－い adj.)
ヒーター	heater

SHORT DIALOGUE

やまだ：　コピーを　しましょうか。

スミス：　はい、おねがいします。

やまだ：　なんまい　しましょうか。

スミス：　3まい　おねがいします。

Yamada: Shall I make a copy?
Smith: Yes, please.
Yamada: How many copies shall I make?
Smith: Three copies, please.

❏ **Vocabulary**

コピー   photocopy

QUIZ

I Read this lesson's opening dialogue and answer the following questions.

  1. クラークさんの　そうべつかいは　いつですか。
  2. スミスさんは　クラークさんの　そうべつかいに　いきますか、いきませんか。
  3. たなかさんは　どこで　クラークさんの　そうべつかいを　しますか。
  4. たなかさんの　うちは　どこに　ありますか。
  5. たなかさんは　スミスさんに　ちずを　かきますか。

II Put the appropriate particles in the parentheses. (If a particle is not required, put an X in the parentheses.)

  1. らいしゅうの　どようび（　　）おくさんと　いっしょ（　　）うち（　　）きませんか。
     ええ、ぜひ。
     いっしょ（　　）ばんごはん（　　）たべましょう。
  2. テニス（　　）いきませんか。いい　てんきですから。
     ざんねんです（　　）、つごう（　　）わるいです。
  3. あついですね。まど（　　）あけましょうか。
     はい、おねがいします。

III Translate into Japanese.

  1. Won't you come to my house on Sunday?
  2. We're having a farewell party for Mr. Clark at our house on Friday. Won't you come?
     Yes, I'd like to.
  3. Won't you have a meal with me?
  4. It's cold, isn't it? Shall I close the window?
     Yes, please.
  5. Shall I draw you a map?

LESSON
18

えいがの　きっぷが　2まい　あります
OWNERSHIP AND EVENTS

Mr. Hayashi and Mr. Smith are making a date to go to the movies.

はやし　：　えいがの　きっぷが　2まい　あります。こんばん
　　　　　　　いっしょに　いきませんか。

スミス　：　ざんねんですが、こんばん　7じに　たいしかんに
　　　　　　　いきます。たいしかんで　パーティーが　ありま
　　　　　　　すから。

はやし　：　そうですか。あしたは　どうですか。

スミス　：　あしたは　じかんが　あります。

はやし　：　じゃ、あした　いきませんか。

スミス　：　ええ、あした　おねがいします。

■スミスさんは　こんばん　たいしかんで　パーティーが
　ありますから、あした　はやしさんと　えいがに　いきま
　す。

Hayashi:　I have two tickets for the movies. Wouldn't you like to go with me tonight?
Smith:　I'm sorry, but I'm going to the embassy tonight at 7:00. There's a party at the embassy.
Hayashi:　I see. What about tomorrow?
Smith:　I'm free tomorrow.
Hayashi:　Well then, would you like to go tomorrow?
Smith:　Yes, let's make it tomorrow.

■ There is a party at the embassy tonight, so Mr. Smith is going to the movies with Mr. Hayashi tomorrow.

❑ **Vocabulary**

あります（ある）	have
じかん	time

GRAMMAR VIII

Lesson 18 Ownership and Events

1. person は　noun が　あります
2. place で　event が　あります

- Grammar III covers the main uses of the verb あります. The following are additional uses.
  1. To have, to own
     ex. くるまが　ありますから、いっしょに　いきましょう。 "I have a car, so let's go together."
     ex. たなかさんは　こどもが　ふたり　あります。 "Mr. Tanaka has two children."
  2. To take place, to happen
     ex. ここで　2じから　かいぎが　あります。 "There will be a meeting here from 2 o'clock."
  Note: Remember that in the case of "giving a party" or "holding a meeting," etc., the verb します is used. (See Note 1, p. 110.)
  Note also, ここで. When あります means "take place" or "occur," the particle used with the place is で, rather than に.

NOTE

1. あしたは　どうですか。
   The questioner is asking about his friend's arrangements for tomorrow. あした ("tomorrow"), though not the grammatical subject, is the topic in question, so it takes the topic marker は.

PRACTICE

❑ **KEY SENTENCES**

1. ［わたしは］きょう　じかんが　あります。
2. ［わたしは］えいがの　きっぷが　2まい　あります。
3. スミスさんは　こどもが　ふたり　あります。
4. どようびに　たいしかんで　パーティーが　あります。

1. I have time today.
2. I have two tickets for the movie.
3. Mr. Smith has two children.
4. On Saturday there will be a party at the embassy.

EXERCISES

I Practice the following pattern by changing the underlined part as in the example given.

　　ex. ［わたしは］じかんが　あります。

　　　1. かいぎ
　　　2. えいがの　きっぷ
　　　3. こども
　　　4. きょうだい

II Make dialogues by changing the underlined parts as in the examples given.

　A. *ex.* Q: ［あなたは］いま　じかんが　ありますか。
　　　　　A*a*: はい、あります。
　　　　　A*n*: いいえ、ありません。
　　　　1. いま、おかね
　　　　2. あした、かいぎ
　　　　3. こんげつ、やすみ

　B. *ex.* Q: ［あなたは］えいがの　きっぷが　ありますか。
　　　　　A: はい、あります。
　　　　1. くるま
　　　　2. きょうだい

　C. *ex.* Q: はやしさんは　きょう　かいぎが　ありますか。
　　　　　A*a*: はい、あります。3じから　かいしゃで　あります。
　　　　　A*n*: いいえ、ありません。あした　あります。
　　　　1. にほんごの　じゅぎょう
　　　　2. パーティー

　D. *ex.* Q: ［あなたは］いつ　やすみが　ありますか。
　　　　　A: らいげつ　あります。
　　　　1. にほんごの　じゅぎょう、げつようびと　かようびに
　　　　2. かいぎ、9じから　5じまで

　E. *ex.* A: どようびに　パーティーが　あります。
　　　　　B: パーティーは　どこで　ありますか。
　　　　　A: たいしかんで　あります。
　　　　1. かいぎ、かいしゃ
　　　　2. ともだちの　けっこんしき、ホテル

　F. *ex.* Q: スミスさんは　きょうだいが　なんにん　ありますか。
　　　　　A: 3にん　あります。
　　　　1. こども、ふたり
　　　　2. いもうとさん、ひとり

❏ **Vocabulary**

きょうだい	brothers and/or sisters
おかね	money
こんげつ	this month
やすみ	vacation, day off
じゅぎょう	class
けっこんしき	wedding
けっこん	marriage
しき	ceremony
いもうとさん	(your) younger sister

SHORT DIALOGUES

1. やまだ：はやしさん、いま　じかんが　ありますか。
   はやし：いいえ、いま　ちょっと　いそがしいです。いまから　かい
   　　　　ぎが　ありますから。

   Yamada:　Mr. Hayashi, do you have time, now?
   Hayashi:　No, I'm afraid I'm busy now. There's a conference (starting) now.

2. やまだ：　クラークさんの　そうべつかいは　どこで　ありますか。
   ホワイト：はやしさんの　うちで　あります。
   やまだ：　いつ　ありますか。
   ホワイト：きんようびの　ごご　7じからです。

   Yamada:　Where is the farewell party for Mr. Clark being held?
   White:　It's being held at Mr. Hayashi's house.
   Yamada:　When is it?
   White:　On Friday evening, from 7 o'clock.

3. たなか：スミスさん、おこさんが　ありますか。
   スミス：ええ、ふたり　あります。むすこと　むすめです。
   たなか：むすこさんは　なんさいですか。
   スミス：むすこは　15さいです。
   たなか：おじょうさんは？
   スミス：13さいです。

   Tanaka:　Mr. Smith, do you have any children?
   Smith:　Yes, I have two. A son and a daughter.
   Tanaka:　How old is your son?
   Smith:　My son is 15.
   Tanaka:　(And) Your daughter?
   Smith:　(She's) 13.

❏ **Vocabulary**

ちょっと	a little
おこさん	(your) child
むすこ	(my) son
むすめ	(my) daughter
むすこさん	(your) son
なんさい	how many years old
〜さい	years old (used only for people and pets)
おじょうさん	(your) daughter

QUIZ

I Read this lesson's opening dialogue and answer the following questions.

1. はやしさんは　なんの　きっぷが　ありますか。
2. はやしさんは　きっぷが　なんまい　ありますか。
3. スミスさんは　こんばん　えいがに　いきますか、パーティーに　いきますか。
4. こんばん　たいしかんで　なにが　ありますか。
5. はやしさんは　こんばん　ひとりで　えいがに　いきますか。
6. はやしさんは　いつ、だれと　えいがに　いきますか。

II Complete the questions so that they fit the answers.

1. はやしさんは　きょうだいが　（　　　）ありますか。
   3にん　あります。
2. あなたは　（　　　）やすみが　ありますか。
   らいげつ　あります。
3. きょう　たいしかんで　（　　　）が　ありますか。
   パーティーが　あります。
4. ともだちの　けっこんしきは　（　　　）で　ありますか。
   ホテルで　あります。

III Put the appropriate particles in the parentheses. (If a particle is not required, put an X in the parentheses.)

1. たなかさんは　くるま（　　　）あります。
2. たなかさんの　くるまは　あそこ（　　　）あります。
3. きょう　かいぎは　どこ（　　　）ありますか。
4. スミスさんは　こども（　　　）ふたり（　　　）あります。
5. にちようびに　ともだちの　うち（　　　）パーティー（　　　）あります。
6. えいが（　　　）きっぷ（　　　）2まい（　　　）あります。
   あした（　　　）いっしょに　いきませんか。

つごうが　わるいです。しごと（　　）たくさん　ありますから。

IV Translate into Japanese.

1. I have three younger sisters. My sisters are in Tokyo and Osaka.
2. Mr. Tanaka, will you have a vacation in August?
   No, I won't. I'll have (one) in September.
3. There is a meeting at (our) Kyoto branch office next week.

LESSON
19

ならに　いって　おてらを　みます
DOING THIS AND THAT

Mrs. Smith is telling Mr. Hayashi about her friend Linda who had just arrived in Japan.

スミス： きのう　アメリカから　ともだちの　リンダさん
　　　　　が　きました。

はやし： リンダさんは　いつまで　にほんに　いますか。

スミス： こんしゅうの　きんようびまで　とうきょうに
　　　　　います。とうきょうに　みっかだけ　います。そ
　　　　　れから　わたしと　いっしょに　りょこうを　し
　　　　　ます。

はやし： どこに　いきますか。

スミス： きょうとと　ならに　いって、ふるい　おてらや
　　　　　にわを　みます。そして　リンダさんは　らいし
　　　　　ゅうの　もくようびに　アメリカに　かえります。

■スミスさんの　ともだちの　リンダさんは　きのう　アメ
　リカから　きました。らいしゅうの　もくようびまで　に
　ほんに　います。

Smith:　　My friend Linda came from America yesterday.
Hayashi:　How long (*lit.* "until when") is Linda staying in Japan?
Smith:　　She'll be in Tokyo until this Friday. She'll only be in Tokyo three days. Then she's taking a trip with me.
Hayashi:　Where are you going?
Smith:　　We'll go to Kyoto and Nara and see (things like) old temples and gardens. Then Linda returns to America on Thursday of next week.

■ Mrs. Smith's friend Linda arrived yesterday from America. She is staying in Japan unitl Thursday of next week.

❏ **Vocabulary**

リンダ	Linda
います（いる）	stay
こんしゅう	this week
みっか	(for) 3 days
だけ	only
それから	after that
なら	Nara (city and prefecture)
おてら	temple

GRAMMAR IX

Lessons 19-27 ーて Form, ーない Form, and Model Verb Conjugation

- All the verbs presented so far have been in, or derived from, the ーます form. Here are two other important verb forms, the ーて form and the ーない form.

    1. ーて Form

Regular I					
buy	かいます	かって	go	いきます	いって*
return	かえります	かえって	read	よみます	よんで
wait	まちます	まって	call	よびます	よんで
write	かきます	かいて	push	おします	おして
Regular II					
eat	たべます	たべて	see	みます	みて
show	みせます	みせて	get off	おります	おりて
Irregular					
come	きます	きて	do	します	して

*いきます, irregular change

- As shown above, the ーて form can be made from the ーます form, although most Regular I verbs undergo a phonetic change.

- Use of － て form: The － て form of the verb occurs in the middle of sentences or combined with く だ さ い to form the polite imperative. It is used extensively and has various meanings which should be learned. Particular uses are explained in Lessons 19-25.

2. － な い Form

Regular I					
buy	かいます	かわない	write	かきます	かかない
return	かえります	かえらない	go	いきます	いかない
wait	まちます	またない			
Regular II					
eat	たべます	たべない	see	みます	みない
show	みせます	みせない	get off	おります	おりない
Irregular					
come	きます	こない	do	します	しない

- Use of the － な い form: A negative verb when used in mid-sentence usually takes the － な い form, rather than the － ま せ ん form it has at the end of a sentence. In this book, only the following use of the － な い form is given: verb － な い で く だ さ い, "Please do not ..."

  This verb － な い ＋ で ＋ く だ さ い is a polite prohibition. (While not included in this book, it should be noted that the － な い form does end negative sentences in familiar speech, which uses the dictionary form for present and future and the － た form for the past tense.)

- Model Verb Conjugation

  As can be inferred from the above, the conjugation of Japanese verbs falls into the following three categories:

  Regular I: Five-vowel conjugation

  Regular II: Single-vowel conjugation

  Irregular: There are only two irregular verbs, し ま す and き ま す.

- Regular I verbs are conjugated according to the Japanese vowel order: あ, い, う, え, お. Regular II verbs are based on the vowels **i** and **e** only. From the － な い form it can be seen whether a verb is Regular I or Regular II. If the vowel preceding － な い is **a**, it is a Regular I verb. If it is **i** or **e**, it is a Regular II verb.

	Regular I	Regular II
－ない form	かかない	たべない
－ます form	かきます	たべます
dictionary form	かく	たべる
conditional form	かけば	たべれば
volitional form	かこう	たべよう
－て form	かいて	たべて
－た form	かいた	たべた

- Of the seven forms above, this book includes the －ない, －ます and －て forms. These three forms, the dictionary form, and the － た form are given comprehensively in Appendix E.

NOTES

1. きのう　アメリカから　リンダさんが　きました。
   リンダさんは　いつまで　にほんに　いますか。
   Since we hear about Linda for the first time in the first sentence, she takes the subject marker が. As soon as the existence of Linda is understood by both speaker and listener, she becomes the topic, and then takes the topic marker は.

2. きょうとと　ならに　いって、ふるい　おてらや　にわを　みます。
   When one acton is followed by another, the first clause is terminated by the verb － て form. The subject of the first clause and the second clause is the same. This cannot be done unless the mood and the tense of both sentences are the same. The following two sentences cannot be connected by the verb － て form.
   A. Statement: わたしは　きっぷが　2まい　あります。"I have two tickets."
   B. Suggestion: あした　いっしょに　えいがに　いきましょう。"Let's go to the movies tomorrow."

PRACTICE

❏ KEY SENTENCES

1. ［わたしは］きのう　しごとの　あとで　ともだちと　しょくじを　して、9じに　うちに　かえりました。
2. クラークさんは　きょねんの　5がつから　にほんに　います。そして　らいねんの　3がつまで［にほんに］います。
3. たなかさんは　まいにち　2じかん　べんきょうを　します。
4. はやしさんは　あさごはんの　まえに　ラジオで　ニュースを　ききます。しょくじの　あとで　しんぶんを　よみます。

1. Yesterday, after work, I had a meal with my friends, and returned home at 9 o'clock.
2. Mr. Clark has been in Japan since last May and will stay until next March.
3. Mr. Tanaka studies two hours every day.
4. Mr. Hayashi listens to the news on the radio before breakfast. After the meal, he reads the newspaper.

❏ **Vocabulary**

しごとの　あとで	after work
の　あとで	after
2じかん	(for) 2 hours
〜じかん	(counter)
〜かん	for
あさごはんの　まえに	before breakfast
の　まえに	before

EXERCISES

I Verbs: Memorize the following －て forms:

meet	あいます	あって	see	みます	みて
go	いきます	いって	do	します	して
read	よみます	よんで	come	きます	きて
eat	たべます	たべて			

II Connect the sentences using the －て form as in the example given.

　　ex. ほんやに　いきます。じしょを　かいます。

　　　　ほんやに　いって、じしょを　かいます。

　　　1. たなかさんに　あいます。いっしょに　えいがに　いきます。
　　　2. かぶきを　みます。しょくじを　します。タクシーで　かえります。
　　　3. えいがを　みましょう。しょくじを　しましょう。
　　　4. うちに　きませんか。おちゃを　のみませんか。
　　　5. スミスさんに　あいました。いっしょに　テニスを　しました。

III Practice the following patterns by changing the underlined parts as in the examples given.

　　A. *ex.* クラークさんは　<u>きょねんの　5がつ</u>から　にほんに　います。
　　　　　　そして　<u>らいねんの　3がつ</u>まで　います。

　　　　　1. ことしの　1がつ、らいねんの　8がつ

2. せんしゅう、らいげつの　25にち

B. *ex.* ［わたしは］しごとの　まえに　しんぶんを　よみます。
    1. かいぎ
    2. しょくじ

C. *ex.* ［わたしは］しごとの　あとで　たなかさんに　あいます。
    1. パーティー
    2. かいもの

IV Make dialogues by changing the underlined parts as in the examples given.

A. *ex.* Q: ［あなたは］どようびに　どのぐらい　しごとを　します
          か。
       A: 3じかんだけ　します。
          1. べんきょう、します、30ぷん
          2. ほん、よみます、1じかん

B. *ex.* Q: きのう　しごとの　あとで　なにを　しましたか。
       A: たなかさんに　あって、いっしょに　ばんごはんを　たべ
          ました。
          1. ほんやに　いきます。じしょを　かいます。
          2. テニスを　します。うちに　かえります。

C. *ex.* Q: にちようびに　なにを　しましょうか。
       A: ぎんざに　いって、かいものを　しませんか。
          1. かぶきを　みます。ぎんざで　しょくじを　します。
          2. こうえんに　いきます。はなを　みます。

D. *ex.* Q: ホワイトさんは　いつから　にほんに　いますか。
       A: きょねんの　8がつから　います。
       Q: いつまで　にほんに　いますか。
       A: らいねんの　10がつまで　います。
          1. 1980ねん、らいねん
          2. せんげつの　15にち、あさって

❏ **Vocabulary**

どのぐらい　　　　　　　　　how long

---

1. やまだ：　ホワイトさんは　どのぐらい　にほんごの　べんきょうを
         しましたか。

ホワイト：　4しゅうかんだけ　しました。まいにち　2じかん　しまし
　　　　　　た。
やまだ：　　にほんごの　べんきょうは　どうでしたか。
ホワイト：　すこし　むずかしかったですが、おもしろかったです。

Yamada:　　How long did you study Japanese?
White:　　　Only 4 weeks, 2 hours a day.
Yamada:　　How did you find Japanese?
White:　　　It was a little difficult but fun.

2. たなか：　おさけは　いかがですか。
　　はやし：　きょうは　けっこうです。
　　たなか：　どうしてですか。
　　はやし：　くるまで　きましたから。

Tanaka:　　Will you have some sake?
Hayashi:　　No, thank you, not today. (lit. "As for today, no thank you.")
Tanaka:　　Why?
Hayashi:　　Because I came by car (and thus I'm driving).

❏ **Vocabulary**

4しゅうかん	4 weeks
〜しゅうかん	(counter)
すこし	a little

QUIZ

I　Read this lesson's opening dialogue and answer the following questions.

1. リンダさんは　スミスさんの　ともだちですか、はやしさんの　と
   もだちですか。
2. リンダさんは　いつ　にほんに　きましたか。
3. リンダさんは　いつまで　にほんに　いますか。
4. リンダさんは　どのぐらい　とうきょうに　いますか。
5. リンダさんは　とうきょうから　どこに　いきますか。
6. リンダさんと　スミスさんは　きょうとや　ならに　いって　なに
   を　しますか。

II　Convert the following verbs into their　－て　form.

1. たべます
2. いきます
3. よみます

4. きます

5. かきます

6. かえります

7. います

8. みます

9. します

10. のみます

11. あいます

12. ききます

III Complete the quesions so that they fit the answers.

1. たなかさんは　アメリカに（　　　）から（　　　）まで　いました
か。
1979ねんの　5がつから　1982ねんの　3がつまで　いました。

2. おおさかに（　　　）いましたか。
1しゅうかん　いました。

3. （　　　）スミスさんに　あいますか。
しごとの　あとで　あいます。

IV Circle the correct words in the parentheses.

1. きょねん　にほんに　きました。（そして、と）らいねん　かえり
ます。

2. あした　きょうとに　（いきますと、いって）、どようびに　とう
きょうに　かえります。

3. ともだちは　とうきょうに（どのぐらい、どう）いましたか。

4. きのう　テニスを　1じかん（ごろ、ぐらい）しました。

5. その　ほんは　（どのぐらい、どう）ですか。
おもしろいです。

6. かいしゃに（なん、どう）で　いきますか。
ちかてつで　いきます。
かいしゃまで（どう、どのぐらい）ですか。
25ふん（ごろ、ぐらい）です。

V Translate into Japanese.

1. Every morning I listen to the news and then go to the office.

2. I met Mr. Tanaka and had dinner with him. And then I went home.

3. How long do you study Japanese at home?
Only 30 minutes. (*lit.* "(I) only do it for 30 minutes.")

4. I didn't go anywhere yesterday. I was at home.

LESSON
20

ビールを　とどけてください
REQUESTS AND ORDERS

Mr. Hayashi telephones a liquor store and orders some beer to be delivered.

はやし　：　もしもし、はやしですが、ビールを　20ぽん　も
　　　　　　ってきてください。
さかや　：　なんじまでに　とどけましょうか。
はやし　：　3じまでに　うちに　とどけてください。
さかや　：　はい、わかりました。ごじゅうしょを　おねがい
　　　　　　します。
はやし　：　あざぶ　2ちょうめ　2の1です。
さかや　：　すみません、もう　いちど　いってください。
はやし　：　あざぶ　2ちょうめ　2の1です。
さかや　：　まいど　ありがとうございます。

■ はやしさんは　さかやに　でんわを　しました。さかやは
　　はやしさんの　じゅうしょを　きいて、はやしさんの　う
　　ちに　ビールを　とどけました。

Hayashi:　Hello, this is Mr. Hayashi. Please bring me 20 bottles of beer.
Clerk:　　By what time should we deliver it?
Hayashi:　Please deliver it to my house by 3:00.
Clerk:　　Certainly, sir. Please give me your address.
Hayashi:　It's 2-1 Azabu 2-chome.
Clerk:　　Excuse me, would you repeat that, please?
Hayashi:　It's 2-1 Azabu 2-chome.
Clerk:　　Thank you, sir.

■ Mr. Hayashi telephoned the liquor store. The liquor store clerk asked Mr. Hayashi for his address and delivered the beer to his house.

❏ **Vocabulary**

もってきて　ください	please bring
もってきます（もってくる）	bring
なんじまでに	by what time
〜までに	by
とどけましょうか	Shall we deliver?
とどけます（とどける）	deliver
とどけて　ください	Please deliver ...
2ちょうめ　2の1	2-*chome* 2-1
2ちょうめ	2-*chome*
〜ちょうめ	*chome*
いちど	once (*lit.* "one time")
〜ど	time (counter)
いって　ください	Please say.
いいます（いう）	say
まいど　ありがとう　ございます	Thank you (for your patronage) each time.
まいど	each time

NOTES

1. 3じまでに

   Do not confuse 3じまで and 3じまでに。

   ex. 15にちまで　とうきょうに　いてください。 "Please stay in Tokyo until the 15th."

   15にちまでに　とうきょうに　きてください。 "Please come to Tokyo by the 15th."

2. うちに　とどけてください。

   Requests are formed by verb −て＋ください.

3. あざぶ　2ちょうめ　2の1

   Japanese city addresses are typically made up of a place name (often combined with ま ち or ちょう, "town, community") ＋ちょうめ＋ばんち＋ごう. ちょうめ are sections of the まち. They may be regular in shape, like a city block, or irregular, their borders being formed by streets or natural features such as rivers. ちょうめ are sub-divided into ばんち, and the ごう is the individual house or building number. In the address above, 2の1 is ばんち number 2, house number 1. The words ばんち and ご う are frequently omitted both in speaking and in writing (except in legal documents).

PRACTICE

❏ KEY SENTENCES

1. ちょっと　まってください。
2. つぎの　かどを　みぎに　まがってください。
3. タイプを　おねがいします。

1. Just a moment, please.
2. Turn right at the next corner.
3. Please type this.

❏ Vocabulary

まって　ください	please wait
つぎ	next
かど	corner
みぎ	right
まがって　ください	please turn
まがります（まがる）	turn
タイプ	typing

EXERCISES

I　Verbs: Memorize the following verbs and their －て form.

	－ます form	－て form		－ます form	－て form
wait	まちます	まって	deliver	とどけます	とどけて
turn	まがります	まがって	show	みせます	みせて
bring	もってきます	もってきて	stop, park	とめます	とめて
say	いいます	いって			

II　Practice the following pattern by changing the －ます form to the －て form.

　　ex. ちょっと　まちます。→ちょっと　まってください。

　　　1. メニューを　みせます。
　　　2. ゆっくり　いいます。
　　　3. ビールと　ジュースを　とどけます。

III Practice the following patterns by changing the underlined parts as in the examples given.

    A. *ex.* <u>タイプ</u>を　おねがいします。
          1.　コピー
          2.　ケーキ
          3.　サンドイッチと　サラダ

    B. *ex.* <u>コピー</u>を　<u>3まい</u>　おねがいします。
          1.　ケーキ、よっつ
          2.　ビール、2ほん

    C. *ex.* つぎの　<u>かど</u>を　<u>みぎ</u>に　まがってください。
          1.　しんごう、みぎ
          2.　こうさてん、ひだり

IV Make dialogues by changing the underlined parts as in the examples given.

    A. *ex.* A:　<u>まどを</u>　<u>あけましょう</u>か。
            B:　はい、<u>あけて</u>ください。
          1.　ドア、しめます
          2.　テレビ、つけます
          3.　ラジオ、けします
          4.　じゅうしょと　なまえ、かきます
          5.　でんわばんごう、いいます

    B. *ex.* A:　あした　<u>でんわを</u>　<u>してください</u>。
            B:　どこに　<u>でんわを</u>　<u>しましょう</u>か。
            A:　かいしゃに　[でんわを]　してください。
            B:　なんじに　[でんわを]　<u>しましょう</u>か。
            A:　10じまでに　おねがいします。
          1.　はなを　とどけます

❑ **Vocabulary**

メニュー	menu
ゆっくり	slowly
ケーキ	cake
しんごう	traffic light
こうさてん	intersection
ひだり	left

ウエイトレス：いらっしゃいませ。
やまだ：　　　こうちゃと　ケーキを　おねがいします。
ウエイトレス：はい、しょうしょう　おまちください。

Waitress:	Good afternoon, madam.
Yamada:	(A cup of) Tea and some cake, please.
Waitress:	Certainly, madam. (Wait) Just a moment, please.

❑ **Vocabulary**

ウエイトレス　　　　　　　waitress

QUIZ

I Read this lesson's opening dialogue and answer the following questions.

1. はやしさんは　どこに　でんわを　しましたか。
2. さかやは　どこに　ビールを　とどけますか。
3. さかやは　ビールを　なんぼん　とどけますか。
4. さかやは　なんじまでに　ビールを　とどけますか。
5. はやしさんは　さかやに　じゅうしょを　おしえましたか。

II Convert the following verbs into their －て form.

1. いいます
2. います
3. まちます
4. ききます
5. まがります
6. みせます
7. もってきます
8. いきます
9. しめます
10. あいます
11. のみます
12. します

III Put the appropriate particles in the parentheses. (If a particle is not required put an X in the parentheses.)

1. これ（　　　）ください。
2. ビール（　　　）5ほん（　　　）ください。

3. あした　8じはんまで（　　）きてください。

4. コピー（　　）おねがいします。

5. ジュース（　　）5ほん（　　）ビール（　　）12ほん　うち
   （　　）もってきてください。

6. つぎの　かど（　　）ひだり（　　）まがってください。

IV Translate into Japanese.

1. Please show me the menu.
   Certainly. Here you are.

2. Excuse me, but could you please deliver 12 bottles of beer to my house.
   Yes, certainly. It's Mr. Clark, isn't it?
   Yes, that's right.

3. Please give me this small TV set.
   Yes, certainly, sir. Shall I deliver it?
   No, that's all right. (Because) I came by car.

LESSON
21

よやくを　おねがいします
HAVING THINGS DONE

Giving directions to a taxi driver.

はやし　：　　　とうきょうえきの　ちかくに　いってくだ
　　　　　　　　さい。
うんてんしゅ：　はい。

はやし　：　　　つぎの　しんごうを　みぎに　まがって、
　　　　　　　　まっすぐ　いってください。

はやし　：　　　あの　こうさてんの　てまえで　とめてく
　　　　　　　　ださい。

うんてんしゅ：　1,200えんです。
はやし　：　　　5,000えんで　おねがいします。
うんてんしゅ：　3,800えんの　おつりです。
はやし　：　　　どうも。

Hayashi:　(I want to) go to the neighborhood of Tokyo Station, please.
Driver:　Yes, sir.

Hayashi:　Please turn right at the next traffic light and go straight ahead.

Hayashi:　Please stop just before that crossing.

Driver:　That's ¥1,200.
Hayashi:　Please take it out of this ¥5,000.
Driver:　Here's (your) change, ¥3,800.
Hayashi:　Thanks.

133

うんてんしゅ	driver
まっすぐ	straight ahead
てまえ	just before
とめて　ください	Please stop.
とめます（とめる）	stop
おつり	change
どうも	thanks (colloquial)

Making a reservation at a restaurant by telephone.

レストランの　ひと：レストランとうきょうでございます。

はやし：　　　　　　　よやくを　おねがいします。

レストランの　ひと：はい、ありがとうございます。いつで
　　　　　　　　　　　すか。

はやし：　　　　　　　あしたの　ばんです。7じごろ　おね
　　　　　　　　　　　がいします。

レストランの　ひと：なんにんさまですか。

はやし：　　　　　　　6にんです。

レストランの　ひと：はい、わかりました。おなまえと　お
　　　　　　　　　　　でんわばんごうを　どうぞ。

Restaurant employee:	This is Restaurant Tokyo.
Hayashi:	I'd like to make a reservation.
Restaurant employee:	Thank you. When would you like it for?
Hayashi:	Tomorrow evening, about 7 o'clock.
Restaurant employee:	For how many?
Hayashi:	Six.
Restaurant employee:	Certainly, sir. May I have your name and telephone number, please?

❏ **Vocabulary**

レストランとうきょう	Restaurant Tokyo
よやく	reservation
なんにんさま	how many people (shopkeeper's expression)
～さま	politer form of ～さん

Having things cleaned.

はやし： クリーニングを　おねがいします。いつ
できますか。
クリーニングや：すいようびの　ごご　できます。

■はやしさんは　すいようびの　ごご　クリーニングやに
いきました。

はやし： もう　できましたか。
クリーニングや：すみません。まだです。4じごろ　できま
す。
はやし： じゃ、また　きます。

Hayashi:　I'd like to have this (these) cleaned. When will it (they) be done?
Clerk:　It (they) will be done on Wednesday afternoon.

■Mr. Hayashi went to the cleaner's on Wednesday afternoon.

Hayashi:　Is it (are they) ready?
Clerk:　I'm sorry, it's (they're) not finished yet. It (they) will be ready about 4:00.
Hayashi:　I'll come back, then.

❏ Vocabulary

クリーニング	dry cleaning
できます（できる）	be ready (finished, done)
クリーニングや	dry cleaner
まだです	not yet
まだ	yet

LESSON
22

どうやって　いきましたか
PUBLIC TRANSPORTATION

Mrs. Tanaka went to visit Haruko at the hospital. Mrs. Hayashi is going to visit her tomorrow and is asking how to get to Tokyo Hospital.

たなか： せんしゅう　とうきょうびょういんに　いきました。

はやし： はるこさんは　どうでしたか。

たなか： あまり　げんきではありませんでした。

はやし： どうやって　とうきょうびょういんに　いきましたか。わたしも　あした　いきます。

たなか： とうきょうえきで　80ばんの　バスに　のりました。あざぶで　おりて、びょういんまで　5ふんぐらい　あるきました。

はやし： そうですか。とうきょうえきから　あざぶまで　どのぐらい　かかりますか。

たなか： バスで　30ぷん　かかります。

■ たなかさんの　おくさんは　せんしゅう　とうきょうびょういんに　いきました。たなかさんの　おくさんは　とうきょうえきで　バスに　のって、あざぶで　おりました。とうきょうえきから　あざぶまで　30ぷん　かかりました。それから　びょういんまで　5ふんぐらい　あるきました。

136

Tanaka: I went to Tokyo Hospital last week.
Hayashi: How was Haruko?
Tanaka: She wasn't feeling very well.
Hayashi: How did you get to Tokyo Hospital? I'm going, too, tomorrow.
Tanaka: I took a No. 80 bus from Tokyo Station. I got off at Azabu and walked about 5 minutes to (get to) the hospital.
Hayashi: I see. How long does it take from Tokyo Station to Azabu?
Tanaka: It takes 30 minutes by bus.

■ Mrs. Tanaka went to Tokyo Hospital last week. She took a bus from Tokyo Station and got off at Azabu. It took 30 minutes from Tokyo Station to Azabu. Then she walked about 5 minutes to Tokyo Hospital.

❏ **Vocabulary**

とうきょうびょういん	Tokyo Hospital
どうやって	how
に	on (particle)
のりました	took, got on
のります（のる）	take, get on
おりて	get/got off (and)
おります（おりる）	get off
まで	to, as far as
あるきました	walked
あるきます（あるく）	walk
かかります（かかる）	(it) takes

NOTES

1. とうきょうえきで　バスに　のりました。あざぶで（バスを）おりました。
   Note the particles used: バスに　のります, "take/get on a bus"
   バスを　おります, "get off the bus"
   とうきょうえきで, "at Tokyo Station"
   あざぶで, "at Azabu"

2. 5ふんぐらい
   An approximate time period is expressed by the suffix 〜ぐらい.
   ex. 5ふんぐらい, "about 5 minutes"
   2じかんぐらい, "about 2 hours"
   3しゅうかんぐらい, "about 3 weeks"
   Do not confuse with ごろ, which expresses an approximate specific time. (See Note 5, p. 76.)

3. なんぷん、なんじかん、なんにち
   How many minutes, hours, days.
   ex. なんじかん　かかりますか。 "How long (*lit.* "how many hours") does it take?"

To ask in a more general way, どのぐらい, "how long," may be used.

ex. どのぐらい　かかりますか。"How long does/will it take?"
　　　どのぐらい is also used to ask how much something will cost.

ex. どのぐらい／いくら　かかりますか。"How much will it cost?"

PRACTICE

❑ KEY SENTENCES

1. ひこうきは　ごぜん　8じ10ぷんに　なりたくうこうを　でます。
2. スミスさんは　ごご　3じに　なりたくうこうに　つきました。
3. とうきょうえきで　バスに　のって、ぎんざで　バスを　おりてください。
4. ［わたしの］うちから　えきまで　バスで　10ぷん　かかります。

1. The airplane leaves Narita Airport at 8:10 A.M.
2. Mr. Smith arrived at Narita Airport at 3:00 P.M.
3. Take the bus from Tokyo Station and get off at the Ginza.
4. It takes 10 minutes by bus from my house to the station.

❑ Vocabulary

を	from (particle)
でます（でる）	leave
つきました	arrived
つきます（つく）	arrive

EXERCISES

I Verbs: Memorize the following verbs and their　－て　form.

	－ ます form	－ て form		－ ます form	－ て form
go out, leave	でます	でて	get off	おります	おりて
arrive	つきます	ついて	walk	あるきます	あるいて
take, get on	のります	のって	take	かかります	かかって

II Practice the following patterns by changing the underlined parts as in the examples given.

A. *ex.* ［わたしは］でんしゃに　のります。でんしゃを　おります。

　　　1. バス
　　　2. タクシー

B. *ex.* たなかさんは　<u>ひる　おおさか</u>を　でました。<u>ゆうがた　とうきょう</u>に　つきました。

    1.　6じに、うち、7じに、かいしゃ
    2.　あさ、きょうと、11じごろ、とうきょうの　うち

III Make dialogues by changing the underlined parts as in the examples given.

  A.　*ex.*　Q:　<u>ひこうき</u>は　なんじに　<u>おおさか</u>を　でますか。
          A:　<u>ごぜん　7じ</u>に　でます。
          Q:　[ひこうきは]　なんじに　とうきょうに　つきますか。
          A:　<u>ごぜん　8じ</u>に　つきます。
            1.　しんかんせん、ごご　1じ、ごご　4じ10ぷん
            2.　たなかさん、ごぜん　10じ、ごご　1じはん
  B.　*ex.*　Q:　<u>うえのえき</u>で　なにに　のりましたか。
          A:　<u>でんしゃ</u>に　のりました。
          Q:　どこで　<u>でんしゃ</u>を　おりましたか。
          A:　<u>とうきょうえき</u>で　おりました。
            1.　バス、こうえんの　まえ
            2.　タクシー、うちの　ちかく

❏ **Vocabulary**

ゆうがた	late afternoon, early evening
うえの	Ueno (place name)

SHORT DIALOGUE

ホワイト：やまださんは　どうやって　かいしゃに　いきますか。

やまだ：　あざぶで　バスに　のって、あおやま　1ちょうめで　おります。あおやま　1ちょうめから　ちかてつに　のって、にほんばしで　おります。そして　かいしゃまで　5ふんぐらい　あるきます。

ホワイト：おたくから　かいしゃまで　どのぐらい　かかりますか。

やまだ：　1じかんぐらい　かかります。

White:　　How do you go to (your) office?

Yamada:　I take a bus from Azabu and get off at Aoyama 1-*chome*, I take the subway from Aoyama 1-*chome* and get off at Nihombashi and walk about 5 minutes to my office.

White:　　How long does it take from your house to your office?

Yamada:　It takes about one hour.

QUIZ

I　Read this lesson's opening dialogue and answer the following questions.

　　1. たなかさんの　おくさんは　いつ　とうきょうびょういんに　いき
　　　　ましたか。

　　2. はやしさんの　おくさんは　たなかさんの　おくさんと　いっしょ
　　　　に　とうきょうびょういんに　いきましたか。

　　3. はやしさんの　おくさんは　いつ　とうきょうびょういんに　いき
　　　　ますか。

　　4. たなかさんの　おくさんは　どこで　バスを　おりましたか。

　　5. とうきょうえきから　あざぶまで　バスで　1じかんぐらい　かか
　　　　りましたか。

II　Complete the questions so that they fit the answers.

　　1. かいしゃに　（　　　）で　いきますか。
　　　　ちかてつで　いきます。

　　2. （　　　）で　バスを　おりますか。
　　　　とうきょうえきの　まえで　おります。

　　3. （　　　）に　のりましょうか。
　　　　タクシーに　のりませんか。てんきが　わるいですから。

　　4. とうきょうから　おおさかまで　しんかんせんで（　　　）かかりま
　　　　すか。
　　　　3じかんぐらい　かかります。

　　5. （　　　）ここに　きましたか。
　　　　とうきょうえきで　でんしゃを　おりて、バスに　のりました。そ
　　　　して　こうえんの　ちかくで　おりて、あるいて　きました。

III Put the appropriate particles in the parentheses. (If a particle is not required,
　　put an X in the parentheses.)

　　1. とうきょうえき（　　　）バス（　　　）のって、ぎんざ（　　　）バス（　　　）
　　　　おりて　ください。

　　2. あさ　きょうと（　　　）でて、5じ（　　　）とうきょう（　　　）つ
　　　　きました。
　　　　なん（　　　）きましたか。
　　　　くるまで　きました。

　　3. うちから　えき（　　　）バス（　　　）15ふん（　　　）かかります。

IV Translate into Japanese.

1. There was a farewell party for a friend (of mine) at a hotel in the Ginza yesterday.
2. I left the office at 6 o'clock, took a bus, and got off at the Ginza.
3. How long did it take you from the office to the hotel?
   It took about 35 minutes.

LESSON
23

テレビを　つけても　いいですか
ASKING PERMISSION

Mr. Smith went to an electrical appliance store.

スミス：　この　テレビを　つけても　いいですか。

でんきや：はい、どうぞ。つけてください。

スミス：　この　テレビの　カタログは　ありますか。

でんきや：はい、その　ケースの　うえに　あります。

スミス：　もらっても　いいですか。

でんきや：はい、どうぞ。

スミス：　どうも　ありがとう。

■スミスさんは　でんきやで　テレビの　カタログを　もら
　いました。

Smith:　　May I turn this TV set on?
Salesman: Certainly, sir. (Please turn it on.)
Smith:　　Do you have a brochure about this set?
Salesman: Yes. (They're) On top of that showcase.
Smith:　　May I have one?
Salesman: Certainly, sir.
Smith:　　Thank you very much.

■ Mr. Smith got a TV set brochure at an electrical appliance store.

❏ Vocabulary

つけても　いいですか	May I turn it on?
でんきや	electrical appliance store or clerk
カタログ	catalogue, brochure
ケース	showcase

1. テレビを　つけても　いいですか。
   （テレビの　カタログを）もらっても　いいですか。

   Asking permission to do something is done using the following sentence construction.
   　　Verb －て form ＋も　いいですか

   Permission is given as follows. The first is politer than the second.
   　　1.　はい、どうぞ。 "Yes, please (do)."
   　　2.　はい、いいです。 "Yes, you may."

   For refusal of permission, see Note 1, p. 148.

PRACTICE

❏ KEY SENTENCES

1. ここで　しゃしんを　とっても　いいですか。
2. この　へやを　つかっても　いいです。

1. May (I) take a photograph here?
2. You may use this room.

❏ Vocabulary

しゃしんを　とっても　いいですか	May (I) take a photograph?
しゃしんを　とります（とる）	take a photograph
つかっても　いいです	You may use it.
つかいます（つかう）	use

EXERCISES

I Verbs: Memorize the following verbs and their －て form.

	－ます form	－て form
take (a photograph)	（しゃしんを）とります	とって
use	つかいます	つかって
go in, enter	はいります	はいって

II Practice the following patterns.

A. *ex.* しゃしんを　とります。→しゃしんを　とっても　いいです。
　　　　　　　　　　　　　　　→しゃしんを　とっても　いいですか。

　　1. この　へやを　つかいます
　　2. この　みずを　のみます
　　3. ラジオを　つけます
　　4. まどを　あけます
　　5. だいどころに　はいります

III Make dialogues by changing the underlined parts as in the examples given.

A. *ex.* A: この　カタログを　もらっても　いいですか。
　　　　 B: はい、どうぞ。
　　1. カメラの　カタログを　もらいます
　　2. この　ペンを　つかいます
　　3. おてあらいを　つかいます
　　4. ここで　しゃしんを　とります
　　5. この　みずを　のみます
　　6. だいどころに　はいります

B. *ex.* A: まどを　あけても　いいですか。
　　　　 B: はい、どうぞ。あけてください。
　　1. ラジオ、つけます
　　2. ドア、しめます

❏ **Vocabulary**

ペン　　　　　　　　　　　　pen

SHORT DIALOGUES

1. やまだ：あした　2じごろ　でんわを　しても　いいですか。
　 はやし：すみませんが、2じごろ　うちに　いませんから、6じごろ　お
　　　　　　ねがいします。
　 やまだ：はい、わかりました。

　 Yamada:　May I call you about 2 o'clock tomorrow?
　 Hayashi:　I'm sorry, but I won't be at home about 2:00, so call me about 6:00.
　 Yamada:　I see.

2. てんいん：ごじゅうしょと　おなまえを　おねがいします。
　 はやし：　すみません。ペンが　ありません。この　ペンを　つかっ
　　　　　　ても　いいですか。

てんいん：はい、どうぞ。

Clerk:　　Your name and address, please.

Hayashi:　I'm afraid I don't have a pen. May I use this pen?

Clerk:　　Certainly. Please do.

3. たなか：ここは　ゆうめいな　おてらです。なかに　はいりましょう。

スミス：すばらしい　にわですね。この　にわの　しゃしんを　とっても　いいですか。

たなか：さあ、わかりません。あの　ひとに　ききましょう。

Tanaka:　This is a famous temple. Let's go inside.

Smith:　　What a wonderful garden. May I take a picture of this garden?

Tanaka:　Well, I don't know. Let's ask that man over there.

❏ **Vocabulary**

すばらしい	wonderful (－い adj.)
さあ	well ...

QUIZ

I　Read this lesson's opening dialogue and answer the following questions.

　1. スミスさんは　どこで　カタログを　もらいましたか。
　2. スミスさんは　なんの　カタログを　もらいましたか。
　3. カタログは　ケースの　なかに　ありましたか。
　4. カタログは　どこに　ありましたか。

II　Convert the following verbs into their －て form.

　1. はいります　　4. みます　　　7. します　　　10. いきます
　2. きます　　　　5. つかいます　8. とります　　11. います
　3. たべます　　　6. のみます　　9. ききます　　12. いいます

III Complete the sentences with the appropriate form of the verbs indicated.

　1. ここで　しゃしんを　（　　）も　いいですか。　（とります）
　2. いっしょに　テニスを　（　　）ませんか。（します）
　　　ええ、（　　）ましょう。　（します）
　3. まどを　（　　）ましょうか。　　　（あけます）
　　　はい、（　　）ください。　（あけます）
　4. この　でんわを　（　　）も　いいですか。（つかいます）
　　　すみません、ちょっと　（　　）ください。（まちます）
　5. あした　なんじに　（　　）ましょうか。　（きます）

8じはんに（　　）ください。　　　（きます）
6. この　カタログを（　　）も　いいですか。　　（もらいます）
7. ほんを（　　）、うちに　かえりました。　（かいます）

IV Translate into Japanese.
1. Shall I turn on the light?
   Yes, please.
2. May I use this telephone?
   Yes, of course. (*lit.* "please.")
3. Is it O.K. to stay here till 3 o'clock ?

ここに　くるまを　とめないでください
REFUSAL

A man parked his car in a "No Parking" area.

けいかん：　　　もしもし、ここは　ちゅうしゃきんしです
　　　　　　　　から、くるまを　とめないでください。

おとこのひと：すみません。この　ちかくに　ちゅうしゃ
　　　　　　　　じょうが　ありますか。

けいかん：　　　ええ、つぎの　かどを　ひだりに　まがっ
　　　　　　　　てください。ひだりがわに　ちゅうしゃじ
　　　　　　　　ょうが　あります。

おとこのひと：どうも　ありがとう。

■けいかんは　おとこのひとに　ちゅうしゃじょうを　おし
えました。

Policeman: I say, this is a "No Parking" (area), so don't park (your) car here.
Man:　　　I'm sorry. Is there a place to park nearby?
Policema: Yes. Turn left at the next corner. There's a parking lot on the left-hand side.
Man:　　　Thank you very much.

■ A policeman directed the man to a parking lot.

❏ **Vocabulary**

けいかん	policeman
もしもし	I say
ちゅうしゃきんし	No Parking
とめないで　ください	Do not park.
とめます（とめる）	park

ちゅうしゃじょう	parking lot
ひだりがわ	left-hand side

NOTE

1. とめないで　ください

   The "please do not ..." construction is formed as follows: verb ない + で + ください
   (For explanation of the －ない form, see Grammar IX, p. 120).

   For refusal of permission, いいえ、だめです, "No, you can't," is sometimes used.

   だめ, "no good, useless, hopeless, out of the question," is a frequently used word in Japanese. Straightforward prohibitive requests such as this are seldom used in politer society. Instead, one says, すみませんが, "Excuse me, but ..." "I'm sorry, but ..." and simply gives the reason for not wanting something done,

   ex. おたくに　くるまで　いっても　いいですか。 "Is it all right to go to your house by car?"

   すみませんが、ちゅうしゃじょうが　ありませんから…。 "I'm sorry, but there's no parking place."

PRACTICE

❏ KEY SENTENCES

1. ここで　たばこを　すわないでください。
2. ここは　ちゅうしゃきんし　ですから、くるまを　とめないでください。

1. Please don't smoke here.
2. This is a "No parking" (area), so don't park (your) car here.

❏ Vocabulary

たばこ	tobacco, cigarette
すわないで　ください	Do not smoke.
すいます（すう）	smoke, inhale

EXERCISES

I Verbs: Memorize the following verbs and their －ない form.

	－ます form	－て form	－ない form
inhale	すいます	すって	すわない
stop, park	とめます	とめて	とめない
take (a photograph)	（しゃしんを）とります	とって	とらない
use	つかいます	つかって	つかわない
open	あけます	あけて	あけない
close	しめます	しめて	しめない

II Practice the following pattern.

    ex. たばこを　すいます ──────→ たばこを　すわないでください。

      1. くるまを　とめます
      2. しゃしんを　とります
      3. この　へやを　つかいます
      4. まどを　あけます
      5. ドアを　しめます

III Make dialogues by changing the underlined part as in the examples given.

    A.　*ex.*　A: ドアを　しめても　いいですか。
           B: いいえ、しめないでください。あついですから。
           1. まど
           2. この　ドア
    B.　*ex.*　A: ここは　いりぐちですから、くるまを　とめないでくださ
             い。
           B: どうも　すみません。
           1. でぐち
           2. みせの　まえ

❏ **Vocabulary**

    でぐち   exit

SHORT DIALOGUES

1. おとこの　ひと: ここで　たばこを　すっても　いいですか。
   スミス:　　　　すみませんが、すわないでください。

   Man:　　　May I smoke here?

Smith: I'm afraid not. (*lit.* "I'm sorry, please don't.")

2. おんなの　ひと：でんきを　けしましょうか。
   たなか：　　　いいえ、いまから　この　へやを　つかいますから、
   　　　　　　　けさないでください。

Woman: Shall I turn off the light?
Tanaka: No, we are going to use this room (from now), so don't turn it off.

QUIZ

I Read this lesson's opening dialogue and answer the following questions.
   1. だれが　おとこの　ひとに　ちゅうしゃじょうを　おしえました
      か。
   2. おとこの　ひとは　どこを　ひだりに　まがりますか。
   3. おとこの　ひとは　つぎの　かどを　ひだりに　まがって、どこに
      いきますか。

II Convert the following verbs into their －ない form.
   1. たべます   6. よみます   11. けします
   2. みます   7. します   12. つけます
   3. いきます   8. すいます   13. つかいます
   4. きます   9. あけます   14. しめます
   5. いいます   10. まがります   15. とります

III Complete the sentences with the appropriate form of the verbs indicated.
   1. ここで　たばこを　（　　）も　いいですか。　　　（すいます）
      いいえ、すみませんが、（　　）ください。　　　（すいます）
   2. まどを　（　　）も　いいですか。　（あけます）
      はい、（　　）も　いいです。　（あけます）
   3. あした　おたくに　（　　）も　いいですか。　　　（いきます）
      はい、どうぞ　（　　）ください。　（きます）
   4. ドアを　（　　）ましょうか。　　　（しめます）
      いいえ、（　　）ください。あついですから。　　　（しめます）

IV Put the appropriate particles in the parentheses. (If particle is not required, put
   an X in the parentheses.)
   1. ここ（　　）ちゅうしゃきんしです（　　）、くるま（　　）とめ
      ないでください。
   2. つぎの　かど（　　）ひだり（　　）まがってください。
   3. でんしゃ（　　）たばこ（　　）すわないでください。
   4. きのうの　あさ　8じごろ　うち（　　）でて、よる　10じ（　　）
      かえりました。

V Translate into Japanese.

1. Please do not go into that room now.
2. Please do not smoke here.
3. Turn right at the next traffic light.

LESSON
25

かいぎを　しています
NOW IN PROGRESS

Mr. Hayashi is looking for Mr. Smith. He knocks on the door.

はやし：　すみません、スミスさんは　いますか。
ひしょ：　いいえ、いません。3がいの　かいぎしつに　います。
　　　　　す。
はやし：　かいぎを　していますか。
ひしょ：　いいえ、スライドを　みています。
はやし：　どうも。

■スミスさんは　かいぎしつで　スライドを　みています。

Hayashi:　　Excuse me, is Mr. Smith here?
Secretary: No, he isn't. He's in the conference room on the third floor.
Hayashi:　　Is he in conference?
Secretary: No. He's looking at (some) slides.
Hayashi:　　Thanks.

■ Mr. Smith is looking at slides in the conference room.

❏ **Vocabulary**

かいぎしつ	conference room
～しつ	room
かいぎを　して　います	is in conference
（して　いる）	
スライド	slide
みて　います（みて　いる）	is looking

---

1. かいぎを　しています。
   スライドを　みています。
   The present progressive is expressed as follows: verb －て＋います.
   This construction expresses either action that is presently going on or action that regularly takes place.

   ex. スミスさんは　まいしゅう　タイムを　よんでいます。"Mr. Smith reads *Time* every week."
   There is also the past progressive.

   ex. きのうの　ごご　なにを　していましたか。"What were you doing yesterday afternoon?"

2. どうも
   A colloquial shortening of どうも　ありがとう, "Thank you so much." It is also widely used as an abbreviation of どうも　すみません, "I'm sorry." It is not especially polite.

PRACTICE

❑ KEY SENTENCES

1. やまださんは　いま　でんわを　しています。
2. ホワイトさんは　いま　しごとを　しています。

1. Mr. Yamada is making a telephone call now.
2. Ms. White is working now.

❑ Vocabulary

でんわを　して　います　is telephoning
しごとを　して　います　is working

EXERCISES

I Verbs: Memorize the following －ています forms.

		Present Progressive	
		aff.	*neg.*
	－ます form	－ています	－ていません
talk	はなしを　します	はなしを　しています	はなしを　していません
read	よみます	よんでいます	よんでいません
listen	ききます	きいています	きいていません
write	かきます	かいています	かいていません

	Past Progressive	
	aff.	*neg.*
	－ていました	－ていませんでした
talk	はなしを　していました	はなしを　していませんでした
read	よんでいました	よんでいませんでした
listen	きいていました	きいていませんでした
write	かいていました	かいていませんでした

II Practice the following pattern.

  ex. ほんを　よみます→たなかさんは　ほんを　よんでいます。

   1. ラジオを　ききます→たなかさんは

   2. てがみを　かきます→たなかさんは

   3. ともだちと　はなしを　します→たなかさんは

III Make dialogues by changing the underlined parts as in the examples given.

  A. *ex.* Q: いま　ほんを　よんでいますか。

    A*a*: はい、よんでいます。

    A*n*: いいえ、よんでいません。

    1. コーヒー、のみます

    2. てがみ、かきます

    3. しごと、します

  B. *ex.* Q: だれが　でんわを　していますか。

    A: ホワイトさんが　[でんわを]　しています。

    1. テレビを　みます、やまださん

    2. てがみを　かきます、スミスさん

C. *ex.* Q: やまださんは　なにを　していますか。

     A: しんぶんを　よんでいます。

     1. ホワイトさん、でんわを　します

     2. いちろうさん、テレビを　みます

     3. たなかさん、ビールを　のみます

D. *ex.* Q: やまださんは　どこで　しゃしんを　とっていますか。

     A: にわで　[しゃしんを]　とっています。

     1. でんわを　します、となりの　へや

     2. ほんを　よみます、いま

E. *ex.* Q: やまださんは　いま　コーヒーを　のんでいますか。

     A: いいえ、しんぶんを　よんでいます。

     1. でんわを　します、てがみを　かきます

     2. かいぎを　します、しょくじを　します

     3. しゃしんを　とります、ホワイトさんと　はなしを　します

❏ **Vocabulary**

はなしを　します（する）　　talk
いちろう　　　　　　　　　　a given name (male)

SHORT DIALOGUE

はやし：　やまださんは　いま　どこに　いますか。
ホワイト：となりの　へやに　います。
はやし：　[やまださんは]　いま　なにを　していますか。
ホワイト：おきゃくさんと　はなしを　しています。

Hayashi:	Where is Ms. Yamada now?
White:	[She's] In the next room.
Hayashi:	What's she doing now?
White:	[She's] Talking with a client.

❏ **Vocabulary**

おきゃくさん　　　　　　　　client

I Read this lesson's opening dialogue and answer the following questions.

    1. スミスさんは　2かいに　いますか、3がいに　いますか。

    2. スミスさんは　3がいの　どこに　いますか。

    3. スミスさんは　なにを　していますか。

II Complete the questions so that they fit the answers.

    1. たなかさんは　いま（　　　）に　いますか。

       2かいに　います。

       2かいで（　　　）を　していますか。

       てがみを　かいています。

    2. はやしさんは（　　　）で　しゃしんを　とっていますか。

       あそこで　とっています。

    3. スミスさんは（　　　）と　はなしを　していますか。

       スミスさんの　ひしょと　はなしを　しています。

    4. ホワイトさんは（　　　）に　でんわを　していますか。

       かいしゃに　しています。

III Translate into Japanese.

    1. Mr. Hayashi will telephone Mr. Smith.

    2. Mr. Hayashi is telephoning Mr. Smith.

    3. What is that girl over there doing?

       She is waiting for a friend.

    4. Ms. White is not working now.

LESSON
26

たんじょうびの　パーティー
READING REVIEW

■すずきさんが　ブラウンさんの　うちに　でんわを　しました。すずきさんは　ブラウンさんの　ともだちです。

すずき：　もしもし、すずきですが、ブラウンさんの　おたくですか。

ブラウン：あ、すずきさん、こんばんは。

すずき：　ブラウンさん、らいしゅうの　どようびの　ばん、わたしの　うちで　パーティーを　します。わたしの　たんじょうびの　パーティーです。おくさんと　いっしょに　きませんか。

ブラウン：どうも　ありがとうございます。よろこんでいきます。

すずき：　では、どようびに。

ブラウン：おでんわ　どうも　ありがとうございました。

■きょうは　パーティーの　ひです。
ブラウンさんと　おくさんが　すずきさんの　うちに　つきました。

すずき：　よく　いらっしゃいました。こちらへ　どうぞ。

ブラウン：おまねき　ありがとうございます。これを　どうぞ。

すずき：　　きれいな　はなですね。どうも　ありがとうご
　　　　　　ざいます。
ブラウン：この　ワインも　どうぞ。
すずき：　　みなさんに　ごしょうかい　しますから、どう
　　　　　　ぞ　こちらへ。

■とても　にぎやかな　パーティーです。

■12じです。みんなは　かえります。

すずきさんの　ともだち：ブラウンさん、くるまで　きまし
　　　　　　　　　　　　たか。
ブラウン：　　　　　　　いいえ、でんしゃで　きました。
すずきさんの　ともだち：おそいですから　わたしの　くる
　　　　　　　　　　　　まで　かえりませんか。
ブラウン：　　　　　　　そうですか。ありがとうございま
　　　　　　　　　　　　す。おねがいします。
みんな：　　　　　　　　とても　たのしかったです。きょ
　　　　　　　　　　　　うは　どうも　ありがとうござい
　　　　　　　　　　　　ました。
すずき：　　　　　　　　どういたしまして。わたしも　た
　　　　　　　　　　　　のしかったです。また　きてくだ
　　　　　　　　　　　　さい。
すずきさんの　おくさん：どうぞ　きをつけて。
みんな：　　　　　　　　おやすみなさい。
すずき：　　　　　　　　おやすみなさい。

■ Mr. Suzuki telephoned the Browns' house. Mr. Suzuki is a friend of Mr. Brown's.

Suzuki:　　Hello. This is Suzuki. Is this the Browns' residence?
Brown:　　Ah, Mr. Suzuki! Good evening.
Suzuki:　　Mr. Brown, we're having a party at my house next Saturday evening. It's my birth-
　　　　　day party. Won't you come, together with Mrs. Brown?

Brown: Thank you very much. We'll be happy to come.
Suzuki: Well then, (see you) on Saturday.
Brown: Thank you for your telephone call.

■ Today is the day of the party. Mr. and Mrs. Brown have arrived at Mr. Suzuki's house.

Suzuki: How nice of you to come. This way, please.
Brown: Thank you for your invitation. These are for you.
Suzuki: What lovely flowers! Thank you very much.
Brown: This wine is for you, too.
Suzuki: Come this way and I'll introduce you to everybody.

■ It is a very lively party.

■ (Now) It is 12 o'clock. Everyone is leaving.

Mr. Suzuki's friend: Mr. Brown, did you come by car?
Brown: No, we came by train.
Mr. Suzuki's friend: Since it's late, can't I drive you home? (*lit.* "Won't you go home in my car?")
Brown: Oh, would you (do that)? Thank you. (*lit.* "I'm happy to accept your offer.")
All: It was very enjoyable. Thank you very much for today.
Suzuki: You're welcome. I enjoyed it too. Please come again.
Mrs. Suzuki: Please be careful (on your way home).
All: Good-night!
The Suzukis: Good-night!

❏ **Vocabulary**

すずき	a surname
よろこんで	(I'd) be happy to.
ひ	day
おまねき　ありがとうございます	Thank you for your invitation.
ワイン	wine
みなさん	everyone (excluding the speaker and his or her group)
みんな	everyone
おそい	late (− い adj.)
きを　つけて	take care, be careful

LESSON
27

とうきょうに　すんでいます
PRESENT CONDITION

Mr. Smith tells Mr. Hayashi that his brother has arrived in Japan.

スミス：　せんしゅう　あにが　アメリカから　にほんに
　　　　　きました。
はやし：　おにいさんは　おくさんと　いっしょに　きまし
　　　　　たか。
スミス：　いいえ、しごとですから　ひとりで　きました。
　　　　　いま　きょうとに　いっています。あには　りょ
　　　　　こうがいしゃに　つとめています。
はやし：　おにいさんは　いつまで　きょうとに　いますか。
スミス：　こんしゅうの　すいようびまで　います。それか
　　　　　ら　ホンコンに　いって、アメリカに　かえりま
　　　　　す。
はやし：　アメリカの　どこに　すんでいますか。
スミス：　ニューヨークに　すんでいます。

■スミスさんの　おにいさんは　りょこうがいしゃに　つと
　めています。せんしゅう　にほんに　きました。いま　き
　ょうとに　いっています。

Smith:　　My (older) brother came to Japan from America last week.
Hayashi:　Did your brother come with his wife?
Smith:　　No, he came on business, so he came alone. He's in Kyoto now. My brother works
　　　　　for a travel agency.

Hayashi: How long will your brother be in Kyoto?
Smith: He'll be there until this week Wednesday. After that he'll go to Hong Kong, then
            return to America.
Hayashi: Where does he live in America?
Smith: He lives in New York (City).

■ Mr. Smith's (older) brother works for a travel agency. He came to Japan last week. Now he
  is in Kyoto.

❏ Vocabulary

あに	(my) older brother
おにいさん	(your) older brother
りょこうがいしゃ	travel agency
つとめて　います	be employed, work for
つとめます（つとめる）	serve, hold a post
ホンコン	Hong Kong
すんで　います	live (*lit.* "is living")
すみます（すむ）	live
ニューヨーク	New York

NOTES

1. いま　きょうとに　いっています。
   Verb －ています is used here. The sentence literally means, "Having gone to Kyoto,
   he is there now." Other common examples of this usage are, たなかさんは　けっこ
   んしています. "Mr. Tanaka is married." (*lit.* "Mr. Tanaka, having got married, is married.") And べんごしは　もう　きましたか. "Has the lawyer come yet?" はい、
   きています. "Yes, he has."

2. あには　りょこうがいしゃに　つとめています。
   The particle used wiht the verb つとめる is に. Here again the －て form is used.
   When asked what kind of work they do, Japanese usually reply by giving their place of
   work rather than the type of work. Note also that in Japanese siblings are always
   referred to as older or younger brothers or sisters, for which there are separate words.
   Namely, あに, "my older brother," おとうと, "my younger brother," おにいさん,
   "your older brother," おとうとさん, "your younger brother," etc. Note the following
   terms for one's own and for other person's relatives.

	Related to the Speaker	Related to Others
family	かぞく	ごかぞく
husband	しゅじん	ごしゅじん
wife	かない	おくさん
child	こども	こどもさん／おこさん
son	むすこ	むすこさん／ぼっちゃん
daughter	むすめ	むすめさん／おじょうさん
parents	りょうしん	ごりょうしん
father	ちち	おとうさん
mother	はは	おかあさん
grandfather	そふ	おじいさん
grandmother	そぼ	おばあさん
brothers and sisters	きょうだい	ごきょうだい
older brother	あに	おにいさん
older sister	あね	おねえさん
younger brother	おとうと	おとうとさん
younger sister	いもうと	いもうとさん
grandchild	まご	おまごさん
uncle	おじ	おじさん
aunt	おば	おばさん
nephew	おい	おいごさん
niece	めい	めいごさん
cousin	いとこ	おいとこさん

3. ニューヨークに　すんでいます。

In describing where people live, the verb －て form is used. うる, the verb meaning "sell" and しる, "know," similarly use the －て form.

❏ KEY SENTENCES

1. スミスさんの　おにいさんは　いま　にほんに　きています。
2. クラークさんは　とうきょうに　すんでいます。
3. はやしさんは　にほんぎんこうに　つとめています。
4. わたしは　たなかさんを　よく　しっています。
5. ちか1かいで　にくや　さかなを　うっています。

1. Mr. Smith's older brother is in Japan now.
2. Mr. Clark lives in Tokyo.
3. Mr. Hayashi works for the Bank of Japan.
4. I know Mr. Tanaka well.
5. They sell meat, fish (and other things) in the first basement.

❏ Vocabulary

しって　います（しる）	know
ちか　1かい	first basement
ちか	basement (*lit.* "underground")
うって　います	sell (*lit.* "is selling")
うります（うる）	sell

EXERCISES

I Verbs: Memorize the following verbs and their　－ています　forms.

	－ます form	－ています form	
		aff.	*neg.*
live	すみます	すんでいます	すんでいません
work for	つとめます	つとめています	つとめていません
know	*	しっています	しりません**
sell	うります	うっています	うっていません

    * The form しります is never used; しっています replaces it.
    ** The negative of しっています is the irregular しりません.

II Practice the following pattern by changing the underlined part as in the example given.

    ex. ［わたしは］とうきょうに　すんでいます。

1. とうきょうの　あざぶ
2. かいしゃの　ちかく

III Make dialogues by changing the underlined parts as in the examples given.

A. *ex.* Q: ホワイトさんは　いま　<u>にほんに</u>　<u>きています</u>か。
Aa: はい、<u>きています</u>。せんげつ　[<u>にほんに</u>]　<u>きました</u>。
An: いいえ、<u>きていません</u>。らいげつ　[<u>にほんに</u>]　<u>きます</u>。
1. とうきょう、きます
2. がいこく、いきます

B. *ex.* Q: <u>たなかさん</u>を　しっていますか。
Aa: はい、しっています。
An: いいえ、しりません。
1. ホワイトさん
2. やまださんの　じゅうしょ
3. はやしさんの　あたらしい　でんわばんごう
4. いい　にくや

C. *ex.* Q: たなかさんの　ともだちは　どこに　つとめていますか。
A: <u>たいしかん</u>に　つとめています。
1. デパート
2. がっこう
3. りょこうがいしゃ

D. *ex.* Q: <u>かさ</u>は　どこで　うっていますか。
A: <u>1かい</u>で　うっています。
1. セーター、4かい
2. くつ、6かい
3. きって、あの　みせ

❏ **Vocabulary**

がいこく	foreign country
セーター	sweater

SHORT DIALOGUE

すずき：　スミスさんは　どこに　つとめていますか。
スミス：　ABCに　つとめています。
すずき：　じゃあ、きょうとししゃの　さとうさんを　しっていますか。
スミス：　ええ、しっています。

Suzuki:　　Where do you work, Mr. Smith?

Smith: I work for ABC.

Suzuki: Then, do you know Mr. Sato in the Kyoto branch?

Smith: Yes, I do.

❏ **Vocabulary**

さとう   a surname

QUIZ

I Read this lesson's opening dialogue and answer the following questions.

1. だれと　だれが　はなしを　していますか。
2. せんしゅう　だれが　アメリカから　にほんに　きましたか。
3. スミスさんの　おにいさんは　いま　とうきょうに　いますか。
4. スミスさんの　おにいさんは　どこに　つとめていますか。
5. スミスさんの　おにいさんは　どこに　すんでいますか。

II Complete the questions so that they fit the answers.

1. （　　　）で　きってを　うっていますか。
   あの　みせで　うっています。
2. あの　ひとは（　　　）に　つとめていますか。
   デパートに　つとめています。
3. （　　　）が　はやしさんの　あたらしい　でんわばんごうを　しっ
   ていますか。
   はやしさんの　ひしょが　しっています。
4. ホワイトさんは　いま（　　　）に　いっていますか。
   ぎんこうに　いっています。

III Put the appropriate particles in the parentheses. (If particle is not required, put
an X in the parentheses.)

1. こちらは　とうきょうでんき（　　　）たなかさんです。
2. たなかさんは　どこ（　　　）つとめていますか。
   とうきょうでんき（　　　）つとめています。
3. スミスさんは　いま　とうきょう（　　　）しごとを　しています。
4. ブラウンさんは　どこ（　　　）すんでいますか。
   うえのえき（　　　）ちかく（　　　）すんでいます。
5. どこ（　　　）えいご（　　　）しんぶん（　　　）うっていますか。
   あそこ（　　　）うっています。

IV Translate into Japanese.

1. Do you know Mr. Tanaka?
   No, I don't know (him).
2. I live near (my) office. It's a 15-minute walk.
3. Mr. Smith works for ABC.

にほんの　かぐが　すきです

EXPRESSING PREFERENCES

Mr. Smith wants to buy some antique furniture. He is asking Ms. Yamada where to find some.

スミス： わたしは　にほんの　ふるい　かぐが　すきです。
せんげつ　たんすを　かいました。つぎは　つくえを　かいたいです。いい　みせを　しっていますか。

やまだ： さあ、しりません。はやしさんは　いろいろな
ことを　よく　しっていますから　はやしさんに
きいてください。

■スミスさんは　ふるい　かぐが　すきです。スミスさんは
やまださんに　ふるい　かぐの　みせについて　ききました。

Smith: I like antique Japanese furniture. Last month I bought a *tansu*. Next, I want to buy
            a table. Do you know a good store?
Yamada: Let me see ... No, I don't. Mr. Hayashi knows a lot about various things, so ask him.

■ Mr. Smith likes antique furniture. Mr. Smith asked Ms. Yamada about stores that sell
antique furniture.

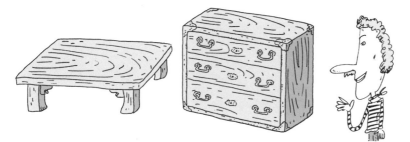

❏ **Vocabulary**

かぐ	furniture
たんす	*tansu* (chest of drawers)
つくえ	table
いろいろな　こと	various things
いろいろな	various (－な adj.)
こと	thing
みせに　ついて	about stores
〜に　ついて	about, concerning

GRAMMAR X

Desire, Preference, Like and Dislike

1. person は　noun が　すきです
2. person は　noun が　いいです
 (person は)　noun は　noun が　いいです
3. わたしは　verb －たいです

- Particle が is used with
 すきです（－な adj.）
 いいです（－い adj.）

- In "I like bananas," "like" is a verb and "bananas" is the object, but in Japanese, "bananas" takes the particle が, and they are described as being "likable," using an adjective rather than a verb.
 ex. バナナが　すきです。"I like bananas." (*lit.* "Bananas are likable.")
 あなたが　すきです。"I love you." (*lit.* "You are lovable.")

- The same construction is used with the adjective いい, "good, preferable," etc.
 ex. コーヒーが　いいです。"I'd like coffee." (*lit.* "Coffee is preferable.") Note the following constructions, all of which mean "I'd like coffee."
 1. わたしは　コーヒーが　いいです。"I'd like coffee." (*lit.* "As for me, coffee is preferable.")
 2. のみものは　コーヒーが　いいです。"I'd like coffee." (*lit.* "As for something to drink, coffee is my choice.")
 3. わたしは　のみものは　コーヒーが　いいです。"I'd like coffee." (*lit.* "As for me, regarding something to drink, coffee is my choice.")
 In this last sentence, the speaker first talks about himself, "わたし," then he chooses the category of drinks, "のみもの," and talks about it.

- The verb わかります also takes が (see Note 2, p. 93.), as does the verb できます, expressing possibility, ability, etc.
 ex. わたしは　タイプが　できます。"I can type." (*lit.* "As far as I'm concerned, typing (is something) I can do.")
 Note: できます also has the meaning "be done" or "be ready," (See Lesson 21.)

- Verb －たいです

Constructions expressing desire can be made from the －ます form as follows:

いきます　　いきたい
たべます　　たべたい

The verb －たい form is inflected like an －い adjective.

ex. いきたいです。 "(I) want to go."
いきたくないです。 "(I) don't want to go."
いきたかったです。 "(I) wanted to go."
いきたくなかったです。 "(I) didn't want to go."

- Verb －たい expresses the speaker's desire.

ex. タクシーで　いきたいです。 "(I) want to go by taxi."
It can be made into a quesion by adding the question marker か.
But asking a person, especially someone senior, what he wishes to do in this form is often considered not polite, and simple questions are preferable.

ex. タクシーで　いきますか。 "Do you (want to) go by taxi?"
This form cannot be used to refer to a third person.
The particle が is sometimes used instead of を.
スライドを／が　みたいです。 "(I) want to see the slides."

NOTES

1. しっています、 "(I) know," always takes the verb －て form. The reply is irregular:
   A*a*: はい、しっています。 "Yes, (I) know."
   A*n*: いいえ、しりません。 "No, (I) don't know."

2. さあ、しりません。
   さあ…("Let me see ...") is an expression often used in Japanese when thinking about an answer.

PRACTICE

❏ KEY SENTENCES

1. たなかさんは　ゴルフが　じょうずです。
2. ［わたしは］りんごが　すきです。
3. ［わたしは］タイプが　できます。
4. ［わたしは］あたまが　いたいです。
5. ［わたしは］ヨーロッパに　いきたいです。
6. ［わたしは］いま　なにも　たべたくないです。

1. Mr. Tanaka is good at golf.
2. I like apples.
3. I can type.
4. I have a headache.
5. I'd like to go to Europe.
6. I don't want to eat anything now.

❏ **Vocabulary**

じょうずな	good at (－な adj.)
できます	can (do)
（できる）	
あたま	head
いたい	aching (－い adj.)
ヨーロッパ	Europe

EXERCISES

I Memorize the following adjectives and verb.

		Present Form		Past Form	
		aff.	*neg.*	*aff.*	*neg.*
－な adj.	skilled in	じょうず です	じょうず ではあり ません	じょうず でした	じょうずでは ありません でした
	like, love	すきです	すきでは ありません	すきでした	すきではあり ませんでした
verb	be able to (do)	できます	できません	できました	できません でした
－い adj.	be painful	いたい です	いたくない です	いたかった です	いたくなかった です

II Practice the following patterns by changing the underlined part as in the examples given.

A. *ex.* たなかさんは　ゴルフが　じょうずです。

　　　1. ドイツご

　　　2. りょうり

B. *ex.* ［わたしは］あたまが　いたいです。

　　　1. のど

　　　2. おなか

　　　3. は

III Make dialogues by changing the underlined parts as in the examples given.

A. *ex.* Q: ［あなたは］<u>くだもの</u>が　すきですか。
   A*a*: はい、とても　すきです。
   A*n*: いいえ、あまり　すきではありません。
   1. えいが
   2. りょこう
   3. はるこさん

B. *ex.* Q: ［あなたは］<u>にほんご</u>が　できますか。
   A*a*: はい、すこし　できます。
   A*n*: いいえ、ぜんぜん　できません。
   1. フランスご
   2. タイプ

C. *ex.* Q: ［あなたは］<u>あたま</u>が　いたいですか。
   A*a*: はい、いたいです。
   A*n*: いいえ、いたくないです。
   1. のど
   2. おなか
   3. は

D. *ex.* Q: ［あなたは］どんな　<u>くだもの</u>が　すきですか。
   A: <u>りんご</u>が　すきです。
   1. やさい、トマト
   2. りょうり、にくの　りょうり

IV Memorize the following －たいです form.

	Present Form		Past Form	
	aff.	*neg.*	*aff.*	*neg.*
want to go	いきたい です	いきたくない です	いきたかった です	いきたくなかった です
want to send	おくりたい です	おくりたくない です	おくりたかった です	おくりたく なかったです

V Practice the following －たいです form.
   1. えいがに　いきます
      ［わたしは］えいがに　いきたいです。
      　　　　　　　　　　　いきたくないです。
      　　　　　　　　　　　いきたかったです。
      　　　　　　　　　　　いきたくなかったです。

2. テレビを　みます

　　［わたしは］テレビを　みたいです。

　　　　　　　　　　みたくないです。

　　　　　　　　　　みたかったです。

　　　　　　　　　　みたくなかったです。

3. たなかさんに　あいます

　　［わたしは］たなかさんに　あいたいです。

　　　　　　　　　　あいたくないです。

　　　　　　　　　　あいたかったです。

　　　　　　　　　　あいたくなかったです。

VI　Practice the following pattern by changing the underlined part as in the example given.

　A.　*ex.*　［わたしは］やまに　いきたいです。

　　　　1.　としょかん

　　　　2.　おんせん

　　　　3.　きょうとの　まつり

　B.　*ex.*　［わたしは］いま　テレビを　みたくないです。

　　　　1.　えいが

　　　　2.　スライド

VII　Make dialogues by changing the underlined parts as in the examples given.

　A.　*ex.*　Q:　［あなたは］どこに　いきたいですか。

　　　　　　A:　やまに　いきたいです。

　　　　1.　うみ

　　　　2.　おんせん

　B.　*ex.*　Q:　［あなたは］なにを　かいたいですか。

　　　　　　A:　かぐを　かいたいです。

　　　　1.　ネクタイ

　　　　2.　くつした

　　　　3.　つくえ

　C.　*ex.*　Q:　［あなたは］いま　なにを　したいですか。

　　　　　　A:　テニスを　したいです。

　　　　1.　ほんを　よみます

　　　　2.　えいがに　いきます

　　　　3.　りょこうを　します

　D.　*ex.*　Q:　［あなたは］なにを　したいですか。

A: なにも　したくないです。

1. たべます
2. のみます
3. かいます

E. ex. Q: ［あなたは］どこに　いきたいですか。

A: どこにも　いきたくないです。

1. だれに、あいます

❏ Vocabulary

ドイツご	German language
のど	throat
おなか	stomach
は	tooth
おくりたい	want to send
おくります（おくる）	send
やま	mountain
としょかん	library
くだもの	fruit
フランスご	French language
トマト	tomato
おんせん	hot spring
まつり	festival
くつした	socks

SHORT DIALOGUES

1. たなか： 　この　りょうりは　とても　おいしいです。

ホワイト：そうですか。もう　すこし　いかがですか。

たなか： 　ありがとうございます。いただきます。ホワイトさんは
　　　　　　りょうりが　じょうずですね。

Tanaka:　This dish is very good.

White:　Is it? Would you like some more?

Tanaka:　Thank you. I'd love some more. You're a good cook.

2. いしゃ：どう　しましたか。

やまだ：きのうから　きぶんが　わるいです。

いしゃ：ねつが　ありますか。

やまだ：ええ、39ど　あります。あたまも　いたいです。

いしゃ：のども　いたいですか。

やまだ：はい、いたいです。

いしゃ：くすりを　あげますから　しょくじの　あとで　のんでくだ
　　　　さい。どうぞ　おだいじに。

Doctor: What's the matter?

Yamada: I haven't felt well since yesterday.

Doctor: Do you have a fever?

Yamada: Yes. My temperature is 39 degrees (C.). I have a headache.

Doctor: Do you have a sore throat too?

Yamada: Yes, I do.

Doctor: (After the examination.) I'll give you some medicine. Take it after meals.
            Look after yourself.

(Note: Parts of the body are given in Appendix F.)

3. たなか： つぎの　にちようびに　なにを　したいですか。

   はやし： テニスを　したいです。ほんも　よみたいです。たなかさん
            は　なにを　したいですか。

   たなか： ［わたしは］えいがに　いきたいです。

Tanaka: What would you like to do next Sunday?

Hayashi: I'd like to play tennis. I'd like to read a book, too. What would you like to
            do?

Tanaka: I'd like to go to a movie.

4. ホワイト：　　　　　　　　　この　にもつを　アメリカに　おくりたい
                            です。どのぐらい　かかりますか。

   ゆうびんきょくの　ひと：　こうくうびんですか、ふなびんですか。

   ホワイト：　　　　　　　　　ふなびんで　おねがいします。

   ゆうびんきょくの　ひと：　そうですね。いっかげつぐらい　かかりま
                            す。

White: I'd like to send this parcel to the United States. How long will it
                    take?

Post office clerk: By airmail or sea mail?

White: By sea mail, please.

Post office clerk: Let me see ... It'll take about one month.

5. はやし： せんしゅうの　にちようびに　ハイキングに　いきましたか。

   たなか： いいえ。いきたかったですが、あたまが　いたかったですか
            ら、いきませんでした。

Hayashi: Did you go hiking last week Sunday?

Tanaka: No. I wanted to, but I had a headache, so I didn't go.

❏ **Vocabulary**

いしゃ	doctor
どう　しましたか	What's the matter?
きぶん	feeling

ねつ	fever
39ど	39 degrees (Centigrade)
〜ど	degree
どうぞ　おだいじに	Look after yourself.
にもつ	parcel
こうくうびん	airmail
ふなびん	sea mail
そうですね	Let me see ...
いっかげつ	(for) one month
〜かげつ	month (see Appendix G.)

QUIZ

I Read this lesson's opening dialogue and answer the following questions.

1. スミスさんは　どんな　かぐが　すきですか。
2. スミスさんは　もう　たんすを　かいましたか。
3. やまださんは　にほんの　ふるい　かぐの　いい　みせを　しっていますか。
4. スミスさんは　はやしさんに　なにについて　ききますか。

II Complete the questions so that they fit the answers.

1. しゅうまつに　（　　）を　したいですか。
   えいがを　みたいです。
2. つぎの　にちようびに　（　　）に　いきたいですか。
   どこにも　いきたくないです。うちに　いたいです。
3. （　　）くだものが　すきですか。
   りんごが　すきです。
4. いっしょに　しょくじに　いきませんか。
   ざんねんですが、[わたしは]　いま　（　　）も　たべたくないです。

III Put the appropriate particles in the parentheses. (If a particle is not required, put an X in the parentheses.)

1. クラークさん（　　）テニス（　　）じょうずです（　　）、わたし（　　）じょうずではありません。
2. あの　ひと（　　）にほんご（　　）できます。とても　じょうずです。
3. きのうから　のど（　　）いたいですから、ひるやすみ（　　）びょういん（　　）いきたいです。
4. いま　なに（　　）のみたくないです。
5. きょう　どこに（　　）いきたくないです。うち（　　）いたいです。うち（　　）ほん（　　）よみたいです。

IV Translate into Japanese.

1. Ms. White likes apples.

2. Can you ski?
   Yes, I can.
3. I want to meet a friend tomorrow and play tennis (together).
4. I wanted to write a letter yesterday, but there wasn't time.
5. My throat is sore, so I don't want to eat anything.

LESSON
29

のみものは　ビールが　いいです
DINING OUT

Mr. Tanaka has invited Mr. Brown to a meal. They are in a restaurant looking at the menu and conversing.

たなか：　　　　すみません、メニューを　みせてください。

ウエイトレス：　はい、どうぞ。

たなか：　　　　のみものは　なにが　いいですか。

ブラウン：　　　ビールが　いいです。

たなか：　　　　りょうりは　すきやきが　いいですか、しゃぶしゃぶが　いいですか。

ブラウン：　　　すきやきは　せんしゅう　たべましたから、しゃぶしゃぶが　いいです。

たなか：　　　　しょくじの　あとで　コーヒーは　いかがですか。

ブラウン：　　　はい、いただきます。

たなか：　　　　ビールを　2ほんと　しゃぶしゃぶを　おねがいします。デザートは　メロンが　いいです。

ウエイトレス：　はい、わかりました。

■たなかさんと　ブラウンさんは　レストランで　しょくじを　しました。ビールを　のんで、しゃぶしゃぶを　たべました。しょくじの　あとで　コーヒーを　のみました。

Tanaka:	Excuse me, could we see the menu, please? (*lit.* "Please show us the menu.")
Waitress:	Cerainly, sir. Here you are.
Tanaka:	What would you like to drink?
Brown:	I'd like some beer.
Tanaka:	As for dinner, would you like *sukiyaki* or (would you like) *shabushabu*?
Brown:	I had *sukiyaki* last week, so I'd like *shabushabu*.
Tanaka:	After the meal, how about some coffee?
Brown:	Yes, I'd love some.
Tanaka:	Two bottles of beer and some *shabushabu*, please. For dessert, we'd like some melon.
Waitress:	I see.

■ Mr. Tanaka and Mr. Brown has a meal in a restaurant. They drank beer and ate *shabushabu*. After the meal they had coffee.

❏ **Vocabulary**

のみもの	beverage
すきやき	*sukiyaki*
しゃぶしゃぶ	*shabushabu*
デザート	dessert
メロン	melon

NOTES

1. のみものは　なにが　いいですか。
   ビールが　いいです。
   See Grammar X (p. 168) for replies when a choice is offered.

2. りょうりは　すきやきが　いいですか、しゃぶしゃぶが　いいですか。
   When offering a choice between two possibilities, the key word is replaced and the predicate is repeated. Note the difference between this and the usual English construction.
   ex. きょうとに　いきますか、おおさかに　いきますか。 "Are you going to Kyoto or (are you going to) Osaka?"

3. すきやきは　せんしゅう　たべましたから
   Although すきやき is the object, it is also the topic and therefore takes the particle は.

PRACTICE

❏ **KEY SENTENCES**

1. わたしは　ジュースが　いいです。
2. のみものは　ジュースが　いいです。

1. I'll have fruit juice.
2. (As for something) to drink, I'll have fruit juice.

EXERCISES

I Practice the following pattern by changing the underlined part as in the example given.

　　ex. ［わたしは］りょこうは　<u>きょうと</u>が　いいです。

　　　1. げつようび
　　　2. らいげつ
　　　3. おんせん

II Make dialogues by changing the underlined parts as in the examples given.

　A. *ex.* A: ビールが　いいですか、<u>ワイン</u>が　いいですか。
　　　　B: <u>ビール</u>が　いいです。
　　　1. コーヒー、こうちゃ
　　　2. にくの　りょうり、さかなの　りょうり
　　　3. やま、うみ
　　　4. どようび、にちようび

　B. *ex.* A: <u>のみもの</u>は　<u>コーヒー</u>が　いいですか、<u>こうちゃ</u>が　いいですか。
　　　　B: <u>コーヒー</u>が　いいです。
　　　1. デザート、おかし、くだもの
　　　2. ドライブ、こんしゅう、らいしゅう
　　　3. かいぎ、9じから、10じから

　C. *ex.* A: <u>デザート</u>は　なにが　いいですか。
　　　　B: <u>アイスクリーム</u>が　いいです。
　　　1. りょうり、すきやき
　　　2. ひるごはん、サンドイッチ

❏ Vocabulary

アイスクリーム　　　　　　ice cream

SHORT DIALOGUES

1. はやし：　りょうりは　にくが　いいですか、さかなが　いいですか。
　ホワイト：にくが　いいです。
　はやし：　では、すきやきは　いかがですか。
　ホワイト：ええ、すきやきを　おねがいします。

Hayashi:	(As for the meal) Would you like meat or fish?
White:	I'd like meat.
Hayashi:	Then how about *sukiyaki*?
White:	Yes, *sukiyaki* please.

2. たなか： しょくじは　なんじごろが　いいですか。
   ホワイト： 6じが　いいです。
   たなか： では、しょくじの　まえに　にわで　しゃしんを　とりま
   せんか。
   ホワイト： ええ、とりましょう。

Tanaka:	What time would you like to eat? (*lit.* "What time would you like the meal?")
White:	Six o'clock would be nice.
Tanaka:	Well then, wouldn't you like to take some pictures in the garden before dinner?
White:	Yes, let's take some.

3. はやし： しゅうまつに　ドライブに　いきませんか。
   ホワイト： ええ、いいですね。
   はやし： どようびが　いいですか、にちようびが　いいですか。
   ホワイト： どようびが　いいです。
   はやし： どこに　いきましょうか。うみは　どうですか。
   ホワイト： ええ、わたしは　うみが　すきです。うみに　いきたいで
   す。

Hayashi:	Wouldn't you (like to) go for a drive this weekend?
White:	Yes. How nice.
Hayashi:	Would you like to go on Saturday or (would you prefer) Sunday?
White:	Saturday would be fine.
Hayashi:	Where shall we go? What about the seaside?
White:	Yes. I like the sea. I'd like to go to the seaside.

QUIZ

I Read this lesson's opening dialogue and answer the following questions.

  1. たなかさんと　ブラウンさんは　いま　どこに　いますか。
  2. たなかさんと　ブラウンさんは　なにを　のみますか。
  3. たなかさんと　ブラウンさんは　すきやきを　たべますか、しゃぶ
     しゃぶを　たべますか。

II Complete the questions so that they fit the answers.

  1. のみものは　（　　　）が　いいですか。
     コーヒーが　いいです。

2. りょうりは　さかなが　いいですか、（　　　）が　いいですか。
にくが　いいです。
3. しょくじは（　　　）からが　いいですか。
11じからが　いいです。
4. りょこうは（　　　）が　いいですか。
きょうとが　いいです。

III Put the appropriate particles in the parentheses. (If particle is not required, put an X in the parentheses.)

1. らいげつの　やすみに　きょうと（　　　）いきたいです。あなた（　　　）？
わたし（　　　）おおさか（　　　）いいです。
2. デザート（　　　）くだもの（　　　）いいです（　　　）、アイスクリーム（　　　）いいです（　　　）。
アイスクリーム（　　　）いいです。
3. しょくじ（　　　）あとで、くだもの（　　　）おねがいします。
4. かいぎ（　　　）まえ（　　　）、わたし（　　　）へや（　　　）きてください。

IV Translate into Japanese.

1. What would you like for dessert?
   Some fruit, please.
2. I wanted to drink some coffee before the meeting, but there wasn't time, so I drank some after the meeting.

LESSON
30

おげんきですか
READING REVIEW

■ ブラウンさんと　おくさんは　アメリカで　にほんごの
べんきょうを　していました。そして　きょう　ブラウン
さんは　アメリカの　さとうせんせいに　にほんごで　て
がみを　かきました。

さとうせんせい、おげんきですか。
　とうきょうは　とても　あついですが、わたしたちは　げ
んきです。わたしは　まいにち　ちかてつで　かいしゃに
いきます。うちから　かいしゃまで　20ぷんぐらいです。と
うきょうの　ちかてつは　べんりですが、あさ　8じころか
ら　9じころまでと　ごご　5じごろから　6じはんごろまで、
とても　こんでいます。しゅうまつには　ドライブを　した
いですが、わたしたちは　くるまが　ありませんから、でん
しゃで　おもしろい　ところに　いきます。
　しごとは　とても　いそがしいです。せんしゅう　おおさ
かと　きょうとの　ししゃに　いきました。きょうとの　か
いぎの　あとで　ちいさい　おてらに　いきました。しずか
でした。にわが　きれいでした。ほかの　おてらも　みたか
ったですが、じかんが　ありませんでした。ざんねんでした。
　かないは　にほんじんの　ともだちや　アメリカじんの
ともだちと　ちいさい　べんきょうの　グループを　つくり

ました。グループの　ひとは　まいつき　15にちに　あって
にほんと　アメリカの　しゃかいや　ぶんかや　かんがえか
たや　けいざいや　せいじについて　はなしを　します。
　かないは　じかんが　ありますから、いろいろな　べんき
ょうを　しています。そして　にほんじんの　ともだちが
たくさん　あります。かないは　にほんごが　じょうずです。
かんじも　よみます。さいきん　かないは　まいあさ　にほ
んごの　べんきょうを　しています。わたしは　かようびに
だけ　にほんごの　べんきょうを　しています。らいげつか
ら　きんようびにも　したいです。いまの　テキストは　も
うすぐ　おわりますから、らいげつから　あたらしいのを
つかいます。わたしは　あたらしい　テキストを　たのしみ
に　しています。
　では　また　てがみを　かきます。
　みなさまに　どうぞ　よろしく。おげんきで。さようなら。

8がつ　いつか

ジョン・ブラウン

■ Mr. and Mrs. Brown studied Japanese in America. And today Mr. Brown wrote a letter in Japanese to their teacher in America, Sato *Sensei*.

Dear Sato *Sensei,*

　How are you? It is very hot in Tokyo, but we are well.

　I go to my office every day by subway. It takes (*lit.* is) about 20 minutes from my house to the office. Tokyo subways are convenient, but they are very crowded from about 8:00 in the morning till about 9:00 and from about 5:00 in the afternoon till about 6:30. On weekends, we'd like to go driving, but since we don't have a car, we visit interesting places by train.

　I'm very busy with work. I visited our Osaka and Kyoto branches last week. After a meeing in Kyoto I went to a small temple. It was quiet, and the garden was beautiful. I wanted to see other temples but, sorry to say, did not have time.

　My wife has formed a small study group with Japanese and American friends. The people in the group meet on the 15th of each month and talk about Japanese and American community life and social conditions, culture, ways of thinking, economy, politics, etc.

　My wife has time, so she is studying various things. And she has many Japanese friends. My wife's Japanese is good. She reads *kanji*, too. Nowadays my wife has a Japanese lesson every morning. I have a Japanese lesson only on Tuesday. From next month, I want to have one on

Friday, too. I'll soon finish my present textbook, so I will use a new one from next month. I am looking forward to the new textbook. I'll write a letter again (soon).

Please give my best regards to everyone. Take care of yourself.

Good-bye,

August 5

John Brown

❏ Vocabulary

さとうせんせい	Professor Sato
せんせい	(term of respect for professors, doctors, lawyers, etc.)
こんで います	be crowded
こみます（こむ）	be crowded
ところ	place
ほか	other
グループ	group
つくりました	formed
つくります（つくる）	form
まいつき	every month
しゃかい	society, social conditions
ぶんか	culture
かんがえかた	way of thinking
けいざい	economy
せいじ	politics
さいきん	nowadays
テキスト	text
もう すぐ	very soon
おわります（おわる）	finish
あたらしいの	new one
の	one
たのしみに して います	be looking forward to
みなさまに どうぞ よろしく	Best regards to everyone.
みなさま	everyone (politer than みなさん)
～に よろしく	Best regards to ...
おげんきで	Take care of yourself. (*lit.* "(Keep) well.")
ジョン	John.

APPENDICES

A. Particles

Particles		Examples	Lesson
は	1.	わたしは　スミスです。	1
	2.	はやしさんは　きょうとに　いきます。	6
	3.	おおさかには　いきません。	6
	4.	きのうは　スミスさんの　うちに　いきました。	11
	5.	すきやきは　せんしゅう　たべました。	29
の	1.	とうきょうでんきの　たなかです。	1
	2.	わたしの　めいしです。	2
	3.	わたしのです。	2
	4.	あたらしいのを　つかいます。	30
	5.	にほんの　くるまです。	5
	6.	100えんの　きってを　ください。	5
	7.	きょうとの　ししゃに　いきました。	6
	8.	テーブルの　うえに　はなと　しんぶんが　あります。	8
	9.	きょねんの　5がつ18にちに　いきました。	7
	10.	しょくじの　あとで　しんぶんを　よみます。	19
	11.	つぎの　しんごうを　みぎに　まがってください。	20
	12.	ともだちの　クラークさんに　もらいました。	15
	13.	わたしの　すきな　いろです。	15
か	1.	スミスさんですか。	1
	2.	べんごしですか、かいしゃいんですか。	1
	3.	どなたですか。	1
	4.	そうですか。	12
から	1.	10じからです。	3
	2.	10じから　6じまでです。	3
	3.	アメリカから　きました。	6
	4.	とうきょうえきから　あざぶまで　30ぷん　かかりました。	22
	5.	きょうは　どようびですから、びょういんは　12じまでです。	9

に	9.	にっこうに／へ　スキーに　いきます。	16
	10.	りょこうがいしゃに　つとめています。	27
	11.	ニューヨークに　すんでいます。	27
や	1.	いまに　いすや　テーブルが　あります。	8
ね	1.	あそこに　うけつけが　ありますね。	8
よ	1.	ええ、ありますよ。	9
までに	1.	3じまでに　とどけてください。	20
…は…が	1.	わたしは　えいがの　きっぷが　2まい　あります。	18
	2.	わたしは　タイプが　できます。	28
	3.	スミスさんは　にほんの　ふるい　かぐが　すきです。	28
	4.	わたしは　あたまが　いたいです。	28
	5.	わたしは　スライドを／が　みたいです。	28
	6.	わたしは　ジュースが　いいです。	29
	7.	（わたしは）のみものは　ビールが　いいです。	29

B. Interrogatives

Interrogatives	Examples	Lesson
どなた／だれ	こちらは　どなた／だれですか。	1, 5
どなた／だれの	これは　どなた／だれの　ほんですか。	2
だれと	スミスさんは　だれと　なりたくうこうに　いきますか。	6
だれが	だれが　きょう　たいしかんに　いきますか。	6
	にわに　だれが　いますか。	8
だれに	だれに　でんわを　しますか。	12
	だれに　あいますか。	12
なん	これは　なんですか。	2
なんじ	いま　なんじですか。	3
なんで	スミスさんは　たなかさんの　うちに　なんで　いきましたか。	7
	スミスさんは　なんで　えいごの　せつめいを　ききましたか。	14
なにが	いまに　なにが　ありますか。	8
	こんばん　たいしかんで　なにが　ありますか。	18
	りょうりは　なにが　いいですか。	29
なにを	しゅうまつに　なにを　しますか。	10

C. Sentence Patterns

Sentence patterns	Sample Sentences	Lesson
1. …は…です	1. わたしは　たなかです。	1
	2. これは　かいしゃの　でんわばんごうです。	2
	3. ぎんこうは　9じから　3じまでです。	3
	4. この　りんごは　とても　おいしいです。	13
	5. きょうは　いい　てんきですね。	13
	6. かぶきは　とても　おもしろかったです。	14
2. …は…が…です	1. わたしは　りんごが　すきです。	28
	2. わたしは　あたまが　いたいです。	28
	3. のみものは　ジュースが　いいです。	29
	4. わたしは　すいようびが　いいです。	29
3. ―たいです	1. にほんの　ふるい　かぐを　かいたいです。	28
4. …に…が あります／います	1. いっかいに　いまが　あります。	8
	2. にわに　たなかさんが　います。	8
5. …は…に あります／います	1. たなかさんは　となりの　へやに　います。	9
	2. タクシーのりばは　えきの　まえに　あります。	9
6. …を おねがいします	1. サンドイッチと　サラダを　おねがいします。	20
7. …を　ください	1. これを　ください。	4
	2. 100えんの　きってを　10まい　ください。	5
8. …に／へ ―ます	1. わたしは　あした　ぎんこうに　いきます。	6
9. …で…を ―ます	1. わたしは　らいしゅう　ぎんざで　かぶきを　みます。	10
10. …に…を ―ます	1. わたしは　ともだちに　てがみを　かきます。	12
	2. スミスさんは　はやしさんに　ほんを　もらいました。	15

D. Adjectives

Included in the following list of adjectives are some which do not appear in the text.

－い adjectives

あかるい, bright	からい, hot, spicy	つまらない, boring
あたたかい, warm	かるい, light	つめたい, cold
あたらしい, new, fresh	きたない, dirty	とおい, far
あつい, hot	くらい, dark	ながい, long
あぶない, dangerous	さむい, cold	はやい, fast, early
あまい, sweet	しおからい, salty	ひくい, low
いい, good	すくない, few, a little	ひろい, wide
いそがしい, busy	すずしい, cool	ふるい, old
いたい, painful	すっぱい, sour	みじかい, short
おいしい, delicious	せまい, narrow	むずかしい, difficult
おおい, many, much	たかい, high, expensive	やさしい, easy
おおきい, large	ただしい, correct	やすい, cheap
おそい, slow, late	たのしい, pleasant	わかい, young
おもい, heavy	ちいさい, small	わるい, bad
おもしろい, interesting	ちかい, near	

－な adjectives

あんぜんな, safe	じょうずな, skillful	ひまな, free
いろいろな, various	しんせつな, kind	ふしんせつな, unkind
きらいな, unlikeable	すきな, likeable	ふべんな, inconvenient
きれいな, clean, pretty	だいじな, important	へたな, unskillful
げんきな, well, healthy	だめな, no good	べんりな, convenient
しずかな, quiet	ていねいな, polite	ゆうめいな, famous
しつれいな, rude	にぎやかな, lively	

Color words

あおい, blue, green	しろい, white
あかい, red	ちゃいろい, ちゃいろの,* brown
きいろい, きいろの,* yellow	みどりいろの,* green
くろい, black	むらさきいろの,* purple

*Note that these words are nouns and are followed by the particle の.

E. Verb Conjugation

The following are the －ます，－て，－ない, plain dictionary and －た forms of Regular I, Regular II and Irregular verbs. (See also Model Verb Conjugation in Lesson 19.)

Regular I					
－ます	－て	－ない	dictionary	－た	
あいます	あって	あわない	あう	あった	meet
あります	あって	ない	ある	あった	be, have
あるきます	あるいて	あるかない	あるく	あるいた	walk
いいます	いって	いわない	いう	いった	say
いきます	いって	いかない	いく	いった	go
いただきます	いただいて	いただかない	いただく	いただいた	accept
いらっしゃいます	いらっしゃって	いらっしゃらない	いらっしゃる	いらっしゃった	go, be
うります	うって	うらない	うる	うった	sell
おくります	おくって	おくらない	おくる	おくった	send
おします	おして	おさない	おす	おした	push
おわります	おわって	おわらない	おわる	おわった	finish
かいます	かって	かわない	かう	かった	buy
かえります	かえって	かえらない	かえる	かえった	return
かかります	かかって	かからない	かかる	かかった	(it) takes
かきます	かいて	かかない	かく	かいた	write
がんばります	がんばって	がんばらない	がんばる	がんばった	do one's best
ききます	きいて	きかない	きく	きいた	listen
けします	けして	けさない	けす	けした	turn off
こみます	こんで	こまない	こむ	こんだ	be crowded
*しっています	しって	しらない	しる	しった	know
すいます	すって	すわない	すう	すった	smoke (cigarettes)
すみます	すんで	すまない	すむ	すんだ	live
ちがいます	ちがって	ちがわない	ちがう	ちがった	be wrong
つかいます	つかって	つかわない	つかう	つかった	use
つきます	ついて	つかない	つく	ついた	arrive
つくります	つくって	つくらない	つくる	つくった	make
とります	とって	とらない	とる	とった	take (a picture)

*See Lesson 27.

のみます	のんで	のまない	のむ	のんだ	drink
のります	のって	のらない	のる	のった	ride, get on
はいります	はいって	はいらない	はいる	はいった	enter
まちます	まって	またない	まつ	まった	wait
まがります	まがって	まがらない	まがる	まがった	turn
もちます	もって	もたない	もつ	もった	have, hold
もらいます	もらって	もらわない	もらう	もらった	receive
よみます	よんで	よまない	よむ	よんだ	read
わかります	わかって	わからない	わかる	わかった	understand

Regular II

－ます	－て	－ない	dictionary	－た	
あけます	あけて	あけない	あける	あけた	open
あげます	あげて	あげない	あげる	あげた	give
います	いて	いない	いる	いた	be
おしえます	おしえて	おしえない	おしえる	おしえた	tell
おります	おりて	おりない	おりる	おりた	get off
かけます	かけて	かけない	かける	かけた	sit down
しめます	しめて	しめない	しめる	しめた	close
たべます	たべて	たべない	たべる	たべた	eat
つけます	つけて	つけない	つける	つけた	turn on
（きを）つけます	つけて	つけない	つける	つけた	be careful
つとめます	つとめて	つとめない	つとめる	つとめた	work for
できます	できて	できない	できる	できた	be able
でます	でて	でない	でる	でた	leave
とどけます	とどけて	とどけない	とどける	とどけた	deliver
とめます	とめて	とめない	とめる	とめた	stop, park
みせます	みせて	みせない	みせる	みせた	show
みます	みて	みない	みる	みた	see

Irregular					
－ます	－て	－ない	dictionary	－た	
きます	きて	こない	くる	きた	come
もってきます	もってきて	もってこない	もってくる	もってきた	bring
します	して	しない	する	した	do
（べんきょうを）					
します	して	しない	する	した	study
おねがい	おねがい	おねがい	おねがい	おねがい	beg a favor
します	して	しない	する	した	
しつれい	しつれい	しつれい	しつれい	しつれい	be rude
します	して	しない	する	した	

The following is a selection of compounds that are formed with する and are conjugated in the same way as べんきょうを　します.

うんてんを　します, drive

かいぎを　します, have a meeting
かいものを　します, shop
クリーニングを　します, dry clean
コピーを　します, make a copy
ゴルフを　します, play golf

しごとを　します, work
しゅっちょうを　します, go on a business trip
しょうかいを　します, introduce
スキーを　します, ski
せつめいを　します, explain

そうべつかいを　します, give a farewell party

タイプを　します, type
テニスを　します, play tennis
でんわを　します, telephone
ドライブを　します, go for a drive/driving

パーティーを　します, give a party
はなしを　します, talk

よやくを　します, make a reservation

りょこうを　します, take a trip

F. こ-そ-あ-ど

	こ - words	そ - words	あ - words	ど - words
direction	こちら here, this way	そちら there, that way	あちら over there	どちら where
people	こちら this person	そちら that person	あちら that person over there	どなた、だれ who
thing	これ this	それ that	あれ that over there	どれ which
place	ここ here	そこ there	あそこ over there	どこ where
demonstrative	この　カメラ this camera	その　カメラ that camera	あの　カメラ that camera over there	どの　カメラ which camera

G. Country, Nationality, Language

	Country	Nationality	Language
Australia	オーストラリア	オーストラリアじん	えいご
Brazil	ブラジル	ブラジルじん	ポルトガルご
Canada	カナダ	カナダじん	えいご／フランスご
China	ちゅうごく	ちゅうごくじん	ちゅうごくご
Egypt	エジプト	エジプトじん	アラビアご
France	フランス	フランスじん	フランスご
Germany	ドイツ	ドイツじん	ドイツご
Indonesia	インドネシア	インドネシアじん	インドネシアご
Italy	イタリア	イタリアじん	イタリアご
Japan	にほん	にほんじん	にほんご
New Zealand	ニュージーランド	ニュージーランドじん	えいご
Russia	ロシア	ロシアじん	ロシアご
Spain	スペイン	スペインじん	スペインご
Switzerland	スイス	スイスじん	ドイツご／フランスご／イタリアご
Thailand	タイ	タイじん	タイご
United Kingdom	イギリス	イギリスじん	えいご
United States	アメリカ	アメリカじん	えいご

The question words are: どこのくに, belonging to or coming from "What country?" (This is often shortened to どこ?) なにご, "What language?" and なにじん, "What nationality?"

H. Common Japanese Names (Source: Nippon Univac Kaisha, Ltd., 1975.)

Family Names	Male Given Names	Female Given Names
1. かとう	1. ひろし	1. よしこ
2. すずき	2. としお	2. けいこ
3. わたなべ	3. よしお	3. かずこ
4. たなか	4. かずお	4. ひろこ
5. いとう	5. あきら	5. ようこ

I. Counters

The abstract numbers (いち, に, さん) are given on p. 10 (0-20), p. 17 (20, 30, ...) and p. 25 (100, 200, ...). The ひとつ, ふたつ, みっつ system is given on p. 33. Two counters (〜まい and 〜ほん) appear on p. 30. Below are other counters used in this book.

1. Floors of a house or building: 〜かい. Which/how many floors, なんかい／なんがい.

いっかい, 1st floor	ごかい, 5th floor	きゅうかい, 9th floor
にかい, 2nd floor	ろっかい, 6th floor	じゅっかい, 10th floor
さんがい, 3rd floor	ななかい, 7th floor	じゅういっかい, 11th floor
よんかい, 4th floor	はちかい, 8th floor	じゅうにかい, 12th floor

   Also: ちか　いっかい, (1st) basement, ちか　にかい, 2nd basement, etc.

2. Liquid measure (cupful, glassful): 〜はい, 〜ばい, 〜ぱい. How many, なんばい.

いっぱい, 1 cupful	ごはい, 5 cupfuls	きゅうはい, 9 cupfuls
にはい, 2 cupfuls	ろっぱい, 6 cupfuls	じゅっぱい, 10 cupfuls
さんばい, 3 cupfuls	ななはい, 7 cupfuls	じゅういっぱい, 11 cupfuls
よんはい, 4 cupfuls	はっぱい, 8 cupfuls	じゅうにはい, 12 cupfuls

3. People: 〜にん. How many people, なんにん.

ひとり, 1 person	ろくにん, 6 people	くにん, 9 people
ふたり, 2 people	しちにん, 7 people	じゅうにん, 10 people
さんにん, 3 people	ななにん, 7 people	じゅういちにん, 11 people
よにん, 4 people	はちにん, 8 people	じゅうににん, 12 people
ごにん, 5 people	きゅうにん, 9 people	

4. Times: 〜かい, 〜ど. Generally speaking, these two counters may be used interchangeably. How many times, なんかい. How many times/degrees, なんど.

いっかい, いちど, once	ななかい, ななど, 7 times
にかい, にど, twice	はちかい, はちど, 8 times
さんかい, さんど, 3 times	きゅうかい, きゅうど, 9 times
よんかい, よんど, 4 times	じゅっかい, じゅうど, 10 times
ごかい, ごど, 5 times	じゅういっかい, じゅういちど, 11 times
ろっかい, ろくど, 6 times	じゅうにかい, じゅうにど, 12 times

J. Extent, Frequency, Quantity

1. Extent

100% ┬
　├ とても　　　　　　　　　　　　　　very, extremely

　├ あまり　－ない／－ません　　　　not very
0% ┴ ぜんぜん　－ない／－ません　　　not at all

ex. この　のみものは　<u>とても</u>　おいしいです。"This drink is very good."

　　この　のみものは　<u>あまり</u>　おいしくないです。"This drink is not very good."

　　この　のみものは　<u>ぜんぜん</u>　おいしくないです。"This drink is not good at all."

2. Frequency

100% ┬ いつも　　　　　　　　　　always
　　├ よく　　　　　　　　　　　often

　　├ ときどき　　　　　　　　　sometimes

　　├ たまに　　　　　　　　　　occasionally
　　├ あまり　－ません　　　　　not very often
0% ┴ ぜんぜん　－ません　　　　never

ex. ばんごはんの　あとで　<u>いつも</u>　テレビを　みます。

"(I) always watch TV after supper."

ばんごはんの　あとで　<u>よく</u>　テレビを　みます。

"(I) often watch TV after supper."

ばんごはんの　あとで　<u>ときどき</u>　テレビを　みます。

"(I) sometimes watch TV after supper."

ばんごはんの　あとで　<u>たまに</u>　テレビを　みます。

"(I) occasinally watch TV after supper."

ばんごはんの　あとで　<u>あまり</u>　テレビを　<u>みません</u>。

"(I) don't often watch TV after supper."

ばんごはんの　あとで　<u>ぜんぜん</u>　テレビを　<u>みません</u>。

"(I) never watch TV after supper."

3. Quantity

100% ┬
　├ たくさん　　　　　　　　　　　a lot, many

　├ すこし　　　　　　　　　　　　few, a little
0% ┴ ぜんぜん　－ません　　　　　　none at all

ex. みせが <u>たくさん</u> あります。 "There are a lot of stores."

みせが <u>すこし</u> あります。 "There are a few stores."

みせが <u>ぜんぜん</u> あり<u>ません</u>。 "There are no stores."

K. Time Expressions

1. Every, まい〜

   まいにち, every day

   まいばん, every evening, every night

   まいあさ, every morning

   まいしゅう, every week

   まいつき／まいげつ, every month

   まいねん／まいとし, every year

2. Period of Time

   Minutes, 〜ふん, 〜ぷん. How many minutes, なんぷん (かん).

   いっぷん (かん), (for) 1 minute

   にふん (かん), (for) 2 minutes

   さんぷん (かん), (for) 3 minutes

   よんぷん (かん), (for) 4 minutes

   ごふん (かん), (for) 5 minutes

   ろっぷん (かん), (for) 6 minutes

   ななふん (かん), (for) 7 minutes

   はっぷん (かん), (for) 8 minutes

   はちふん (かん), (for) 8 minutes

   きゅうふん (かん), (for) 9 minutes

   じゅっぷん (かん), (for) 10 minutes

   じゅういっぷん (かん), (for) 11 minutes

   じゅうにふん (かん), (for) 12 minutes

   Hours, 〜じかん. How many hours, なんじかん.

   いちじかん, (for) 1 hour

   にじかん, (for) 2 hours

   さんじかん, (for) 3 hours

   よじかん, (for) 4 hours

   ごじかん, (for) 5 hours

   ろくじかん, (for) 6 hours

   ななじかん, (for) 7 hours

   しちじかん, (for) 7 hours

   はちじかん, (for) 8 hours

   くじかん, (for) 9 hours

   じゅうじかん, (for) 10 hours

   じゅういちじかん, (for) 11 hours

   じゅうにじかん, (for) 12 hours

   Days, 〜にち (かん). How many days, なんにち (かん).

   いちにち (かん), (for) 1 day

   ふつか (かん), (for) 2 days

   みっか (かん), (for) 3 days

   よっか (かん), (for) 4 days

   いつか (かん), (for) 5 days

   むいか (かん), (for) 6 days

   なのか (かん), (for) 7 days

   ようか (かん), (for) 8 days

   ここのか (かん), (for) 9 days

   とおか (かん), (for) 10 days

   じゅういちにち (かん), (for) 11 days

   じゅうににち (かん), (for) 12 days

Weeks, 〜しゅうかん. How many weeks, なんしゅうかん.

いっしゅうかん, (for) 1 week   ななしゅうかん, (for) 7 weeks

にしゅうかん, (for) 2 weeks   はっしゅうかん, (for) 8 weeks

さんしゅうかん, (for) 3 weeks   きゅうしゅうかん, (for) 9 weeks

よんしゅうかん, (for) 4 weeks   じゅっしゅうかん, (for) 10 weeks

ごしゅうかん, (for) 5 weeks   じゅういっしゅうかん, (for) 11 weeks

ろくしゅうかん, (for) 6 weeks   じゅうにしゅうかん, (for) 12 weeks

Months, 〜かげつ (かん). How many months, なんかげつ (かん).

いっかげつ (かん), (for) 1 month   しちかげつ (かん), (for) 7 months

にかげつ (かん), (for) 2 months   はっかげつ (かん), (for) 8 months

さんかげつ (かん), (for) 3 months   きゅうかげつ (かん), (for) 9 months

よんかげつ (かん), (for) 4 months   じゅっかげつ (かん), (for) 10 months

ごかげつ (かん), (for) 5 months   じゅういっかげつ (かん), (for) 11 months

ろっかげつ (かん), (for) 6 months   じゅうにかげつ (かん), (for) 12 months

ななかげつ (かん), (for) 7 months

Years, 〜ねん （かん）. How many years, なんねん （かん）.

いちねん (かん), (for) 1 year   しちねん (かん), (for) 7 years

にねん (かん), (for) 2 years   はちねん (かん), (for) 8 years

さんねん (かん), (for) 3 years   きゅうねん (かん), (for) 9 years

よねん (かん), (for) 4 years   じゅうねん (かん), (for) 10 years

ごねん (かん), (for) 5 years   じゅういちねん (かん), (for) 11 years

ろくねん (かん), (for) 6 years   じゅうにねん (かん), (for) 12 years

ななねん (かん), (for) 7 years

Note: Except for 〜じかん and 〜しゅうかん the suffix かん may be considered optional and need be added only when one needs to be specific.

3. Relative Time

Day   Week

おととい, day before yesterday   せんせんしゅう, week before last

きのう, yesterday   せんしゅう, last week

きょう, today   こんしゅう, this week

あした, tomorrow   らいしゅう, next week

あさって, day after tomorrow   さらいしゅう, week after next

Morning	Month
おとといの　あさ, morning before last	せんせんげつ, month before last
きのうの　あさ, yesterday morning	せんげつ, last month
けさ, this morning	こんげつ, this month
あしたの　あさ, tomorrow morning	らいげつ, next month
あさっての　あさ,	さらいげつ, month after next
morning of the day after tomorrow	

Evening	Year
おとといの　ばん／よる,	おととし, year before last
evening/night before last	きょねん, last year
きのうの　ばん／よる,	ことし, this year
yesterday evening/night	らいねん, next year
こんばん, this evening	さらいねん, year after next
あしたの　ばん／よる,	
tomorrow evening/night	
あさっての　ばん／よる,	
evening/night of the day after tomorrow	

4. Seasons

はる, spring　　なつ, summer　　あき, autumn　　ふゆ, winter

L. Parts of the Face and Body

1. Face, かお, and head, あたま

あご, chin, jaw	は, tooth	まぶた, eyelid
かみ, hair	はな, nose	まゆ／まゆげ, eyebrow
くち, mouth	ひたい, forehead	みみ, ear
くちびる, lip	ほほ, cheek	め, eye
した, tongue	まつげ, eyelash	

2. Body, からだ

あし, foot, leg	くび, neck	のど, throat
うで, arm	こし, hip	ひふ, skin
おしり, buttock	せなか, back	むね, chest
おなか, stomach, abdomen	つめ, nail	ゆび, finger, toe
かた, shoulder	て, hand	

M. Kanji

Each かんじ conveys an idea, and most of them have at least two readings. The numbers in parentheses indicate the number of strokes.

Counters, Day of the Week, Date

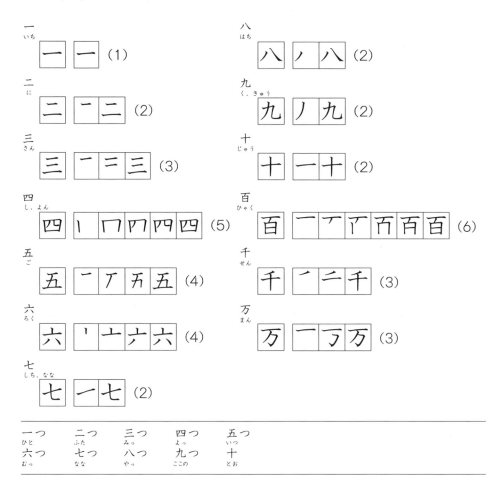

一 | 二 | 三 | 四 | 五
ひと | ふた | みっ | よっ | いっ
六 | 七 | 八 | 九 | 十
むっ | なな | やっ | ここの | とお

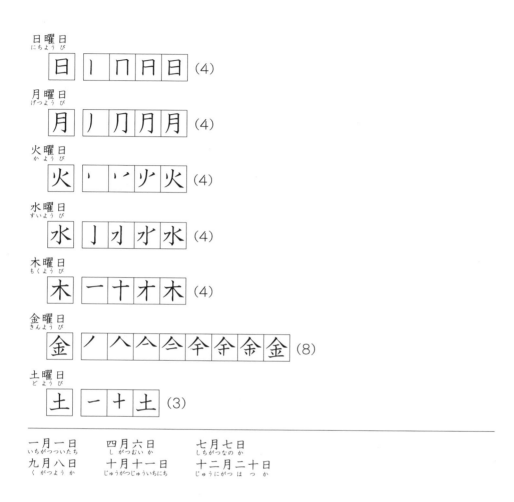

日曜日
にちようび
日 | ⊓ ⿵ 日 (4)

月曜日
げつようび
月) ⼏ 月 月 (4)

火曜日
かようび
火 ヽ ⺌ ⺌ 火 (4)

水曜日
すいようび
水 丿 刂 氺 水 (4)

木曜日
もくようび
木 一 十 才 木 (4)

金曜日
きんようび
金 ノ 人 亼 𠆢 全 仐 金 金 (8)

土曜日
どようび
土 一 十 土 (3)

一月一日　　　四月六日　　　七月七日
いちがつついたち　し　がつむいか　　しちがつなのか

九月八日　　　十月十一日　　　十二月二十日
く　がつようか　じゅうがつじゅういちにち　じゅうにがつはつか

QUIZ ANSWERS

Lesson 1
I 1. スミスです。 2. いいえ、にほんじんではありません。 3. べんごしです。

II 1. スミスさん 2. ドイツじん 3. べんごし 4. どなた

III 1. は 2. か、か 3. の

IV 1. スミスです。 2. はじめまして。どうぞ よろしく。 3. やまださん、こちらは とうきょうでんきの たなかさんです。 4. スミスさんは アメリカじんですか、ドイツじんですか。

Lesson 2
I 1. めいしです。 2. はい、かいしゃの なまえです。 3. かいしゃの [じゅうしょ] です。 4. いいえ、うちの でんわばんごうではありません。 5. ゼロさんの さんよんゼロゼロの きゅうゼロさんいちです。

II 1. かいしゃ 2. だれ／どなた 3. なん 4. なんばん

III 1. は 2. は、か、の、は、の 3. は、の、の

IV 1. こちらは たなかさんです。 2. これは たなかさんの めいしです。 3. これは たなかさんの うちの でんわばんごうではありません。かいしゃのです。 4. [あなたの]かいしゃの でんわばんごうは なんばんですか。

Lesson 3
I 1. いいえ、10じではありません。 2. 10じからです。 3. いいえ、7じまででは ありません。

II 1. なんじ 2. なんようび 3. なんにち

III 1. は 2. の、は 3. は、から、まで

IV 1. どうも ありがとう。 2. どういたしまして。 3. すみません。ゆうびんきょくは なんじまでですか。 4. きょうは 15にちです。あしたは 16にちです。 5. きょうは もくようびです。きのうは すいようびでした。

Lesson 4
I 1. いいえ、[これは]とけいではありません。 2. [あれは]テレビです。 3. [あれは]50,000えんです。 4. いいえ、[それは]50,000えんではありません。 5. [それは]5,000えんです。 6. はい、[これも]5,000えんです。

II 1. なん 2. いくら 3. どなた 4. あれ

III 1. を 2. は、も、も、も、は、は

IV 1. それを みせてください。 2. これを ください。 3. これは いくらですか。 4. いらっしゃいませ。

Lesson 5

I　1.［その　ドイツの　カメラは／それは］　50,000えんです。　2. いいえ、［この　カメラは／これは］　ドイツのではありません。　3.［この　カメラは／これは］　35,000えんです。　4.［あの　ちいさい　ラジオは／あれは］　にほんのです。

II　1. いくら　2. あれ　3. イギリス、どこ

III　1. は、の、も、の　2. を　3. を、×　4. は　5. ×、は、×

IV　1. これは　いくらですか。　2. この　ラジオは　いくらですか。　3. わたしの　とけいは　にほんのではありません。アメリカのです。　4. その　ちいさい　テープレコーダーを　みせてください。　5. フィルムを　みっつ　ください。どの　フィルムですか。その　フィルムです。

Lesson 6

I　1. きょうとの　ししゃに／へ　いきます。　2. かいしゃの　ひとと　いきます。　3. あさって　かえります。

II　1. ぎんこう、ゆうびんきょく　2. いつ　3. どこ、だれ／どなた

III　1. ×、に／へ　2. と、に／へ　3. は、×　4. で　5. に／へ、も、は　6. が

IV　1. すみません、この　バスは　とうきょうえきに／へ　いきますか。　2. たなかさんは　きのう　かいしゃの　ひとと　おおさかに／へ　いきました。そして　あさって　とうきょうに／へ　かえります。　3. スミスさんは　きょねん　ひとりで　にほんに／へ　きました。　4. だれ／どなたが　くうこうに／へ　いきましたか。たなかさんの　ひしょが　いきました。

Lesson 7

I　1. スミスさんが　いきました。　2. にちようびに　いきました。　3. いいえ、でんしゃで　いきませんでした。　4. タクシーで　いきました。

II　1. どこ　2. いつ　3. なんにち、なん、だれ／どなた

III　1. で、に／へ、も　2. ×、に

IV　1. こんにちは。　2. よく　いらっしゃいました。　3. どうぞ　おかけください。

V　1. どうぞ　こちらに／へ。　2. どうぞ　おはいりください。　3. たなかさんは　きのう　タクシーで　うちに／へ　かえりました。　4. ホワイトさんは　きんようびに　おおさかの　ししゃに／へ　いきます。

Lesson 8

I　1. （いまに）　いすや　テーブルや　テレビが　あります。　2. しんぶんと　はがが　あります。　3. たなかさんの　おくさんが　います。　4. だれも　いません。

II　1. だれ／どなた　2. なに　3. だれ／どなた　4. なに

III　1. あります　2. います　3. いません　4. ありません

IV 1. の、に、が　2. の、と、が　3. や、が　4. が、も

V 1. いまに　いすや　テーブルが　あります。　2. にわに　たなかさんと　お
とこの　こが　います。　3. だいどころに　だれが　いますか。だれも　いま
せん。　4. いすの　うえに　なにも　ありません。

Lesson 9

I 1. ゆうびんきょくに　いきます。　2. いいえ、スーパーの　まえではありま
せん。

II 1. どこ　2. なに　3. どこ　4. どうして　5. いくつ　6. なんにん

III 1. は、×、の、に　2. に、×、×　3. に／へ、から　4. は、に

IV 1. さかやは　やおやの　となりです。／さかやは　やおやの　となりに　あり
ます。　2. すみません、おてあらいは　どこですか。／すみません、おてあら
いは　どこに　ありますか。あそこです。／あそこに　あります。　3. ホワイ
トさんは　おおさかに／へ　いきましたから、きょう　かいしゃに　いません。
4. どうして　きょう　びょういんは　12じまでですか。どようびですから。
5. ほんやの　まえに　こどもが　5にん　います。

Lesson 10

I 1. かぶきを　みます。　2. いいえ、ひとりで　みません。　3. せんしゅう
かいました。　4. ぎんざの　プレイガイドで　かいました。

II 1. なんようび　2. どこ　3. なに　4. なに

III 1. に　2. で、に／へ　3. で、を　4. で、も　5. を　6. ×、で、を

IV 1. にちようびに　デパートで　カメラを　かいました。45,000えんでした。
2. きのう　なにを　しましたか。あさ、うちで　にほんごの　テープを　きき
ました。ごご　ぎんざに／へ　いきました。そして、ぎんざで　カメラを　か
いました。　3. ホワイトさんは　あさ　なにも　たべません。

Lesson 12

I 1. かとうさんが　しました。　2. いませんでした。　3. 9じごろ　かえりま
す。　4. はい、します。

II 1. なに、だれ／どなた　2. だれ／どなた　3. だれ／どなた

III 1. いいえ、きません　2. みます、いいえ、みません　3. よく　4. よみます、
よみません

IV 1. に　2. に　3. ×、と　4. に、を　5. が、は

V 1. もしもし、たなかさんの　おたくですか。　2. とうきょうでんきの　たな
かです。はやしさんは　いらっしゃいますか。　3. また　あとで　でんわを
します。　4. クラークさんに　かいしゃの　でんわばんごうを　ききました。
5. クラークさんは　あまり　ともだちに　てがみを　かきませんが、ホワイト
さんは　よく　かきます。

Lesson 13

I 1. はい、たべました。　2. にほんの　おかしを　たべました。　3. おちゃを のみました。

II 1. げんき　2. おもしろい　3. どなた／だれ　4. どんな

III 1. おいしくないです　2. きれいな　3. おもしろくないです　4. よくないです 5. ゆうめいな　6. ちかいです

IV 1. コーヒーは　いかがですか。ありがとうございます。いただきます。　2. コーヒーを　もう　いっぱい　いかがですか。いいえ、もう　けっこうです。 3. わたしたちは　ゆうめいな　レストランで　ばんごはんを　たべました。 4. あの　きっさてんは　きれいですが、しずかではありません。　5. [わたし は]　きょう　いそがしいです。

Lesson 14

I 1. かぶきを　みました。　2. おもしろかったです。　3. イヤホーンで　きき ました。

II 1. やさしい　2. ちかい　3. つまらない　4. おおきい　5. たかい　6. いそがし い　7. あつい　8. しずかな　9. ふるい　10. わるい

III 1. なに、どう、よかった　2. どうして　3. どんな

IV 1. よかったです　2. どう　3. にぎやかでした　4. きれいではありません　5. おもしろくなかったです　6. げんきでした

V 1. きのうの　かいぎは　どうでしたか。　2. きのうの　てんきは　よかった です。　3. あの　レストランの　りょうりは　あまり　おいしくなかったで す。

Lesson 15

I 1. たんじょうびに　もらいました。　2. クラークさんに／から　もらいまし た。　3. クラークさんが　あげました。　4. たなかさんに　あげました。

II 1. だれ／どなた　2. だれ／どなた　3. なに

III 1. に／から　2. が、を　3. に、を　4. に、を、も

IV 1. たなかさんは　クラークさんに　きれいな　かびんを　もらいました。　2. はやしさんは　スミスさんに　きょうとの　ちずを　あげました。　3. あの ひとに　めいしを　あげましたか。はい、あげました。

Lesson 16

I 1. にっこうに　いきます。　2. いいえ、ひとりで　いきません。　3. とうきょ うえき　[の　かいさつぐち]　で　あいます。　4. 7じに　あいます。　5. でん しゃで　いきます。

II 1. どこ、なんじ　2. だれ／どなた

III 1. に、を　2. に、に　3. に、に　4. に、で

IV 1. どようびに　デパートに／へ　かいものに　いきました。　2. いっしょに
しょくじを　しませんか。ええ、しましょう。どこに／へ　いきましょうか。
えきの　ちかくの　あたらしい　レストランに／へ　いきませんか。ええ、そ
うしましょう。

Lesson 17

I 1. どようび [の　ばん] です。　2. いきます。　3. たなかさんの　うちで
します。　4. あざぶに　あります。　5. はい、かきます。

II 1. に、に、に／へ、に、を　2. に、が、が　3. を

III 1. にちようびに　うちに／へ　きませんか。　2. きんようびに　うちで　ク
ラークさんの　そうべつかいを　します。きませんか。ええ、ぜひ。　3. いっ
しょに　しょくじを　しませんか。　4. さむいですね。まどを　しめましょう
か。はい、おねがいします。　5. ちずを　かきましょうか。

Lesson 18

I 1. えいがの　きっぷが　あります。　2. 2まい　あります。　3. パーティーに
いきます。　4. パーティーが　あります。　5. いいえ、いきません。　6. あ
した　スミスさんと　いきます。

II 1. なんにん　2. いつ　3. なに　4. どこ

III 1. が　2. に　3. で　4. が、×　5. で、が　6. の、が、×、×、が

IV 1. わたしは　いもうとが　3にん　あります。いもうとは　とうきょうと　お
おさかに　います。　2. たなかさん、8がつに　やすみが　ありますか。いい
え、ありません。9がつに　あります。　3. らいしゅう　きょうとの　ししゃ
で　かいぎが　あります。

Lesson 19

I 1. スミスさんの　ともだちです。　2. きのう　きました。　3. らいしゅうの
もくようびまで　います。　4. みっか（かん）います。　5. きょうとや　な
らに／へ　いきます。　6. ふるい　おてらや　にわを　みます。

II 1. たべて　2. いって　3. よんで　4. きて　5. かいて　6. かえって　7. いて
8. みて　9. して　10. のんで　11. あって　12. きいて

III 1. いつ／なんねんの　なんがつ、いつ／なんねんの　なんがつ　2. どのぐら
い／なんにち（かん）ぐらい／なんしゅうかんぐらい　3. いつ

IV 1. そして　2. いって　3. どのぐらい　4. ぐらい　5. どう　6. なん、どのぐら
い、ぐらい

V 1. まいあさ　ニュースを　きいて、かいしゃに／へ　いきます。　2. たなか
さんに　あって、いっしょに　ばんごはんを　たべました。そして　うちに／
へ　かえりました。　3. どのぐらい　うちで　にほんごの　べんきょうを　し
ますか。30ぷんだけ　します。　4. きのう　どこに／へも　いきませんでし
た。うちに　いました。

Lesson 20

I 1. さかやに ［でんわを］ しました。　2. はやしさんの うちに とどけます。　3. 20ぽん とどけます。　4. 3じまでに とどけます。　5. はい、おしえました。

II 1. いって　2. いて　3. まって　4. きいて　5. まがって　6. みせて　7. もってきて　8. いって　9. しめて　10. あって　11. のんで　12. して

III 1. を　2. を、×　3. に　4. を　5. を、と、を、に／へ　6. を、に／へ

IV 1. メニューを みせてください。はい、どうぞ。　2. すみませんが、うちに ビールを 12ほん とどけてください。はい、わかりました。クラークさんですね。ええ、そうです。　3. この ちいさい テレビを ください。はい、わかりました。とどけましょうか。いいえ、けっこうです。くるまで きましたから。

Lesson 22

I 1. せんしゅう いきました。　2. いいえ、［いっしょに］ いきませんでした。　3. あした いきます。　4. あざぶで おりました。　5. いいえ、かかりませんでした。

II 1. なん　2. どこ　3. なに　4. どのぐらい／なんじかんぐらい　5. どうやって

III 1. で、に、で、を　2. を、に、に、で　3. まで、で、×

IV 1. きのう ぎんざの ホテルで ともだちの そうべつかいが ありました。　2. かいしゃを 6じに でて、バスに のって、ぎんざで おりました。　3. かいしゃから ホテルまで どのぐらい かかりましたか。35ふんぐらい かかりました。

Lesson 23

I 1. でんきやで もらいました。　2. テレビの カタログを もらいました。　3. いいえ、ケースの なかに ありませんでした。　4. ケースの うえに ありました。

II 1. はいって　2. きて　3. たべて　4. みて　5. つかって　6. のんで　7. して　8. とって　9. きいて　10. いって　11. いて　12. いって

III 1. とって　2. し、し　3. あけ、あけて　4. つかって、まって　5. き、きて　6. もらって　7. かって

IV 1. でんきを つけましょうか。はい、おねがいします。　2. この でんわを つかっても いいですか。はい、どうぞ。　3. 3じまで ここに いても いいですか。

Lesson 24

I 1. けいかんが おしえました。　2. つぎの かどを ひだりに まがります。　3. ちゅうしゃじょうに／へ いきます。

II 1. たべない 2. みない 3. いかない 4. こない 5. いわない 6. よまない
7. しない 8. すわない 9. あけない 10. まがらない 11. けさない 12. つ
けない 13. つかわない 14. しめない 15. とらない

III 1. すって、すわないで 2. あけて、あけて 3. いって、きて 4. しめ、しめ
ないで

IV 1. は、から、を 2. を、に／へ 3. で、を 4. を、に

V 1. いま あの へやに はいらないでください。 2. ここで たばこを す
わないでください。 3. つぎの しんごうを みぎに／へ まがってくださ
い。

Lesson 25

I 1. 3がいに います。 2. かいぎしつに います。 3. スライドを みていま
す。

II 1. どこ／なんがい、なに 2. どこ 3. だれ／どなた 4. どこ

III 1. はやしさんは スミスさんに でんわを します。 2. はやしさんは ス
ミスさんに でんわを しています。 3. あの おんなの こは なにを し
ていますか。ともだちを まっています。 4. ホワイトさんは いま しごと
を していません。

Lesson 27

I 1. スミスさんと はやしさんが はなしを しています。 2. スミスさんの
おにいさんが きました。 3. いいえ、いません。 4. りょこうがいしゃに
つとめています。 5. ニューヨーク／アメリカに すんでいます。

II 1. どこ 2. どこ 3. だれ／どなた 4. どこ

III 1. の 2. に、に 3. で 4. に、の、に 5. で、の、を、で

IV 1. たなかさんを しっていますか。いいえ、しりません。 2. わたしは か
いしゃの ちかくに すんでいます。あるいて 15ふんです。 3. スミスさん
は ABCに つとめています。

Lesson 28

I 1. にほんの ふるい かぐが すきです。 2. はい、もう かいました。 3.
いいえ、しりません。 4. ふるい かぐの みせについて ききます。

II 1. なに 2. どこ 3. どんな 4. なに

III 1. は、が、が、は 2. は、が 3. が、に、に／へ 4. も 5. も、に、で、
を／が

IV 1. ホワイトさんは りんごが すきです。 2. スキーが できますか。はい、
できます。 3. あした ともだちに あって、いっしょに テニスを／が し
たいです。 4. きのう てがみを／が かきたかったですが、じかんが あり
ませんでした。 5. ［わたしは］ のどが いたいですから、なにも たべたく
ないです。

Lesson 29

 I　1. レストランに　います。　2. ビールを　のみます。　3. しゃぶしゃぶを
　　たべます。

 II　1. なに　2. にく　3. なんじ　4. どこ

 III　1. に／へ、は、は、が　2. は、が、か、が、か、が　3. の、を　4. の、に、
　　の、に／へ

 IV　1. デザートは　なにが　いいですか。くだものを　おねがいします。　2. かい
　　ぎの　まえに　コーヒーを／が　のみたかったですが、じかんが　ありません
　　でしたから、かいぎの　あとで　のみました。

JAPANESE-ENGLISH GLOSSARY

あ, Ah, 38

アイスクリーム, ice cream, 179

あいましょうか, shall (we) meet, 104; あいます, あう, meet, 77

あおい, blue, 35

あかい, red, 34

あかちゃん, baby, 107

あけましょうか, shall (I) open; あけます, あける, open, 110

あげました, gave; あげます, あげる, give, 98

あさ, morning, 70

あさごはん, breakfast, morning meal, 70

あさって, the day after tomorrow, 38

あした, tomorrow, 16

あそこ, over there, that place (over there), 55

あたま, head, 170

あたらしい, new, fresh, 89

あちら, over there, that person over there, 195

あつくなかった, was not hot; あつい, hot, 93

あとで, afterwards, later, 76

あなた, you, 3, 5

あに, older brother, 161, 162

あね, older sister, 101, 162

あの, that (over there), 32, 34

あまり　―ない／ません, not very ..., 86

あまり　―ません, does not ... often, 77

アメリカ, America, 5

アメリカじん, an American, 5

アメリカたいしかん, American Embassy, 5

ありがとう　ございます, (I am) grateful, 8

あります, ある, is/are (inanimate), 51

あります, ある, have, 114

ありません, do/does not have, 2

ありませんでした, was/were not, 16

あるきました, walked; あるきます, あるく, walk, 137

あれ, that (one) over there, 23, 32

いい, good, 65

いいえ, no 2, 5

いいえ、だめです, No, you can't, 148

いいえ、もう　けっこうです, No, (thank you). That was enough, 84

いいですね, It's/That's nice/good/all right, 65

いいます, いう, say, speak, 128

いかが, how, 84

いかがですか, How is it, 84, 85

いきます, いく, go, is going, will go, 38

イギリス, United Kingdom, 34

いくつ, how many, 31, 62

いくら, how much, 23, 138

いしゃ, doctor, 174

いす, chair, 51

いそがしい, busy, 89

いたい aching, painful, 170

いただきます, いただく, eat, 84, 85

イタリア, Italy, 34

いち, one, 10

いちおく, one hundred million, 25

1(いち) じはん, half past one, 16

いちど, once, one time, 128

いちまん, ten thousand, 25

いつ, when, 15, 20

いつか, 5th day of the month, 19

1かい (いっかい), first floor, ground floor, 53

いっかげつ, (for) one month, 175

いっしょに, together (with), 104

いつつ, five, 33

いって　ください, Please say/speak, 128

いっぱい, 1 cupful/glassful/bottleful, 84

いとこ, cousin, 162

いま, living room, 51

いま, now, 15

います, いる, is/are (animate), 51

います, いる, stay, 120

いもうと, いもうとさん, younger sister, 116, 162

イヤホーン, earphones, 93

いらっしゃいました, came, 46; いらっしゃいま
　　す, いらっしゃる, is/are, 46, 76
いらっしゃいませ, Come in, Welcome, 22
いりぐち, entrance, 62
いろ, color, 98
いろいろ (な), various, 168

うえ, top, 51
ウエイトレス, waitress, 131
うけつけ, reception, 55
うち, home, house, 8, 76
うって　います, sell, is selling; うります, うる,
　　sell, 163
うみ, sea, ocean, 107
〜うりば, selling place, 62
うるさい, noisy, 111
うんてんしゅ, driver, 134

え, picture, 70
えいが, movie, film, 20
えいご, English language, 93
ええ, yes, 8
えき, station, 40
えん, yen, 23

お〜 (honorific), 55
おい, おいごさん, nephew, 162
おいしい, good, tasty, delicious, 84
おいとこさん, cousin, 162
おおきい, big, large, 34
おかあさん, mother, 80, 162
おかけ　ください, Do sit down, 46
おかし, cake, 84
おかね, money, 116
おきゃくさん, client, customer, guest, 155
おくさん, wife, 51, 162
おくります, おくる, send, 173
おげんきで, Take care of yourself, 184
おこさん, child, 117
おさけ, Japanese rice wine, 71
おじ, おじさん, uncle, 162
おじいさん, grandfather, 162
おしえます, おしえる, tell, show, teach, 79
おします, おす, push, 120
おじょうさん, daughter, 117, 162

おそい, late, slow, 159
おたく, residence, 76
おちゃ, tea, 70
おつり, change, 134
おてあらい, lavatory, toilet, 55
おてら, temple, 120
おとうさん, father, 80, 162
おとうと, おとうとさん, younger brother, 162
おとこ, man, male; おとこの　ひと, man, 43
おとこの　こ, boy, 51
おととい, the day before yesterday, 48
おなか, stomach, abdomen, 173
おにいさん, older brother, 161, 162
おねえさん, older sister, 162
おねがいします, Please (do) ..., 76
おば, おばさん, aunt, 162
おばあさん, grandmother, 162
おはいり　ください, Do come in, 46
おまちください, Please wait, 80
おまねき　ありがとうございます, Thank you
　　for your invitation, 159
おもしろい, entertaining, interesting, 89
おりて, get off (and); おります　おりる, get
　　off, 120, 137
おわります, おわる, finish, end, 184
おんがく, music, 70
おんせん, hot spring, spa, 173
おんな, woman, female; おんなの　ひと, woman, 15
おんなの　こ, girl, 53

か (question marker, particle), 2, 5
が (subject marker, particle), 42
が, but (particle), 74
が (particle), 76
〜かい, floor (counter), 53
かいぎ, conference, meeting, 20
かいぎしつ, conference/meeting room, 152
かいぎを　します (する), hold a meeting/confer-
　　ence, 74; かいぎを　して　います, be holding
　　a meeting, be in conference, 152
がいこく, foreign country, 164
かいさつぐち, ticket gate, 62
かいしゃ, company, 8
かいしゃいん, company employee, 5
かいました, bought; かいます, かう, buy, 66

こうくうびん, airmail, 175
こうさてん, intersection, 130
こうちゃ, black tea, 71
こうばん, police box, 62
コーヒー, coffee, 71
ここ, here, this place, 62
ごご, P.M., afternoon, 15
ここのか, 9th day of the month, 19
ここのつ, nine, 33
ごしゅじん, husband, 76
ごじゅっぷん, ごじっぷん, 50 minutes, 15
ごしょうかいします, Let me introduce you, 6
ごぜん, A.M., morning, 16
ごちそうさま, Thank you for a lovely meal, 85
こちら, this one, this person, 1, 3; こちら, here, this way, this direction, 46
コップ, mug, glass, cup, 107
こと, thing, 168
ことし, this year, 74
こども, child, 55, 162
5(ご)にん, 5 people, 59
この, this, 32
ごはん, meal, 67
コピー, photocopy, 112; コピーを　します (する), 111
ごりょうしん, parents, 162
ゴルフ, golf, 95
これ, this (one), 8, 23, 32
ごろ, about, 74, 76
こんげつ, this month, 116
こんしゅう, this week, 120
こんで　います, こみます, こむ, be crowded, 184
こんばん, this evening, tonight, 71

さあ, well, let me see, 145, 169
～さい, ... years old (counter), 117
さいきん, nowadays, recently, 184
さかな, fish, 62
さかなや, fish shop/seller, 30, 62
さかや, liquor store, 62
さけ, Japanese rice wine, 71
ざっし, magazine, 71
～さま, Mr., Mrs., Ms., Miss, 134
さむかった, was cold; さむい, cold, 93
サラダ, salad, 70

さん, three, 10
～さん, Mr., Mrs., Ms., Miss, 1
さんぜんえん, 3,000 yen, 23
サンドイッチ, sandwich, 70
39(さんじゅうく)ど, 39 degrees, 175
さんにん, 3 people, 39
ざんねん(な), regrettable; ざんねんですが, I'm sorry, but ..., 107
さんぽ, a walk; さんぽを　します (する), take a walk, 107

し, four, 10
～じ, o'clock, 15
シーディー, CD, compact disc, 70
じかん time, 114
～じかん, (for) ... hours, 123
しき, ceremony, 116
しごと, work, 20; しごとを　します (する), work, 68
ししゃ, branch office, 38
じしょ, dictionary, 101
しずか(な), quiet, calm, 86
した, under, beneath, 55
しち, seven, 10
しつ, room, 152
しって　います (いる), know, 163
しつれい, rudeness, 46; しつれいします, May I, Excuse me, I'm sorry, Good-bye, 46, 76
して　います (いる), be doing, 152, 161
します, する, do, 65
しめます, しめる, close, shut, 111
じゃ, well then, 23
しゃかい, society, community life, social conditions, 184
しゃしん, photograph, 53; しゃしんを　とります (とる), take a photograph, 143; しゃしんを　とっても　いいですか, May I take a photograph, 143
じゅう, ten, 10
11(じゅういち)にち, 11th day of the month, 19
～しゅうかん, weeks (counter), 125
じゅうしょ, address, 11
10(じゅう)じ, 10 o'clock, 15
ジュース, juice, 71
12(じゅうに)ほん, 12 bottles, 34
18(じゅうはち)にち, 18th day of the month, 16, 19
10(じゅう)まい, 10 sheets, 34

しゅうまつ, weekend, 65
じゅうよっか, 14th day of the month, 19
じゅぎょう, class, lesson, 116
しゅじん, husband, 162
しゅっちょう, business trip, 38; しゅっちょうで
　すか, Is it a business trip (you're going on), 38
しょうしょう, a moment, 80
じょうず(な), good at, skillful, 170
ジョギングを　します(する), jog, 80
しょくじ, meal; しょくじを　します(する),
　have a meal, eat, 89
しょくどう, dining room, cafeteria, lunch room,
　restaurant, 55, 74
〜じん, person (suffix), 5
しんごう, traffic light, 130
しんかんせん, Shinkansen, New Trunk Line, 48
しんせつ(な), kind, helpful, 89
しんぶん, newspaper, 11

すいます, すう, smoke, inhale, 148
すいようび, Wednesday, 18
スーパー, supermarket, 58
スープ, soup, 71
スキー, skiing, 104
すき(な), like, likeable, favorite, 98
すきやき, *sukiyaki*, 178
すくない, a little, 191
すこし, a little, 125
すばらしい, wonderful, 145
スプーン, spoon, 107
すみません, Excuse me, I'm sorry, 15, 148
スライド, slide, 152
すわないで　ください, Do not smoke, 148
すんで　います, live, is living; すみます, すむ,
　live, 161

せいじ, politics, 184
セーター, sweater, 164
せつめい, explanation, 93
ぜひ, by all means, 104, 109
ゼロ, zero, 8, 10
せん, one thousand, 25
せんげつ, last month, 42
せんしゅう, last week, 40
せんせい, teacher, professor, 80, 184

ぜんぜん　ーません, never (do), 80
ぜんぜん　ーません, not at all, 92

そうです, That's right, 8
そうですか, I see, 76
そうですね, Let me see, 175
そうべつかい, farewell party, 109
そこ, there, that place, 62
そして, and then, 38
そちら, there, that way, that person, 195
その, that, 30, 32
そふ, grandfather, 162
そぼ, grandmother, 162
それ, that (one), 23, 32
それから, and, and then, after that, 30, 120

たいしかん, embassy, 5
だいどころ, kitchen, 51
タイプ, typing, 77, 129; タイプを　します(する), 194
たかい, expensive, high, 89
たくさん, many, lots of, 59
タクシー, taxi, 46
タクシーのりば, taxi stand, 59
だけ, only, 120
〜たち, (plural suffix for people), 89
たてもの, building, 59
たな, shelf, 53
たのしい, enjoyable, 95
たのしみに　して　います(いる), be looking
　forward to, 184
たばこ, tobacco, cigarette, 148
たべました, ate; たべます, たべる, eat, 67
たまご, egg, 89
だめ, no good, useless, hopeless, out of the question,
　148; だめ(な), 191
だれ, who, 3
だれの, whose, 11
だれも　ーません, nobody is, 51
たんじょうび, birthday, 16
たんす, chest of drawers, 168

ちいさい, small, 30
ちか, basement, underground, 163
ちかい, near, close to, 86
ちか1かい(いっかい), first basement, 163

ちがいます, ちがう, That's/It's wrong/different, 80

ちかく, neighborhood, vicinity; の　ちかくに／へ, near, close to, 53

ちかてつ, subway, underground railway, 42

ちず, map, 71

ちち, father, 101

ちゃ, tea, 70

ちゅうごく, China, 5

ちゅうごくじん, a Chinese, 5

ちゅうしゃきんし, no parking, 147

ちゅうしゃじょう, parking lot, 148

ちょう, town, community, 128

〜ちょうめ (block in an address), 128

ちょっと, a little, 117

ついたち, 1st day of the month, 19

つかっても　いいです, You may use it; つかいます, つかう, use, 143

つぎ, next, 129

つきました, arrived; つきます, つく, arrive, 138

つくえ, desk, table, 168

つくりました, made, formed; つくります, つくる, form, make, build, 184

つけても　いいですか, May I turn (it) on, 142; つけます, つける, switch/turn on, 111

つごう, condition, 107; つごうが　わるいです, conditions are unfavorable, 104, 107

つとめて　います, be employed, work for; つとめます, つとめる, serve, work for, 161

つまらない, boring, uninteresting, 86

つめたい, cold, 191

〜で, at, 66

〜で, by, 46

テープ, tape, 34

テーブル, table, 51

テープレコーダー, tape recorder, 26

てがみ, letter, 71

テキスト, text, 184

できます, できる, be able to, can (do) be ready/finished/done, 135, 168, 170

でぐち, exit, 149

でございます, This is ..., 80

デザート, dessert, 178

でした, was/were, 2, 16

〜です, is/are, 1, 39, 52

テニス, tennis, 71; テニスを　します (する), play tennis, 68, 194

〜では, well then, 23, 27

〜では／じゃ　ありません, is/are not, 2

デパート, department store, 15

てまえ, just before, this side of, 134

でます, でる, leave, start, 138

でも, but, 111

テレビ, television, TV set, 26

てん, (decimal) point, 25

てんいん, store clerk, 22

てんき weather, 90

でんき, (electric) light, 111

でんきや, electrical appliance store/clerk, 142

でんしゃ, (electric) train, 40

でんち, battery, 32

でんわ, telephone, 8

でんわばんごう, telephone number, 8

でんわを　します (する), make a phone call, telephone, 66, 77

と, and (particle), 51

と, with (particle), 38

〜ど, times, 128

〜ど, degree, 175

ドア, door, 111

ドイツ, Germany, 5

ドイツご, German language, 173

ドイツじん, a German, 5

どう, how, 92

どう　いたしまして, Don't mention it, You're welcome, 15

どうして, why, 58, 62

どう　しましたか, What's the matter, 174

どうぞ, please (accept, do), 7, 85

どうぞ　おだいじに, Look after yourself, 175

どうぞ　よろしく, Please favor me, 1, 3

どうでしたか, How was it, 92, 93

どうですか, How is it, 85

どうも, very much, 7

どうも, thanks, 134, 153

どうも　ありがとうございます, Thank you very much, 7

どうやって, how, 137

とお, ten, 33

とおい, far, 86

とおか, 10th day of the month, 19

ときどき, sometimes, 74

とけい, clock, watch, 9

どこ, where, belonging to or coming from what place, 34, 67

どこにも, nowhere, 52

ところ, place, 184

としょかん, library, 173

とだな, closet, cabinet, cupboard, 53

どちら, where, 109

とても, very, 84

とどけましょうか, Shall we deliver; とどけます, とどける, deliver, 128

どなた, who, 3, 5

となり, next to, 58

どの, which, 35

どのぐらい, how long, 124; how much, 138

トマト, tomato, 173

とめて ください, Please stop, 134; とめます, とめる, park, stop, 129, 147; とめないで ください, Do not park, 147

ともだち, friend, 42

どようび, Saturday, 18

ドライブ, driving, a drive, 107

とります, とる, take, 143

とりにく, chicken meat, 89

どれ, which one, 30

どんな, what kind of, 85, 89

ないせんばんごう, extension number, 79

なか inside, 53

なつ, summer, 21

なつやすみ, summer vacation, 21

なな, seven, 10

ななつ, seven, 33

なに／なん, what, 8, 11; なに／なんで, how, by what means, 46

なにも, nothing; なにも ―ません, nothing is, 55

なのか, 7th day of the month, 19

なまえ, name, 8

なんがつ, which month, 15

なんさい, how old, 117

なんじ, what time, 15

なんじかん, how many hours, 137

なんじまでに, by what time, 128

なんにち, which day of the month, how many days, 15, 20, 137

なんにん, how many people, 62

なんねん, what year, 48

なんばん, what number, 9, 11

なんぷん, how many minutes, 137

なんぼん, how many bottles, 62

なんまい, how many sheets, 62

なんようび, which day of the week, 15, 20

に, in, at (particle), 51

に, on (particle), 46, 137

に, to (particle), 38, 104, 105

に, to, from (particle), 66, 76, 98

に, two, 10

にぎやか(な), lively, 88, 93

2(に) キロ, 2 kilograms, 34

にく, meat, 62

にくや, meat store, butcher, 62

2(に) じかん, 2 hours, 123

にじゅう, twenty, 10

にじゅうよっか, 24th day of the month, 19

20(にじゅっ) ぷんぐらい, (for) about 20 minutes, 90

～にち, day, 16

にちようび, Sunday, 18

にちょうめ にの いち, 2ちょうめ 2-1 (address), 128

に ついて, concerning, about 168

にほん, Japan, 5

にほんぎんこう, Bank of Japan, 5

にほんご, Japanese language, 34

にほんじん, a Japanese, 5

にもつ, parcel, 175

ニュース, news, 70

に よろしく, Best regards to, 3, 184

にわ, garden, 51

～にん, person/people (counter), 59

ね, Isn't it/Aren't there, 55, 58

ネクタイ, necktie, 101

ねつ, fever, 175

～ねん, year, 48

ねんがじょう, New Year's card, 79

の (possessive particle), 1, 3

の　あとで, after, 123

のど, throat, 173

の　まえに, before, in front of, 53, 123

のみます, のむ, drink, take (medicine), 68, 71

のみもの, beverage, drink, 168, 178

～のりば, boarding place, 59

のりました, got on; のります, のる, get on, ride, take, 137

は (topic marker, particle), 1, 2

は, tooth, 173

パーティー, party, 20

はい, yes, certainly, 2, 5

～はい, measureful (counter), 84

ハイキング, hiking, 107

はいざら, ashtray, 26

はいります, はいる, enter, go/come in, 46, 143

はがき, postcard, 31, 53

はこ, box, 53

はじめまして, How do you do, 1, 3; はじめる, begin, 3

バス, bus, 42

バスのりば, bus terminal, 62

はち, eight, 10

はつか, 20th day of the month, 19

はな, flower, 51

はなしを　します (する), talk, 155

バナナ, banana, 2

はなや, flower shop, florist, 30

はは, mother, 79, 162

はん, half, 30 minutes after the hour, 16

ばん, evening, 70

～ばん, number, 11

パン, bread, 62

ばんごう, number, 8

ばんごはん, dinner, evening meal, 70

ばんち (part of a block in an address), 128

パンや, bread store, bakery, 62

ひ, day, 159

ヒーター, heater, 111

ビール, beer, 34

ひがし, east, 38

ひこうき, airplane, 62

ひしょ, secretary, 5

ひだり, left, 130

ひだりがわ, left-hand side, 148

ビデオ, video, 111

ひと, person, 15

ひとつ, one, 32

ひとり, 1 person, 62

ひとりで, alone, 38

ひま (な), free, 89

ひゃく, one hundred, 16, 25

びょういん, hospital, 59, 62

ひらがな (Japanese script), 101

ひらきます, ひらく, open, 15

ひる, noon, daytime, 16

ビル, building, 55

ひるごはん, lunch, noon meal, 67

ひるやすみ, lunch time, noon recess, 16

フイルム, film, 23, 30

ふたつ, two, 33

ふたり, 2 people, 62

ふつか, 2nd day of the month, 19

ふなびん, sea mail, 46, 175

フランス, France, 34

フランスご, French language, 173

ふるい, old, not fresh, 89

プレイガイド, theater booking agency, 66

～ふん (～ぷん), minute, 15

ぶん, part, 25

ぶんか, culture, 184

へ, to (particle), 38

へや, room, 62

ペン, pen, 46, 144

べんごし, lawyer, 1

べんきょうを　します (する), study, 67

べんり (な), convenient, 89

ほか, other, 184

ポスト, mail box, post box, 58

ぼっちゃん, son, 162

ホテル, hotel, 79

ほん, book, 11

～ほん (counter), 30, 34

ほんとうに, really, truly, 90

ほんや, book store/seller, 30, 59

まい〜, every, 67
〜まい (counter), 30, 34
まいあさ, every morning, 71
まいしゅう, every week, 71
まいつき, every month, 184
まいど, each (every) time; まいど　ありがとう
　ございます, Thank you (for your patronage) each
　time, 128
まいにち every day, 39, 67
まいねん, every year, 79
まいばん, every evening/night, 71
まえ, in front of, before, 53
まがって　ください, Please turn; まがります,
　まがる, turn, 129
まご, grandchild, 162
また, again, 76
まだです, not yet, 135
まち, town, street, community, 95, 128
まちます, まつ, wait, 80
まっすぐ, straight, straight ahead, 134
まって　ください, Please wait; まちます, まつ,
　wait, 120, 129
まつり, festival, 173
まで, to, as far as (particle), 137
まで, until (particle), 15
までに, by (particle), 128
まど window, 53

みかん, tangerine, 34
みぎ, right, 129
みず, water, 26
みせ, store, shop, 79
みせて　ください, Please show me; みせます, み
　せる, show, 22, 23
みっか, 3rd day of the month, 19
みっか, (for) 3 days, 120
みっつ, three, 30
みて　います (いる), is looking, is watching, 152
みなさま, everyone, 184
みなさまに　どうぞ　よろしく, Best regards to
　everyone, 184
みます, みる, see, watch, look at, 65, 120

ミルク, milk, 71
みんな, みなさん, everyone, 159

むいか, 6th day of the month, 19
むずかしい, difficult, hard, 89
むすこ, むすこさん, son, 117, 162
むすめ, むすめさん, daughter, 117, 162
むっつ, six, 33

めい, めいごさん, niece, 162
めいし, business card, name card, 7
めがね, (eye) glasses, 62
めしあがって　ください, Please eat/have (some), 84
メニュー, menu, 130
メロン, melon, 178

も, too (particle), 23
もう, already, 65, 85
もう, more (another), 84
もうすぐ, very soon, 184
もくようび, Thursday, 16, 18
もしもし, hello, 76; I say , 147
もってきて　ください, Please bring; もってき
　ます, もってくる, bring, 128
もらいました, received; もらいます, もらう,
　receive, 98, 99

や, and (etc.), 51
〜や, store, shop, clerk, seller, 30
やおや, vegetable store, greengrocer, 62
やさい, vegetable, 89
やさしい, easy, 89
やすい, inexpensive, cheap, 89
やすみ, rest (period), vacation, holiday, day off, clos-
　ing day, 16, 62, 116
やっつ, eight, 33
やま, mountain, 173

ゆうがた, late afternoon, early evening, 139
ゆうびんきょく, post office, 20
ゆうめい(な), famous, well known, 84, 89
ゆっくり, slowly, 130

よ, I tell you (particle), 58

よい, good, 86
ようか, 8th day of the month, 19
〜ようび, day of the week, 16
ヨーロッパ, Europe, 170
よく, well, 46
よく, often, 77
よく いらっしゃいました, How nice of you to
  come, 46
よくない, not good, 86
よっか, 4th day of the month, 19
よっつ, four, 33
よびます, よぶ, call, 120
よみます, よむ, read, 66, 71
よやく, reservation, 134
よろこんで (よろこぶ), (I'd) love/be happy to,
  gladly, with pleasure, 159
よろしく, regards, 3, 184
よん, four, 10
4(よん)しゅうかん, 4 weeks 125

らいげつ, next month, 48
らいしゅう, next week, 48
らいねん, next year, 41
ラジオ, radio, 26

りょうしん, parents, 162
りょうり, food, cooking, cuisine, 95
りょこう, trip, travel, 95; りょこうを します
  (する), take a trip, travel, 119, 194
りょこうがいしゃ, travel agency, 161
りんご, apple, 26

れい, zero, 10
れきし, history, 101
レコード, record, 70
レシート, receipt, 26
レストラン, restaurant, 67

ろく, six, 10
6(ろく)がつ, June, 16
6(ろく)じ, 6 o'clock, 15

ワイン, wine, 159
わかりました, Sure, Certainly, I see, 77, 104

わかりました, understood; わかります, わかる,
  understand, 58, 92, 168
わたし, I, 5
わたしたち, we, 89
わたしの, my, 7
わるい, bad, 86

を, from, out of (particle), 138
を (object marker, particle), 22, 66

ENGLISH-JAPANESE GLOSSARY

Note: Idiomatic expressions have been omitted, as well as counters, particles that have no independent meaning and words listed in some appendices. Since equivalents differ in nuance, refer to the pages listed to check context and usage.

about, ごろ, 74, 76; ぐらい, 90, 137
about (concerning), に　ついて, 168
aching, いたい, 170
address, じゅうしょ, 11
after, (の) あとで, 123
afternoon (P.M.), ごご, 15
after that, それから, 120
afterwards, あとで, 76
again, また, 76
airmail, こうくうびん, 175
airplane, ひこうき, 62
airport, くうこう, 42
a little, ちょっと, 117; すこし, 125; すくない, 191
alone, ひとりで, 38
already, もう, 65, 85
and, と, 51; and (etc.), や, 51
and then, それから, 30; そして, 38
apple, りんご, 26
approximately, ぐらい, 90, 137
arm, うで, 201
arrive, つきます (つく), 138
as far as, まで, 137
ashtray, はいざら, 26
ask, ききます (きく), 79
at, に, 51; で, 66
aunt, おば, おばさん, 162

baby, あかちゃん, 107
back, せなか, 201
bad, わるい, 86
bakery, パンや, 62
banana, バナナ, 2
bank, ぎんこう, 5
basement, ちか, 163

battery, でんち, 32
be able, できます (できる), 168, 170
because, から, 58
beef, ぎゅうにく, 89
beer, ビール, 34
before, まえ, 53; (の) まえに, 123
begin, はじめる, 3
be married, けっこんしている, 161
beneath, した, 55
beverage, のみもの, 168, 178
big, おおきい, 34
birthday, たんじょうび, 16
black, くろい, 35
black tea, こうちゃ, 71
blue, あおい, 35
body, からだ, 201
book, ほん, 11
book store/seller, ほんや, 30, 59
boring, つまらない, 86
box, はこ, 53
boy, おとこの　こ, 51
branch office, ししゃ, 38
bread, パン, 62
breakfast, あさごはん, 70
bright, あかるい, 191
bring, もってきます (もってくる), 128
brothers/sisters, きょうだい, 116, 162
brown, ちゃいろい, ちゃいろの, 191
build, つくります (つくる), 184
building, ビル, 55; たてもの, 59
bus, バス, 42
business card, めいし, 7
business trip, しゅっちょう, 38
bus terminal, バスのりば, 62
busy, いそがしい, 89
but, が, 74; でも, 111
butcher, にくや, 62
buy, かいます (かう), 66
by, で, 46; までに, 128
by all means, ぜひ, 104, 109

cabinet, とだな, 53

café, きっさてん, 71

cafeteria, しょくどう, 74

cake, ケーキ, 130; おかし, 84

call, よびます (よぶ), 120

calm, しずか(な), 86

camera, カメラ, 30

camera store/clerk, カメラや, 30

can, できます (できる), 168, 170

car, くるま, 11

catalogue, カタログ, 142

CD (compact disc), シーディー, 70

ceremony, しき, 116

chair, いす, 51

change, おつり, 134

cheap, やすい, 89

cheek, ほほ, 201

chest, むね, 201

chest of drawers, たんす, 168

chicken (meat), とりにく, 89

child, こ, 51; こども, 55, 162; おこさん, 117

chin, あご, 201

Christmas card, クリスマスカード, 79

cigarette, たばこ, 148

class, じゅぎょう, 116

clean, きれい(な), 84

client, おきゃくさん, 155

clock, とけい, 9

close, しめる, 111

close, ちかい, 86

close (to), (の) ちかくに/で, 53

closet, とだな, 53

coffee, コーヒー, 71

coffee shop, きっさてん, 71

cold, さむい, 93; つめたい, 191

color, いろ, 98

come, きます (くる), 41

come back, かえります (かえる), 38

come in, はいります (はいる), 46, 143

company, かいしゃ, 8

concerning, に ついて, 168

condition, つごう, 107

conference, かいぎ, 20

conference room, かいぎしつ, 152

convenient, べんり(な), 89

cookie, クッキー, 85

cooking, りょうり, 95

cool, すずしい, 191

corner, かど, 129

correct, ただしい, 191

cost, かかります (かかる), 137, 138

cousin, いとこ, おいとこさん, 162

crowded (be), こみます (こむ), 184

cuisine, りょうり, 95

culture, ぶんか, 184

cup, コップ, 107

cupboard, とだな, 53

customer, おきゃくさん, 155

dangerous, あぶない, 191

dark, くらい, 111

daughter, むすめ, むすめさん, 117, 162; おじょう さん, 117, 162

day, ひ, 159; 〜にち, 16

day after tomorrow, あさって, 38

day before yesterday, おととい, 48

day off, やすみ, 116

daytime, ひる, 16

decimal point, てん, 25

degree, 〜ど, 175

delicious, おいしい, 84

deliver, とどけます (とどける), 128

department store, デパート, 15

desk, つくえ, 168

dessert, デザート, 178

dictionary, じしょ, 101

difficult, むずかしい, 89

dining room, しょくどう, 55

dinner, ばんごはん, 70

dirty, きたない, 191

do, します (する), 65

doctor, いしゃ, 174

door, ドア, 111

draw, かきます (かく), 77

drink, のみます (のむ), 68, 71

drink, のみもの, 168, 178

drive, うんてんを します (する), 194

drive, driving, ドライブ, 107

driver, うんてんしゅ, 134

drug store, くすりや, 62

dry clean, クリーニングを します (する), 194

dry cleaner, クリーニングや, 135

greengrocer, やおや, 62
group, グループ, 184
guest, おきゃくさん, 155

hair, かみ, 201
half, はん, 16
hand, て, 201
hard, むずかしい, 89
have, あります (ある), 114
have a headache, あたまが　いたい, 170
have a meal, しょくじを　します (する), 89
head, あたま, 170
healthy, げんき (な), 89
hear, ききます (きく), 70
heater, ヒーター, 111
heavy, おもい, 191
hello, もしもし, 76
helpful, しんせつ (な), 89
here, こちら, 46; ここ, 62
high, たかい, 89
hiking, ハイキング, 107
hip, こし, 201
history, れきし, 101
hold a meeting, かいぎを　します (する), 74
holiday, やすみ, 62
home, うち, 8
hospital, びょういん, 59
hot (temperature), あつい, 93; (spicy) からい, 191
hot spring, おんせん, 173
hotel, ホテル, 79
house, うち, 8, 76
how, どう, 92; どうやって, 137; いかが, 84; な
　に／なんで, 46
how long, どのぐらい, 124
how many, いくつ, 31, 62
how much, どのぐらい, 138; いくら, 23
husband, ごしゅじん, 76; しゅじん, 162

I, わたし, 5
ice cream, アイスクリーム, 179
important, だいじ (な), 191
in, に, 51
inconvenient, ふべん (な), 191
inexpensive, やすい, 89
in front of, まえ, 53; (の) まえに, 123
inside, なか, 53

interesting, おもしろい, 89
intersection, こうさてん, 130
introduce, しょうかいを　します (する), 194
is/are (animate), います (いる), 51
is/are (inanimate), あります (ある), 51

Japanese rice wine, さけ, おさけ, 71
jaw, あご, 201
jog, ジョギングを　します (する), 80
juice, ジュース, 71
just before, てまえ, 134

key, かぎ, 11
kind, しんせつ (な), 89
kitchen, だいどころ, 51
know, しっています (しる), 163

large, おおきい, 34
late, おそい, 159
late afternoon, ゆうがた, 139
later, あとで, 76
lavatory, おてあらい, 55
lawyer, べんごし, 1
leave, でます (でる), 138
left, ひだり, 130
left-hand side, ひだりがわ, 148
leg, あし, 201
lesson, じゅぎょう, 116
letter, てがみ, 71
library, としょかん, 173
light, かるい, 191
light (electric), でんき, 111
likeable, すき (な), 98
lip, くちびる, 201
liquor store, さかや, 62
listen, ききます (きく), 70
live, すみます (すむ), 161
lively, にぎやか (な), 88, 93
living room, いま, 51
long, ながい, 191
look at, みます (みる), 65, 120
look forward to, たのしみに　しています, 184
lots of, たくさん, 59
low, ひくい, 191
lunch, ひるごはん, 67
lunch time, ひるやすみ, 16

mail box, ポスト, 58

magazine, ざっし, 71

make, つくります (つくる), 184

make a phone call, でんわを　します (する), 66, 77

make a reservation, よやくを　します (する), 194

man, おとこ, おとこの　ひと, 43

many, たくさん, 59; おおい, 191

map, ちず, 71

marriage, けっこん, 116

marry, けっこんします (する), 161

meal, ごはん, 67; しょくじ, 89

meat, にく, 62

meat store, にくや, 62

medicine, くすり 62

meet, あいます (あう), 77

meeting, かいぎ, 20

meeting room, かいぎしつ, 152

melon, メロン, 178

menu, メニュー, 130

milk, ミルク, 71

minute, 〜ふん (〜ぷん), 15

Monday, げつようび, 18

money, おかね, 116

month(s), 〜がつ, 16

morning, あさ, 70

morning (A.M.), ごぜん, 16

mother, はは, おかあさん, 79

mountain, やま, 173

mouth, くち, 201

movie, えいが, 20

much, おおい, 191

mug, コップ, 107

music, おんがく, 70

my, わたしの, 7

nail, つめ, 201

name, なまえ, 8

narrow, せまい, 191

near, ちかい, 86; (の) ちかくに／で, 53

neck, くび, 201

necktie, ネクタイ, 101

nephew, おい, おいごさん, 162

never (do) ..., ぜんぜん　ーません, 80

new, あたらしい, 89

news, ニュース, 70

New Year's card, ねんがじょう, 79

newspaper, しんぶん, 11

next, つぎ, 129

next to, となり, 58

niece, めい, めいごさん, 162

nine, きゅう, く, 10; ここのつ, 33

no, いいえ, 2, 5

nobody, だれも　ーません, 51

no good, だめ, 148; だめ(な), 191

noisy, うるさい, 111

noon, ひる, 16

no parking, ちゅうしゃきんし, 147

nose, はな, 201

not at all, ぜんぜん　ーません, 92

not good, よくない, 86

nothing, なにも, 55

not often, あまり　ーません, 77

not very, あまり, 86

not yet, まだです, 135

now, いま, 15

nowadays, さいきん, 184

nowhere, どこにも, 52

number, ばんごう, 8

ocean, うみ, 107

often, よく, 77

old, ふるい, 89

older brother, あに, おにいさん, 161, 162

older sister, あね, 101; おねえさん, 162

on, に, 137

once, いちど, 128

one, いち, 10; ひとつ, 32

one hundred, ひゃく, 16, 25

one thousand, せん, 25

one time, いちど, 128

only, だけ, 120

open, あけます (あける), 110; open, ひらきます
　(ひらく), 15

other, ほか, 184

over there, あそこ, 55; あちら, 195

painful, いたい, 170

parcel, にもつ, 175

parents, りょうしん, ごりょうしん, 162

park, こうえん, 84, 89

park, とめます (とめる), 129, 134, 147

parking lot, ちゅうしゃじょう, 148

part, ぶん, 25
party, パーティー, 20
pen, ペン, 46, 144
person, ひと, 15
pharmacy, くすりや, 62
photocopy, コピー, コピーを　します(する), 111
photograph, しゃしん, 53
picture, え, 70
place, ところ, 184
play golf, ゴルフを　します(する), 193
play tennis, テニスを　します(する), 68, 193
pleasant, たのしい, 191
police box, こうばん, 62
policeman, けいかん, 147
polite, ていねい(な), 191
politics, せいじ, 184
postage stamp, きって, 34
post box, ポスト, 58
postcard, はがき, 53
post office, ゆうびんきょく, 20
pretty, きれい(な), 84
professor, せんせい, 80, 184
purple, むらさきの, 191
push, おします(おす), 120

quiet, しずか(な), 86

radio, ラジオ, 26
read, よみます(よむ), 66, 71
really, ほんとうに, 90
receipt, レシート, 26
receive, もらいます(もらう), 98, 99
recently, さいきん, 184
reception, うけつけ, 55
record, レコード, 70
red, あかい, 34
reservation, よやく, 134; make a reservation, よや
　くを　します(する), 193
residence, おたく, 76
rest (period), やすみ, 16
restaurant, レストラン, 67; しょくどう, 55, 74
return, かえります(かえる), 38
ride, のります(のる), 137
right, みぎ, 129
room, へや, 62; しつ, 152
rude, しつれい(な), 191

safe, あんぜん(な), 191
salad, サラダ, 70
salty, しおからい, 191
sandwich, サンドイッチ, 70
Saturday, どようび, 18
say, いいます(いう), 128
school, がっこう, 11
sea, うみ, 107
sea mail, ふなびん, 46, 175
secretary, ひしょ, 5
see, みます(みる), 65, 120
sell, うります(うる), 163
send, おくります(おくる), 173
seven, なな, しち, 10; ななつ, 33
shabu-shabu, しゃぶしゃぶ, 178
shelf, たな, 53
shoes, くつ, 71
shop, かいものを　します(する), 68
shop, みせ, 79
shopping, かいもの, 71
short, みじかい, 191
shoulder, かた, 201
show, みせます(みせる), 22, 23; おしえます(お
　しえる), 79
showcase, ケース, 142
shut, しめます(しめる), 111
siblings, きょうだい, 116, 162
sisters/brothers, きょうだい, 116, 162
sit, かけます(かける), 46
six, ろく, 10; むっつ, 33
ski, スキーを　します(する), 198
skiing, スキー, 104
skillful, じょうず(な), 170
skin, ひふ, 201
slide, スライド, 152
slow, おそい, 159
slowly, ゆっくり, 130
small, ちいさい, 30
smoke たばこを　すいます(すう), 148
so, から, 58
society, しゃかい, 184
socks, くつした, 173
sometimes, ときどき, 74
son, むすこ, むすこさん, 117, 162; ぼっちゃん, 162
soup, スープ, 71
sour, すっぱい, 191

too, も, 23
tooth, は, 173
top, うえ, 51
town, まち, 95, 128
traffic light, しんごう, 130
train (electric), でんしゃ, 40
travel, りょこうを　します (する), 119
travel agency, りょこうがいしゃ, 161
tree, き, 90
trip, りょこう, 95
truly, ほんとうに, 90
Tuesday, かようび, 18
turn, まがります (まがる), 129
turn off, けします (けす), 111
turn on, つけます (つける), 111
TV set, テレビ, 26
two, に, 10; ふたつ, 33
type, タイプを　します (する), 194
typing, タイプ, 77, 129

umbrella, かさ, 23, 26
uncle, おじ, おじさん, 162
under, した, 55
underground, ちか, 163
underground railway, ちかてつ, 42
understand, わかります (わかる), 58
uninteresting, つまらない, 86
unkind, ふしんせつ(な), 191
unlikeable, きらい(な), 191
unskillful, へた(な), 191
until, まで, 15
use, つかいます (つかう), 143
useless, だめ, 148

vacation, やすみ, 116
various, いろいろ(な), 168
vase, かびん, 98
vegetable, やさい, 89
vegetable store, やおや, 62
vehicle, くるま, 11
very, とても, 84
very much, どうも, 7
very soon, もう　すぐ, 184
video, ビデオ, 111

wait, まちます (まつ), 80

waitress, ウエイトレス, 131
walk, さんぽ, 107; あるきます (あるく), 137
warm, あたたかい, 191
watch, みます (みる), 65, 120
watch, とけい, 9
water, みず, 26
way of thinking, かんがえかた, 184
we, わたしたち, 89
weather, てんき, 90
wedding, けっこんしき, 116
Wednesday, すいようび, 18
weekend, しゅうまつ, 65
welcome party, かんげいかい, 111
well, げんき(な), 89
well known, ゆうめい(な), 84, 89
what, なに／なん, 8, 11
what kind of, どんな, 85, 89
when, いつ, 15, 20
where, どこ, 34, 67; どちら, 109
which, どの, 35
which one, どれ, 30
white, しろい, 191
who, だれ, 3; どなた, 3, 5
whose, だれの, 11
why, どうして, 58, 69
wide, ひろい, 191
wife, かない, 101, 162, おくさん, 51, 162
window, まど, 53
wine, ワイン, 159
with, と, 38
woman, おんな, おんなの　ひと, 15
wonderful, すばらしい, 145
work, しごと, 20; しごとを　します (する), 68
write, かきます (かく), 77
wrong, ちがう, 80

yen, えん, 23
yellow, きいろい, きいろの, 191
yes, ええ, 8; はい, 5
yesterday, きのう, 16
you, あなた, 35, 5
young, わかい, 191
younger brother, おとうと, おとうとさん, 162
younger, sister, いもうと, いもうとさん, 116, 162

zero, れい, 10; ゼロ, 8, 10

INDEX

コミュニケーションのための日本語　第1巻　かな版テキスト
JAPANESE FOR BUSY PEOPLE I　Kana Version

1995年12月　第 1 刷発行
2004年12月　第12刷発行

著　者　　社団法人　国際日本語普及協会
発行者　　畑野文夫
発行所　　講談社インターナショナル株式会社
　　　　　〒112-8652 東京都文京区音羽 1-17-14
　　　　　電話　03-3944-6493（編集部）
　　　　　　　　03-3944-6492（営業部・業務部）
　　　　　ホームページ　www.kodansha-intl.com
印刷・製本所　大日本印刷株式会社

落丁本・乱丁本は購入書店名を明記のうえ、小社業務部宛にお送りください。送料小社負担にて
お取替えします。本書の無断複写（コピー）、転載は著作権法の例外を除き、禁じられています。

定価はカバーに表示してあります。

© 社団法人 国際日本語普及協会 1995
Printed in Japan
ISBN4-7700-1987-4

JAPANESE LANGUAGE GUIDES

Easy-to-use guides to essential language skills

13 SECRETS FOR SPEAKING FLUENT JAPANESE

日本語をペラペラ話すための13の秘訣   *Giles Murray*

The most fun, rewarding, and universal techniques of successful learners of Japanese that anyone can put immediately to use. A unique and exciting alternative, full of lively commentaries, comical illustrations, and brain-teasing puzzles.

Paperback, 184 pages; ISBN 4-7700-2302-2

BREAKING INTO JAPANESE LITERATURE: Seven Modern Classics in Parallel Text

日本語を読むための七つの物語   *Giles Murray*

Read classics of modern Japanese fiction in the original with the aid of a built-in, customized dictionary, free MP3 sound files of professional Japanese narrators reading the stories, and literal English translations. Features Ryunosuke Akutagawa's "Rashomon" and other stories.

Paperback, 240 pages; ISBN 4-7700-2899-7

READ REAL JAPANESE: All You Need to Enjoy Eight Contemporary Writers

新装版 日本語で読もう   *Janet Ashby*

Original Japanese essays by Yoko Mori, Ryuichi Sakamoto, Machi Tawara, Shoichi Nejime, Momoko Sakura, Seiko Ito, Banana Yoshimoto, and Haruki Murakami. With vocabulary lists giving the English for Japanese words and phrases and also notes on grammar, nuance, and idiomatic usage.

Paperback, 168 pages; ISBN 4-7700-2936-5

ALL ABOUT PARTICLES   新装版 助詞で変わるあなたの日本語   *Naoko Chino*

The most common and less common particles brought together and broken down into some 200 usages, with abundant sample sentences.

Paperback, 160 pages; ISBN 4-7700-2781-8

JAPANESE VERBS AT A GLANCE   新装版 日本語の動詞   *Naoko Chino*

Clear and straightforward explanations of Japanese verbs—their functions, forms, roles, and politeness levels.

Paperback, 180 pages; ISBN 4-7700-2765-6

THE HANDBOOK OF JAPANESE VERBS   日本語動詞ハンドブック   *Taeko Kamiya*

An indispensable reference and guide to Japanese verbs aimed at beginning and intermediate students. Precisely the book that verb-challenged students have been looking for.

• Verbs are grouped, conjugated, and combined with auxiliaries
• Different forms are used in sentences   • Each form is followed by reinforcing examples and exercises

Paperback, 256 pages; ISBN 4-7700-2683-8

THE HANDBOOK OF JAPANESE ADJECTIVES AND ADVERBS

日本語形容詞・副詞ハンドブック   *Taeko Kamiya*

The ultimate reference manual for those seeking a deeper understanding of Japanese adjectives and adverbs and how they are used in sentences. Ideal, too, for those simply wishing to expand their vocabulary or speak livelier Japanese.

Paperback, 336 pages; ISBN 4-7700-2879-2

JAPANESE LANGUAGE GUIDES

Easy-to-use guides to essential language skills

BEYOND POLITE JAPANESE: A Dictionary of Japanese Slang and Colloquialisms

新装版 役に立つ話しことば辞典　*Akihiko Yonekawa*

Expressions that all Japanese, but few foreigners, know and use every day. Sample sentences for every entry.

Paperback, 176 pages; ISBN 4-7700-2773-7

BUILDING WORD POWER IN JAPANESE: Using Kanji Prefixes and Suffixes

新装版 増えて使えるヴォキャブラリー　*Timothy J. Vance*

Expand vocabulary and improve reading comprehension by modifying your existing lexicon.

Paperback, 128 pages; ISBN 4-7700-2799-0

HOW TO SOUND INTELLIGENT IN JAPANESE: A Vocabulary Builder

新装版 日本語の知的表現　*Charles De Wolf*

Lists, defines, and gives examples for the vocabulary necessary to engage in intelligent conversation in fields such as politics, art, literature, business, and science.

Paperback, 160 pages; ISBN 4-7700-2859-8

MAKING SENSE OF JAPANESE: What the Textbooks Don't Tell You

新装版 日本語の秘訣　*Jay Rubin*

"Brief, wittily written essays that gamely attempt to explain some of the more frustrating hurdles [of Japanese].… They can be read and enjoyed by students at any level."
—*Asahi Evening News*

Paperback, 144 pages; ISBN 4-7700-2802-4

LOVE, HATE and Everything in Between: Expressing Emotions in Japanese

新装版 日本語の感情表現集　*Mamiko Murakami*

Includes more than 400 phrases that are useful when talking about personal experience and nuances of feeling.

Paperback, 176 pages; ISBN 4-7700-2803-2

BASIC CONNECTIONS: Making Your Japanese Flow

新装版 日本語の基礎ルール　*Kakuko Shoji*

Explains how words and phrases dovetail, how clauses pair up with other clauses, how sentences come together to create harmonious paragraphs. The goal is to enable the student to speak both coherently and smoothly.

Paperback, 160 pages; ISBN 4-7700-2860-1

JAPANESE CORE WORDS AND PHRASES: Things You Can't Find in a Dictionary

新装版 辞書では解らない慣用表現　*Kakuko Shoji*

Some Japanese words and phrases, even though they lie at the core of the language, forever elude the student's grasp. This book brings these recalcitrants to bay.

Paperback, 144 pages; ISBN 4-7700-2774-5

A HANDBOOK OF COMMON JAPANESE PHRASES

日本語決まり文句辞典　*Sanseido*

Japanese is rich in common phrases perfect for any number and variety of occasions. This handbook lists some 600 of them and explains when, where, and how to use them, providing alternatives for slightly varied circumstances and revealing their underlying psychology.

Paperback, 320 pages; ISBN 4-7700-2798-2

KODANSHA INTERNATIONAL DICTIONARIES

Easy-to-use dictionaries designed for non-native learners of Japanese.

KODANSHA'S FURIGANA JAPANESE DICTIONARY
JAPANESE-ENGLISH / ENGLISH-JAPANESE ふりがな和英・英和辞典

Both of Kodansha's popular furigana dictionaries in one portable, affordable volume. A truly comprehensive and practical dictionary for English-speaking learners, and an invaluable guide to using the Japanese language.
• 30,000-word basic vocabulary   • Hundreds of special words, names, and phrases
• Clear explanations of semantic and usage differences   • Special information on grammar and usage
Hardcover, 1318 pages; ISBN 4-7700-2480-0

KODANSHA'S FURIGANA JAPANESE-ENGLISH DICTIONARY
新装版 ふりがな和英辞典

The essential dictionary for all students of Japanese.
• Furigana readings added to all *kanji*   • 16,000-word basic vocabulary
Paperback, 592 pages; ISBN 4-7700-2750-8

KODANSHA'S FURIGANA ENGLISH-JAPANESE DICTIONARY
新装版 ふりがな英和辞典

The companion to the essential dictionary for all students of Japanese.
• Furigana readings added to all *kanji*   • 14,000-word basic vocabulary
Paperback, 728 pages; ISBN 4-7700-2751-6

KODANSHA'S ROMANIZED JAPANESE-ENGLISH DICTIONARY
新装版 ローマ字和英辞典

A portable reference written for beginning and intermediate students.
• 16,000-word basic vocabulary   • No knowledge of *kanji* necessary
Paperback, 688 pages; ISBN 4-7700-2753-2

KODANSHA'S CONCISE ROMANIZED JAPANESE-ENGLISH DICTIONARY
コンサイス版 ローマ字和英辞典

A first, basic dictionary for beginner students of Japanese.
• 10,000-word basic vocabulary   • Easy-to-find romanized entries listed in alphabetical order
• Definitions written for English-speaking users
• Sample sentences in romanized and standard Japanese script, followed by English translations
Paperback, 480 pages; ISBN 4-7700-2849-0

KODANSHA'S BASIC ENGLISH-JAPANESE DICTIONARY
日本語学習 基礎英日辞典

An annotated dictionary useful for both students and teachers.
• Over 4,500 headwords and 18,000 vocabulary items   • Examples and information on stylistic differences
• Appendices for technical terms, syntax and grammar
Paperback , 1520 pages; ISBN 4-7700-2895-4

THE MODERN ENGLISH-NIHONGO DICTIONARY
日本語学習 英日辞典

The first truly bilingual dictionary designed exclusively for non-native learners of Japanese.
• Over 6,000 headwords   • Both standard Japanese (with *furigana*) and romanized orthography
• Sample sentences provided for most entries   • Numerous explanatory notes and *kanji* guides
Vinyl flexibinding, 1200 pages; ISBN 4-7700-2148-8

KODANSHA INTERNATIONAL DICTIONARIES
Easy-to-use dictionaries designed for non-native learners of Japanese.

KODANSHA'S ELEMENTARY KANJI DICTIONARY
新装版 教育漢英熟語辞典

A first, basic *kanji* dictionary for non-native learners of Japanese.
• Complete guide to 1,006 *Shin-kyōiku kanji*   • Over 10,000 common compounds
• Three indices for finding *kanji*   • Compact, portable format   • Functional, up-to-date, timely
Paperback, 576 pages; ISBN 4-7700-2752-4

KODANSHA'S ESSENTIAL KANJI DICTIONARY
新装版 常用漢英熟語辞典

A functional character dictionary that is both compact and comprehensive.
• Complete guide to the 1,945 essential *jōyō kanji*   • 20,000 common compounds
• Three indices for finding *kanji*
Paperback , 928 pages; ISBN 4-7700-2891-1

THE KODANSHA KANJI LEARNER'S DICTIONARY
新装版 漢英学習字典

The perfect kanji tool for beginners to advanced learners.
• Revolutionary SKIP lookup method   • Five lookup methods and three indices
• 2,230 entries and 41,000 meanings for 31,000 words
Paperback, 1060 pages (2-color); ISBN 4-7700-2855-5

KODANSHA'S EFFECTIVE JAPANESE USAGE DICTIONARY
新装版 日本語使い分け辞典

A concise, bilingual dictionary which clarifies the usage of frequently confused words and phrases.
• Explanations of 708 synonymous terms   • Numerous example sentences
Paperback, 768 pages; ISBN 4-7700-2850-4

KODANSHA'S DICTIONARY OF BASIC JAPANESE IDIOMS
日本語イディオム辞典

All idioms are given in Japanese script and romanized text with English translations. There are approximately 880 entries, many of which have several senses.
Paperback, 672 pages; ISBN 4-7700-2797-4

A DICTIONARY OF JAPANESE PARTICLES
てにをは辞典

Treats over 100 particles in alphabetical order, providing sample sentences for each meaning.
• Meets students' needs from beginning to advanced levels
• Treats principal particle meanings as well as variants
Paperback, 368 pages; ISBN 4-7700-2352-9

A DICTIONARY OF BASIC JAPANESE SENTENCE PATTERNS
日本語基本文型辞典

Author of the best-selling All About Particles explains fifty of the most common, basic patterns and their variations, along with numerous contextual examples. Both a reference and a textbook for students at all levels.
• Formulas delineating basic pattern structure   • Commentary on individual usages
Paperback, 320 pages; ISBN 4-7700-2608-0

The best-selling language course is now even better!

JAPANESE FOR BUSY PEOPLE Revised Edition

改訂版　コミュニケーションのための日本語　全3巻

Association for Japanese-Language Teaching (AJALT)

The leading textbook for conversational Japanese has been improved to make it easier than ever to teach and learn Japanese.

- Transition to advancing levels is more gradual.
- Kana version available for those who prefer Japanese script. Audio supplements compatible with both versions.
- English-Japanese glossary added to each volume.　• Short *kanji* lessons introduced in Volume II.
- Clearer explanations of grammar.　　　　• Shorter, easy-to-memorize dialogues.

Volume I

Teaches the basics for communication and provides a foundation for further study.

- Additional appendices for grammar usage.

Text	paperback, 232 pages	ISBN 4-7700-1882-7
Text / Kana Version	paperback, 256 pages	ISBN 4-7700-1987-4
Cassette Tapes	three cassette tapes (total 120 min.)	ISBN 4-7700-1883-5
Compact Discs	two compact discs (total 120 min.)	ISBN 4-7700-1909-2
The Workbook	paperback, 192 pages	ISBN 4-7700-1907-6
The Workbook Cassette Tapes	two cassette tapes (total 100 min.)	ISBN 4-7700-1769-3
Japanese Teacher's Manual	paperback, 160 pages	ISBN 4-7700-1906-8
English Teacher's Manual	paperback, 244 pages	ISBN 4-7700-1888-6

Volume II

Provides the basic language skills necessary to function in a professional environment.

Text	paperback, 288 pages	ISBN 4-7700-1884-3
Text / Kana Version	paperback, 296 pages	ISBN 4-7700-2051-1
Compact Discs	three compact discs (total 200 min.)	ISBN 4-7700-2136-4
The Workbook	paperback, 260 pages	ISBN 4-7700-2037-6
The Workbook Cassette Tapes	three cassette tapes (total 130 min.)	ISBN 4-7700-2111-9
Japanese Teacher's Manual	paperback, 168 pages	ISBN 4-7700-2036-8

Volume III

Expands vocabulary and structure to bring the student to the intermediate level.

Text	paperback, 256 pages	ISBN 4-7700-1886-X
Text / Kana Version	paperback, 296 pages	ISBN 4-7700-2052-X
Compact Discs	three compact discs (total 200 min.)	ISBN 4-7700-2137-2
The Workbook	paperback, 288 pages	ISBN 4-7700-2331-6
The Workbook Cassette Tapes	two cassette tapes (total 100 min.)	ISBN 4-7700-2358-8
Japanese Teacher's Manual	paperback, 200 pages	ISBN 4-7700-2306-5

Kana Workbook

Straightforward text for quick mastery of *hiragana* and *katakana* utilizing parallel learning of reading, writing, listening and pronunciation.

- Grids for writing practice.　• Reading and writing exercises.
- Optional audio tape aids in pronunciation.

Text	paperback, 80 pages	ISBN 4-7700-2096-1
Cassette Tape	one cassette tape (40 min.)	ISBN 4-7700-2097-X

JAPANESE FOR PROFESSIONALS　ビジネスマンのための実戦日本語

Association for Japanese-Language Teaching (AJALT)

A serious and detailed manual of the language of trade, commerce, and government. Fourteen lessons introduce common business situations with key sentences and a dialogue to illustrate proper usage.

Paperback, 256 pages; ISBN 4-7700-2038-4